INDIA-AFRICA

Building Synergies in Peace, Security and Development

INDIA-AFRICA

Building Synergies in Peace, Security and Development

Editor

Ruchita Beri

MANOHAR PARRIKAR
idsa
MANOHAR PARRIKAR INSTITUTE FOR DEFENCE STUDIES AND ANALYSES
मनोहर पर्रिकर रक्षा अध्ययन एवं विश्लेषण संस्थान

PENTAGON PRESS LLP

First published in 2024 by

PENTAGON PRESS LLP
206, Peacock Lane, Shahpur Jat
New Delhi-110049, India
Contact: 011-26490600

Back Cover Map Courtesy GIS Lab, MP-IDSA
Typeset in AGaramond, 11.5 Point
Printed by **Aegean Offset Printers, Greater Noida, U.P.**

ISBN 978-81-968722-9-8 (HB)

www.pentagonpress.in

Contents

Foreword

Historically, India has enjoyed close ties with the African continent. Our ancient maritime trade, driven by the monsoon winds, brought us together. The presence of a vast Indian diaspora in Africa once included a young Mahatma Gandhi who perfected his ideals of Truth and Non-Violence through years of struggle in South Africa. This had led the late Nelson Mandela to say, "You gave us Mohandas; we returned him to you as Mahatma Gandhi". On the other hand, the Siddis in Gujarat and Karnataka trace their roots to the Bantu people of East Africa. They are part of the cultural splendour of India.

India had long supported Africa's liberation from colonialism and from apartheid, both before and after attaining Independence. We have supported one another in the endeavour to realise our true destinies as free nations.

Today, India's relationship with Africa is driven by the framework of South-South cooperation. Under the dynamic leadership of Prime Minister Narendra Modi, India-Africa ties have been fundamentally transformed.

India has designated Africa as a 'top priority of its foreign and economic policy'. Prime Minister Modi's government has carried out an unprecedented outreach and engagement through high-level visits. The India Africa Forum Summit (IAFS) and the India-Africa Defence Dialogue (IADD) held in 2022 have brought India and the African continent closer.

India continues to be a reliable development partner for Africa through multiple capacity building programmes. The Indian Technical and Economic Cooperation (ITEC) initiative, extension of multiple Lines of Credits and Grant Assistance, success of phase I of the Pan Africa E-Network linking 48 African countries to India and with one another, and the launch of the e-VidyaBharti (Tele-education) and e-ArogyaBharti (Tele-medicine) Project (e-VBAB) in 2019, are notable milestones.

India is actively involved in capacity building, human resource development and bridging the digital divide in Africa. India is a close partner of Africa in achieving the socio-economic transformation of the continent. The India-Africa engagement has been further strengthened during the COVID-19 pandemic. India has extended timely humanitarian and medical assistance on various occasions to African countries.

The India-Africa partnership remains anchored in the principles of equality, mutual respect and mutual benefit with direction provided by African priorities. As Prime Minister Modi had stated while outlining India's 10 guiding principles of African engagement in Uganda in 2018 – 'India's developmental partnership will be on terms that will liberate African potential and not constrain African future'. India remains invested in Africa's prosperity as envisaged in the African Union's 'Agenda 2063'.

India has also made rich contributions to UN Peace Keeping Operations in Africa, and to anti-piracy operations in the Gulf of Aden and the wider Indian Ocean.

Our shared maritime interests remain anchored in developing a blue economy, particularly in the context of SAGAR (Security and Growth for All in the Region), and in ensuring unimpeded commerce and freedom of navigation and over-flight along key sea lanes of communication.

The concept of the Indo-Pacific binds the two great oceans as one seamless strategic space. Several African states are members of the Indian Ocean Naval Symposium (IONS) and Indian Ocean Rim Association (IORA) which promote maritime co-operation among the littoral states of the Indian Ocean Region. Strong India-Africa ties can strengthen multi-polarity in the Indo-Pacific region.

Today, the greatest challenge before the Global South is the fight against poverty, climate change, natural disasters, and food and energy security. These are indivisible and transcend borders. Cooperation on these issues will ensure the achievement of Sustainable Development Goals (SDGs). If we develop a broad consensus on the way forward, we may be in a better position to collectively address our common challenges.

The Manohar Parrikar Institute for Defence Studies and Analyses (MP-IDSA) has the distinction of successfully organising the India-Africa Strategic Dialogue on pertinent themes related to India-Africa ties. The Institute has also published several volumes on various facets of India-Africa ties.

In recent decades, the key challenge confronting the African continent relates to the management of interplay between security and development. India is also a stakeholder in Africa's future in a region in which interdependence is the norm and proximity is both a challenge and an opportunity.

This edited volume titled "India-Africa: Building Synergies in Peace, Security and Development" has been published against the backdrop of these emerging developments. It brings together a wide spectrum of opinions and viewpoints of experts, strategic thinkers and scholars from India and Africa. It covers a range of crucial themes including developmental cooperation, trade and investment, climate change, security and cooperation in counter-terrorism, as well as collaboration in United Nations peacekeeping, among others.

I compliment the authors for their efforts, and hope that the contents of the volume will provide readers a deeper understanding of the India-Africa partnership and the imperative of working together to forge a common destiny of peace and progress.

Sujan R. Chinoy
Director General
MP-IDSA

About the Editor/Contributors

Ruchita Beri is a Consultant with the Manohar Parrikar Institute for Defence Studies and Analyses (MP-IDSA), New Delhi. Earlier, Ms Beri served as Senior Research Associate and Centre Coordinator, Africa, Latin America, Caribbean and United Nations Centre at the MP-IDSA. She has over three decades experience in research on international relations, political economy and security of Sub-Saharan Africa, India–Africa relations and Emerging Powers in Africa and the Indian Ocean region. She is a member of the Africa Committee of the Confederation of Indian Industry (CII). She is also a member of the Africa Experts Group at the Vivekananda International Foundation, New Delhi. She is the former President of African Studies Association of India (ASA). She serves on Editorial Board/ Editorial Advisory Board of journals, such as, *Africa Review*, *Austral: Brazilian Journal of Strategy & International Relations* and the *Development Cooperation Review*. She has authored several research articles and edited and co-edited numerous books including *Food Governance in India: Rights, Security and Challenges in the Global Sphere* (Routledge, 2023) and *India and Africa: Common Security Challenges for the Next Decade* (Pentagon Press, 2016)

Sanjukta Banerji Bhattacharya, currently retired, was a Professor of International Relations at Jadavpur University, Kolkata, India. She has received the prestigious Fulbright Award twice and has four books as well as over seventy articles and chapters in international and national journals and edited volumes. She has also presented over a hundred papers at national and international conferences. Currently, she is a member of Academic Councils, Boards of Studies, and Doctoral Committees etc of various Grade I universities around the country, is an Executive Board member of several prestigious academic bodies and the All India Vice President of the Jadavpur Association of International Relations.

Aparajita Biswas is former Professor and Director, of the Centre for African Studies, University of Mumbai. She has taught at the Centre over 34 years and demonstrated continued commitment to promoting African Studies in India. She is associated with many universities, research institutes and research groups in India and abroad. She has also taught as a Visiting Professor at various universities in Asia, Africa and Europe. Her major research interest is on India-Africa Relations, Africa and Indian Ocean, Africa's international relations, Human Rights Issues in Africa, and the Indian Diaspora in Africa. She is the former President of African Studies Association of India. She has been invited by numerous institutions and universities across the world to share her views on several African issues and, specially, on India-Africa relations .She is the author of many books and articles. Presently she is writing on issues of Indian Foreign policy in various newspapers in India.

Sujan R. Chinoy is the Director General of the Manohar Parrikar Institute for Defence Studies and Analyses (MP-IDSA), New Delhi since 2019. A career diplomat from 1981-2018, he held several important diplomatic assignments, including as Ambassador to Japan and Mexico. A specialist on China, East Asia and politico-security issues, he anchored negotiations and confidence-building measures (CBMs) with China on the boundary issue from 1996-2000. On deputation to the National Security Council Secretariat (NSCS) from 2008-2012, his expertise covered external and internal security issues in the extended neighbourhood of the Indo-Pacific. Among his diverse foreign postings, he also served as Counsellor (Political) in the Embassy in Riyadh, Kingdom of Saudi Arabia. He was the Chair of the Think20 engagement group for India's G20 Presidency and a Member of the high-powered DRDO Review Committee.

Yeshi Choedon was until recently a Professor in International Organization at the Centre for International Politics, Organisation and Disarmament (CIPOD), School of International Studies (SIS), Jawaharlal Nehru University (JNU), New Delhi. She had been a faculty member at JNU since 2004. Before joining JNU, Prof. Choedon held position as Lecturer and later as Reader in Political Science and International Relations at the Sikkim Government College, Gangtok. She was awarded the UGC Career Award from 1995 to 1998 and was a DAAD Fellow at Free University, Berlin in 1997.

Sallie Simba Kayunga, is a senior lecturer, Department of Political Science and Public Administration, Makerere University, Uganda, specialising in security studies. He is also consultant with the Directorate of Doctrine of the Uganda People's Defense Forces (UPDF) as well as a lecturer and member of the Quality Control Board, Senior Command and Staff College, Kimaka, Uganda. He has attended numerous conferences on security sector governance in Africa. He has published articles on Islamic Fundamentalism in Uganda, in particular and Africa in general. He has a PhD from Roskilde University, Denmark, among other qualifications and a certificate in cultural and social studies from the Centre for Studies in the Social Sciences (CSSS), Kolkata, India.

Rajeesh Kumar is an Associate Fellow and Acting Coordinator at the ALAC&UN Centre, MP-IDSA, New Delhi. Dr Kumar was Co-Chair of the T20 India Task Force on 'Reformed Multilateralism: Transforming Global Institutions and Frameworks' to the G20. Prior to joining MP-IDSA in 2016, he held teaching positions at Jamia Millia Islamia, New Delhi and University of Calicut, Kerala. His research interests span both Indian Foreign Policy and Multilateralism. Dr Kumar is the author of *Principled but Evolving: India's Approach to Multilateral Peace and Security* (New Delhi, IDSA, 2021) and *The International Committee of the Red Cross in Internal Armed Conflicts: Is Neutrality Possible* (London, Palgrave Macmillan, 2019). He is also the co-editor of the *Eurozone Crisis and the Future of Europe: Political Economy of Further Integration and Governance* (London, Palgrave Macmillan, 2014). His articles and opinion pieces have appeared in Journals and Newspapers, including Strategic Analysis, India Quarterly, E-International Relations, The Diplomat, The Hindu, Japan Times, Tehran Times and The Outlook.

Sanusha Naidu is a foreign policy and political analyst based in Cape Town. Her work includes democracy, development and the political economy of Africa's international relations and South Africa's Foreign Policy. She has also focused her interests on South-South Cooperation and the footprint of emerging powers (China and India) in Africa. Ms Naidu has a Masters in International Relations from the University of Staffordshire, United Kingdom. Currently she is a Senior Research Associate with the Institute for Global Dialogue. She has previously worked at the Centre for Conflict Resolution based in Cape Town and managed the South African Foreign Policy Initiative (SAFPI) at the Open Society Foundation for South Africa. She also managed Fahamu's (a network for social justice movements) China and Emerging Powers in Africa programme. Ms. Naidu has published extensively including two edited books on Africa-China; China-Africa relations. She has conducted political risk training for the South Africa Department of International Relations and Cooperation (DIRCO) and is a regular media commentator for South African and international media agencies.

Ian Subhash Shanghvi is a Partnership, Membership & Engagement Specialist at the Agricultural Non State Actors Forum (ANSAF), Dar es Salaam, Tanzania. He is a member of the Member of Task Force in developing Tanzania's National Agricultural Research Agenda. He is a former Assistant Research Fellow of the Economic and Social Research Foundation (ESRF) in Dar es Salaam. Ian was a Visiting Fellow at the Africa, Latin America, Caribbean and United Nations Centre, MP-IDSA from September to December 2014. During this period he submitted this paper and another entitled Enhancing Energy Security in Rural Tanzania: Examples of Decentralized Rural Energy Approaches from India to the MP-IDSA for publication

Uttam Kumar Sinha is a Senior Fellow at the Manohar Parrikar Institute for Defence Studies and Analyses (MP-IDSA), New Delhi. He is a leading scholar and commentator on transboundary rivers, climate change and the Arctic. He was Co-Chair of the Think-20 Task Force on 'Accelerating SDGs: Exploring New Pathways to the 2030 Agenda' during India's G20 Presidency. After a brief stint in the print media and a doctoral degree from Jawaharlal Nehru University, he joined the MP-IDSA in 2001, where he coordinates the Non-Traditional Security Centre and is the Managing Editor of *Strategic Analysis* published by Routledge, the institute's flagship journal. He is a recipient of many fellowships and leadership programmes including senior fellow at the Nehru Memorial Museum and Library (2018-2020); US-South Asia Leader Engagement Programme at the Harvard Kennedy School (2015); Chevening 'Gurukul' leadership at the London School of Economics and Political Science (2008) and a visiting fellow at the Peace Research Institute Oslo (2006). His recently published work is *BBIN Sub-Region: Perspectives on Climate-water-Energy Nexus (Pentagon Press, 2023)*, *Indus Basin Interrupted: A History of*

Territory and Politics from Alexander to Nehru (Penguin, 2021). His other works include the *Riverine Neighbourhood: Hydro-politics in South Asia* (Pentagon Press, 2016) and *Climate Change Narratives: Reading the Arctic* (2014). His edited and co-edited volumes include *Modi: Shaping a Global Order in Flux* (Wisdom Tree, 2023).

Hussein Solomon is Professor in the Centre for Gender and Africa Studies at the University of the Free State. His research interests revolve around political Islam and issues of terrorism. His most recent books include *African Security in the Anthropocene* (with Jude Cocodia, Springer, 2023), *The Future of War in Africa* (with Eeben Barlow, Amazon Kindle, 2023), *Intersectionality and LGBTQI Rights: A Comparative Analysis of Iran. Turkey and Egypt* (with Simone Bekker, Nova Publishers, 2023), *Directions in international Terrorism: Theories, Trends and Trajectories* (Palgrave, 2021), *Terrorism in Africa: New Trends and Frontiers* (with Glen Segell and Sergey Kostelyanets, Institute for African Studies, Moscow, 2021), and *Arab MENA Countries: Vulnerabilities and Constraints Against Democracy on the Eve of the Global COVID- 19 Crisis* (with Arno Tausch, Springer 2021).

Introduction

Ruchita Beri

India and Africa have shared a close relationship, and this relationship has gained momentum in recent years. Greater economic engagement has been crucial to boosting ties between Africa and India. India's trade with Africa amounted to US$ 68 billion in 2011-12 and has reached US$ 98 billion in the year 2022-23.[1] The First India-Africa Forum Summit, held in New Delhi in 2008, marked the beginning of a robust and contemporary partnership. The second summit, held in Addis Ababa in May 2011, emphasized the need for India to strengthen and enhance its partnership with countries in the African continent. The third summit held in 2015 called for consolidation of this significant partnership. The numerous high-level visits to the continent, several initiatives such as "Vaccine Maitri" for supply of medicines and vaccines during the COVID-19 pandemic, are a testimony to the growing partnership. The inclusion of the African Union as part of the G-20 grouping during the India's presidency of the G20, added to India's efforts to enhance partnership with African countries. Similarly, expanding defence ties are another area of cooperation. The hosting of the India- Africa Defence Dialogue (IADD), a biennial meeting with defence ministers from the African region, on the sidelines of the Defence Expo 2022 in Gandhinagar in October 2022, is a step in that direction.

India and Africa both recognise that peace, security and development are intimately interwoven. While peace ensures opportunity for development, security enables as well as protects fruits of development. Africa is a continent which has witnessed many conflicts. However, Africa has also witnessed economic growth and political reform in the past decade. Six African countries featured among the top ten fastest growing economies in the last decade. African countries are increasingly moving towards democracy even though some may not have perfected democratic institutions and practices. Like India, Africa is also concerned with the issue of climate change particularly as it impacts its food security. The issue of terrorism is also of deep concern to both India and Africa as political conflicts in Africa have recently been hijacked by terror movements with pan-regional and global agenda. Therefore it is important that India engages with Africa on these issues. The aim is to foster mutual learning and effective engagement. This volume focuses on engagement between India and the African countries on issues of peace, security and development.

Peace, Security and Development

The complex inter-linkage between peace, security and development is well known and recognized. Within Africa, the Constitutive Act of the African Union recognizes "that the scourge of conflicts in Africa constitutes a major impediment to the socio-economic development of the continent." It also often manifests in the blurring of boundaries between peacekeeping and peacebuilding. In this context, Rajeesh Kumar's chapter in the book provides a perspective on the conceptual linkage between peace, security and development. This chapter examines how insecurity affects development and vice-versa. It analyses how the security development discourse impacted on Africa's security and development policies. The chapter also studies the securitization of development policies in the continent.

The book dwells on perspectives on development in Africa with a two-pronged focus on trade and investment as well as development cooperation. It was premised on the view that peace cannot be viewed simply as absence of conflict. Lasting peace can be only achieved in Africa if the focus is on creating a political economy that favours inclusive growth and distributive justice along with political rights to the masses. Therefore, issues of equitable development become very important for Africa. The Busan Partnership for effective development cooperation signed in 2011, introduced a new paradigm for development cooperation. However, during the Busan dialogue, there were wide differences in perceptions of India and the Development Assistance Committee (DAC) members on aid and development cooperation. In this context, Sanusha Naidu's chapter points to the many lacunae in the development aid and cooperation programmes involving external actors in

Africa since the 1970s. She explains how the continent's developmental visions and priorities were lost or compromised due to these assistance programmes. She argues that the there is a need to bring about a convergence in the goals of Agenda 2063 and India's developmental support to Africa to make the relationship sustainable, and the realization of development goals a reality.

Siimilarly, Ruchita Beri's chapter looks into the India-Africa development partnership. She argues that development partnership is the most important pillar of the India-Africa relationship. The chapter suggests three main features of India's development partnership with African countries: consultation, capacity building and collaboration. The chapter also analyses India-Africa development cooperation in key areas –agriculture, construction/infrastructure, solar power, electrification and health. Here, it is important to note that development can only come about through vibrant trade and investment in the continent. In trade and investment, India remains Africa's fourth largest trading partner. Over the years India's investments in the region have grown, though estimates vary. In this context, Aparajita Biswas outlines the existing pattern of trade and investment between India and Africa. She examines India's investments in various sectors including, mining, oil, agriculture and ICT. She points to the challenges that Indian industry faces while doing business in Africa. She contends that there is much scope for increased trade and investment between the two sides in the future.

Conflict Resolution, Peacekeeping, Terrorism

This volume looks into matters of peace and security with a focus on conflict resolution. Conflicts, continue to be a marked feature of Africa. *The Global Peace Index 2022* suggests that five out of ten least peaceful countries in the world are in Africa.[2] Some of the conflict-ridden countries in the region are Sudan, Democratic Republic of Congo, Somalia, Central African Republic and South Sudan. Rising authoritarianism and unconstitutional changes of government have increased the insecurity. The Sahel region faced four coups between 2020 and 2023. They include countries, such as, Mali, Guinea-Bissau, Burkina Faso and Niger. Africa also witnessed a gradual evolution of the African Peace and Security Architecture (APSA) which strives for 'African solutions to African problems'. Yet the APSA and various initiatives by the regional organizations face their own challenges and constraints. Many new issues that are challenging peace on the continent include the problem of State-building in countries like South Sudan, and the new phase of military intervention in Africa that began with the Libyan crisis. India has always deeply engaged with conflict resolution in Africa especially in the United Nations peacekeeping efforts and this engagement can be deepened. In this context, Yeshi Cheodon's chapter looks at Indian participation in peacekeeping in Africa and argues that India accords high significance to its participation in UN peacekeeping in Africa. She argues that initially, the rationale for its participation was to express solidarity with African countries, but now it has more to do with ensuring energy security, and maximizing the opportunity for trade and investment. In pursuance of its aspiration for recognition as a great power, India has been leveraging its contribution to UN peacekeeping operations to lay claim to a permanent seat at the UN Security Council since the early 1990s. She concludes that India's declining participation in peacekeeping may be attributed to the need to reconfigure its participation and to highlight the need to go back to the root of the peacekeeping operations.

The challenge of terrorism to peace and security in Africa is another issue dealt with in the book. There has been a surge in terrorism in the continent in recent years. There is clearly an economic imperative to the rise of Islamist terrorism in some parts of Africa. In others, domestic terrorist groups have forged linkages with the Al Qaeda and the Islamic State (ISIS), thus adding to their lethality. Some terrorist groups are purely ideologically motivated. In some cases there is inter-meshing of violent conflicts with terrorism. In this context, the chapter by Sally Simba Kayunga maps the nature and extent of terrorism in Africa, and based on the ongoing counter-terrorism initiatives, suggests ways in which India can help with military and non-military aspects of counter-terrorism, relying on its own strengths and capabilities. He argues that India is a good example of how to manage diversity that African countries can emulate. Hussein Solomon's chapter seeks to explore some of the internal and external variables fueling terrorism and radicalization in the African continent. These include ethnic fragmentation, governance failure, the deliberate stoking of religious tensions as well as the failure of the international community at large. At the same time, the chapter provides some insights on African responses, specifically that of the African Union and its Regional Economic Communities (RECs). The chapter argues that State actors need to work in partnership with the international community for arriving at a more holistic approach to counter-terrorism. This would include drafting legislation, establishing forensic laboratories, restructuring the armed forces, and economic development. Sanjukta Banerji Bhattacharya outlines the history of terrorism in India and Africa. She makes a case for counter-terrorism cooperation based on the specific requirements of the African countries since there are more divergences than commonalities in their experiences of terrorism. The rise of Islamist terrorism, she contends, is a threat that both sides face and must cooperate to counter it. They both underscore the need for support for Africa's development.

The Climate Change Conundrum

Africa faces severe challenges to its agricultural output, bio-diversity and human health due to climate change. The problem is exacerbated due to under-development and poor adaptive capacity. Additionally, the impact of climate change has amplified existing conflicts and could fuel newer ones. In this context, Uttam Kumar Sinha traces India's engagement with the climate change regime since 1972 and highlights that issues of equity and per capita emissions have been important talking points for India. His chapter begins with a discussion on the science of climate change and its impact on the food, energy and water nexus. The chapter goes on to examine India's recent climate action, particularly at the Conference of the Parties to the UN Framework Convention on climate change. He analyses India's focus on climate values through Prime Minister Modi's Mission LIFE (Lifestyle for Environment) movement, launched in November 2022. He argues that climate change has been one of the issues on the agenda of cooperation since the establishment of India-Africa-Forum Summit in 2008, and that there is space for convergence between India and the African countries on this crucial issue. There is also much scope for the two sides to push for finance and technology transfer to help with adaptation and mitigation. Finally, Ian Subhash Shanghvi dwells on the impact of climate change on human security and welfare in Sub Saharan Africa (SSA). He highlights the impact of climate change on a wide-range of security issues in Africa, including human health, food security, water crisis, displacement and migration, human settlements, the energy sector, and transport. He suggests that India can assist SSA in mitigating several impacts of climate change.

The chapters in this volume include updated versions of select papers presented during the the 3rd India-Africa Strategic Dialogue on 3-4 March 2015, organized by the Manohar Parrikar Institute for Defence Studies and Analyses (MP-IDSA), New Delhi. The objective of this Dialogue is to build on existing partnerships between African countries and India, and to explore new areas of convergence for mutual engagement. While the relationship with Africa has grown substantially over these years, the contributions, reflecting on longer term trends, remain extremely significant, since the issues highlighted by the scholars and policy makers resonate in India's relationship with the African continent even today.

NOTES

1 "Remarks made by External Affairs Minister, Dr. S. Jaishankar at the Business Community Interaction" Ministry of External Affairs, Government of India, 8 July 2023 at https://www.mea.gov.in/Speeches-Statements.htm?dtl/36766 (Accessed 22 July 2023).

2 *The Armed Conflict Survey 2022: Sub-Saharan Africa Regional Analysis,* International Institute of Strategic Studies at https://www.iiss.org/online-analysis/online-analysis//2022/11/acs-2022-sub-saharan-africa (Accessed 12 September 2023).

1

Security-Development Nexus and the Securitization of Development in Africa

Rajeesh Kumar

'Security' and 'Development' are independent yet interdependent concepts. Security means the absence of any form of threats or violence. On the other hand, development denotes growth and progress. However, both are highly contested concepts and have undergone radical change in the past. For instance, security was traditionally understood as primarily connected to the State and the military. However, in recent decades the meaning of security has widened and deepened to include issues on development, environment, human rights, migration, etc. As with the concept of security, there are different definitions for development. The concept has transformed significantly from economic growth to human development and sustainable development.

Over the years, the concept of security has been increasingly linked to development, thus creating the security-development nexus discourse. According to Mark Duffield development is one important domain that has been increasingly merged with and subjected to security concerns.[1] The UNDP's *Human Development Report 1994* offers clear evidence of this shift as it raises the question of human security. The Report equates security with people rather than the State or territories and discusses national and global human security concerns.[2] This change has been reflected in the development and security policies at the discursive and policy levels. For development policy, security issues have moved into the field of direct vision and on the other hand, security policy has increasingly tied up with development matters.

Against this backdrop, this chapter will discuss the linkages between security and development in Africa. It will examine how insecurity affects development and vice-versa. The chapter proceeds as follows: The first section will offer the definitions of development and security and outline the discourse of the security-development nexus. The second part will examine how the security-development nexus discourse impacted Africa's security and development policies. It will also analyze how the security-development nexus resulted in the securitization of development policies in the continent.

I

Linking Security and Development

The term "security" has always been vague in terms of its definition. "Security" denotes different things to different people. Depending on the context, it may even have a different meaning for the same individual. In International Relations (IR), security is traditionally linked to nation-states and the protection of their territory and vital interests. It is based on the assumption that security threats arise primarily from other States or external actors seeking to harm a country's interests through military, political, or economic means. Stephen Walt, for instance, defines security exclusively in terms of the ability of the State to defend its territory and its principal values against a military threat.[3] The security agenda is set by State actors, with a focus on national defence, border security, and strategic alliances with other States. This view assumes that if the State is secure, so too will those living within it. Security, then, means national security. The Cold War era was a perfect example, where security was all about States, strategies, military power and status quo.

In the post-Cold War period, the definition of security broadened to include non-military threats ranging from civil wars and resource conflicts to environmental crisis. 'Security' therefore refers to the search to "avoid, prevent, reduce, or resolve violent conflicts – whether the threat originates from other States, non-State actors, or structural socio-economic conditions."[4] With the introduction of the human security concept, policymakers have encountered increasing pressure to address humanitarian concerns as a security problem. Human security emphasizes the need to address the underlying causes of insecurity and promote people's well-being and dignity. It takes a comprehensive and multi-dimensional approach that considers the economic, social, and political dimensions of security and the protection of human rights.

Likewise the concept of security, development also has different connotations. For many, it is fundamentally associated with economic growth and social progress. In the 1950s and 1960s, for instance, development largely referred to economic growth.[5] For this school of thought, development would come as a natural consequence of economic growth. This narrow approach has been criticized for neglecting social and environmental concerns and for perpetuating inequalities between developed and developing countries. Amartya Sen argues that pure economic growth cannot be treated as development and development has to be more concerned with enhancing people's lives and the freedom they enjoy. He emphasized development as distributive justice.

Consequently, development is linked with modernization or social progress and refers to an actual historical and material occurrence: "a significant change in the economic, social, political, and cultural conditions affecting large groups of people."[6] According to Ruth Pearson, development involves qualitative, quantitative improvement or both, particularly in the use of available resources.[7] In recent years, development is connected more to sustainability – achieving lasting satisfaction of human needs and improving the quality of life. This broad approach was accepted partly because the results of past development policies had been disappointing.

This conceptual widening of the definitions of security and development led to a blurring of the boundaries between security policy and development policy. The link between insecurity and development is a complex, but indisputable one. The security-development nexus illustrates how underdevelopment and insecurity reinforce each other to sustain long cycles of violence and poverty. Persistent economic, political and social ramifications often characterize the vicious cycle. David Chandler notes that before the nexus paradigm, security and development were viewed as separate sectors with distinct ideas and ambitions.[8] According to him, mainly two factors contributed to the change of paradigm. First, the belief that merging security and development will create coherent policies regarding post-conflict assistance. Second, the belief that long-term development requires security and lasting security depends upon development.[9]

At its core, the security-development nexus recognizes that security is a prerequisite for development and long-term security. In other words, it is difficult to achieve sustainable development without security, and it is difficult to achieve lasting security without addressing the root causes of underdevelopment. This link was evident in UN Secretary-General Kofi Annan's statement: "we will not enjoy development without security; we will not enjoy security without development."[10] At the policy level, this was reflected in the form of development-oriented security policies and security became multidimensional, covering military, political, economic, environmental, and societal elements.[11] As a result, major international organizations and governments have emphasized the nexus between security and development and underlined the need to link security and development policies. The Millennium Declaration, where all member states of the UN acknowledged the need for a human-centred approach to security, and its outcome document, *The Millennium Development Goals*, are examples of this perspective shift. The subsequent reports and policies of the UN, including the *In Larger Freedom* and *The Sustainable Development Goals*, are also focused considerably on the development aspects of security.

In 2005, the European Security Strategy and European Consensus on Development acknowledged that "there cannot be sustainable development without peace and security, and without development and poverty eradication, there would be no sustainable peace."[12] Similarly, the Organisation for Economic Co-operation and Development (OECD) also noted that, "the political, security, economic and social spheres are interdependent: failure in one risks failure in all others."[13] The Paris Declaration on Aid Effectiveness and the Accra Agenda for Action are other examples of the translation of security-development nexus concerns into policy actions.

The nexus has also been the basis for aid interventions in developing countries, primarily those that are weak, fragile, incapable, and facing development problems and security threats. This link was reinvented mainly to provide scientific explanations for terrorism after 9/11. For instance, the issue was a central theme of the 2002 US National Security Strategy. Later, it was reflected more nuancedly in the policy statements of the OECD and the World Bank. The creation of the International Network on Conflict and Fragility in 2008 and the *World Development Report* (*WDR*) in 2011 unpacked the link between security and development and recommended implementing strategies related to this nexus. Most recently, the debate over the link between development and security has been renewed in the context of Sustainable Development Goals (SDGs).[14]

The objective of linking security and development was to include development goals under the security head. This was also aimed at holistically viewing development and security and improving both. For example, programmes aimed at reducing poverty, increasing access to education and healthcare, and promoting economic growth can help reduce social unrest and mitigate security risks. Similarly, security programmes and initiatives can support development goals. For instance, peacekeeping operations, conflict resolution and prevention, and counter-terrorism efforts can help create a stable and secure environment conducive to economic development. However, in practice, this process has become the securitization of development policies and security strategies prioritized over development needs. In Africa, this securitization aspect was more evident, where States became stronger, supported by securitization and the enthusiasm of governments and donors to put security above all else. The following section will examine how linking security and development resulted in the securitization of development in Africa.

II

Securitization of Development in Africa

Africa was one of the central focuses of the security-development nexus debate. The continent is home to some of the poorest countries in the world, with high levels of inequality, unemployment, and poverty. These conditions often lead to social and political unrest, resulting in security challenges such as terrorism, conflict, and violence.[15] These diverse security threats and challenges have refocused global policy and scholarly attention on the peace-security-development nexus. As a result, development programmes and initiatives in Africa are often implemented to address these underlying social and economic issues and to promote stability and security. However, a critical analysis of the link between security and development in Africa shows that it has significant ramifications, including the securitization of development in the continent.

The securitization of development refers to the use of security strategies and frameworks to address development challenges and subordination of growth and development objectives to security priorities. It is the process by which actors transform the subject of development from a regular socio-political issue into a matter of 'security'. According to the Copenhagen School, securitization is the "move that takes an issue beyond the established rules of the game and frames the issue either as special sort of politics or above the politics."[16]This approach emphasizes the importance of security in achieving development goals, and often involves prioritizing security concerns over other development priorities.[17]

The securitization of development in Africa often resulted in the militarization of development interventions, with security forces taking on roles traditionally performed by development actors. For instance, in the Lake Chad Basin, which includes parts of Nigeria, Cameroon, Chad, and Niger, the Boko Haram insurgency has displaced millions of people and created a humanitarian crisis. In response, the governments of the region, with the support of international partners, have increased their military presence in the area.[18] However, this has led to the militarization of humanitarian assistance, with aid workers forced to operate in a highly securitized environment. Moreover, it has resulted in the increase of external military presence in these States, which over time, were institutionalized. This has also made it more difficult to deliver aid effectively and to address the underlying causes of the crisis.

Securitization also led African States and international agencies to focus on short-term security goals at the expense of long-term development objectives. Similarly, securitization also resulted in the diversion of resources from development interventions to security-related activities.[19] This led to a lack of investment in the continent's critical development areas, such as health, education, and infrastructure. For instance, in Somalia, the government and international partners have prioritized counter-terrorism efforts in response to the ongoing threat posed by Al-Shabaab. While these efforts have successfully reduced the group's capabilities, they have also diverted resources away from development initiatives.[20] This has led to criticism that the securitization of development in Somalia has come at the expense of mitigation of the root causes of poverty, inequality, and underdevelopment.

Similarly, in the Sahel region, security has become a major concern due to the threat posed by jihadist groups. As a result, several international partners have prioritized security assistance in the region, often at the expense of development initiatives. According to Rita Abrahamsen, the securitization of Sahel has helped "legitimize the 'war on terrorism, which has moved the focus toward a 'risk/fear/threat' project, but has done very little to offer for Africa's developmental problems."[21] In countries like Mali, Chad, Niger, Nigeria, Burkina Faso, securitization has also led to the radicalization of the populations.[22]

Moreover, in several African States, the securitization of development has also played an ambiguous role in the gaining and maintaining of power by political elites. For instance, "the Chadian, Ethiopian, Rwandan and Ugandan regimes have benefited from the securitization of development over a sustained period and have used this process to build semi-authoritarian and illiberal states."[23] In countries like Ethiopia and Uganda, governments have extensively used anti-terror laws to justify the repression of political opposition and civil society organizations. It is also important to note that most countries in Africa's top ten external essential aid recipients are authoritarian regimes that do not allow democratic participation and criminalize political opposition.[24]

In recent years, the issue of migration has become increasingly securitized in Africa, as governments and international partners prioritize border security and counter-smuggling efforts. However, this approach has been criticized for neglecting the underlying factors that drive migration, such as poverty, unemployment, and conflict. Instead, advocates for a more development-focused approach argue that addressing these underlying factors is necessary to reduce migration flows in the long term. In 2016, the European Union (EU) launched the Partnership Framework on Migration, which addresses irregular migration and migrant smuggling from African countries to Europe. The framework focuses on enhancing border security and increasing return of irregular migrants.[25] However, critics argue that the framework neglects the underlying drivers of migration, such as poverty and conflict, and that it prioritizes security concerns over development initiatives.

Conclusion

The security-development nexus refers to the complex relationship between security and development, where security and development are intertwined and influence each other. In the African context, the consequences of the security-development nexus can vary, depending on the specific context and the nature of the regional security and development challenges. One potential consequence of the security-development nexus in Africa is that security challenges can impede development progress. For example, conflicts and instability can disrupt economic growth, discourage foreign investment, and divert resources from development initiatives. This can result in poverty, inequality, and social unrest, further exacerbating security challenges.

Contrarily, development can also have a positive impact on security in Africa. For example, development initiatives such as education, healthcare, and infrastructure can promote social stability, reduce poverty, and improve economic opportunities, which can help to address the root causes of insecurity and conflict. However, there are also risks associated with the security-development nexus in Africa. As discussed above, it can lead to the securitization of development. Similarly, if not tailored to the local context and implemented with sufficient consultation with local communities, development initiatives supported by foreign actors can be counter-productive.

Addressing the adverse implications of securitization of development in Africa requires a comprehensive and coordinated approach. First, a nuanced strategy that recognizes the complex relationship between security and development is to be designed. It is also essential to understand that security and development are not always positively correlated, and efforts to promote one can sometimes undermine the other. Second, African countries need to strengthen their democratic institutions, promote transparency and accountability, and fight corruption. This will create a stable political environment that fosters economic growth and social stability. Third, African countries need to work together to address security challenges that transcend national borders. This includes sharing intelligence, coordinating crisis responses, and promoting regional integration. Finally, investing in peacebuilding initiatives and conflict prevention mechanisms can help prevent and mitigate conflicts, leading to greater stability and economic growth.

NOTES

1 Mark Duffield, *Global Governance and the New Wars: The Merging of Development and Security*, Zed Books, London, 2001.

2 *UNDP Human Development Report 1994* at https://hdr.undp.org/content/human-development-report-1994 (Accessed 15 February 2023).

3 Stephen Walt, 'The Renaissance of Security Studies', *International Studies Quarterly,* 35 (2), 1991, p. 212.

4 IPA Report, 'The Security-Development Nexus: Conflict, Peace and Development in the 21st Century', 2004, p. 2.

5 Walt Whitman Rostow, *The Stages of Economic Growth: A Non-Communist Manifesto,* Cambridge University Press, *Cambridge*, 1991.

6 O.P. Dwivedi, R. Khator and J. Nef, 'A History of Development and Development as History', in O.P. Dwivedi, R. Khator and J. Nef, (Eds) *Managing Development in a Global Context,* Palgrave Macmillan, London, 2007, p.17.

7 Ruth Pearson, 'Rethinking Gender Matters in Development', in T. Allen, and A. Thomas, (Eds.). *Poverty and Development into the 21st Century,* Oxford University Press, Oxford, 2007.

8 David Chandler, 'The Security-development Nexus and the Rise of Anti-Foreign Policy', *Journal of International Relations and Development*, 10 (4), 2007, pp. 362–386.

9 Ibid.

10 Secretary-General's Address to the Commission on Human Rights, 07 April 2005 at https://www.un.org/sg/en/content/sg/statement/2005-04-07/secretary-generals-address-commission-human-rights (Accessed 10 February 2023.)

11 Barry Buzan, Ole Waever and Jaap de Wilde, *Security: A New Framework for Analysis*, Lynne Rienner, London, 1998.

12 'European Security Strategy: A Secure Europe in a Better World, Council of European Union at https://www.consilium.europa.eu/media/30823/qc7809568enc.pdf (Accessed 10 February 2023).

13 OECD, *Principles of Good International Engagement in Fragile States* at https://www.oecd.org/dac/conflict-fragility-resilience/docs/38368714.pdf (Accessed 1 March 2023).

14 'Nexus Between Security Sector Governance/Reform and Sustainable Development Goal 16' at https://www.sdg16hub.org/topic/nexus-between-security-sector-governancereform-and-sustainable- development-goal-16 (Accessed 1 March 2023).

15 Ayodele Odusola *et al.,* 'Inequalities and Conflict in Africa: An empirical investigation', UNDP Africa Economists Working Papers 307334, 2017 at https://www.un-ilibrary.org/content/books/9789210607100s005-c007. (Accessed 16 March 2023).

16 Barry Buzan, Ole Waever and Jaap de Wilde, no. 11, p. 23.

17 Ole Wæver, Securitization, in Christopher W. Hughes, Yew Meng Lai eds. *Security Studies A Reader*, London, Routledge, 2011.

18 Earl Conteh-Morgan, 'Militarization and Securitization in Africa: The Role of Sino-American Geostrategic Presence', *Insight Turkey*, 21 (1), 2019, pp. 77–94.

19 Mark Bradbury and Michael Kleinman, 'Winning hearts and minds? Examining the Relationship between Aid and Security in Kenya' at https://fic.tufts.edu/assets/WinningHearts-in-Kenya.pdf (Accessed 20 February 2023).

20 Stephen Brown and Jörn Grävingholt, 'Security, Development and the Securitization of Foreign Aid', in S. Brown, J. Grävingholt, (Eds.), *The Securitization of Foreign Aid,* Palgrave Macmillan, London, 2016.

21 Rita Abrahamsen, 'Blair's Africa: The Politics of Securitization and Fear', *Alternatives: Global, Local, Political,* 30 (1), 2005, pp. 55–80.

22 Stephen O. Idahosa, Denis A. Degterev and Solomon I. Ikhidero, 'Securitization Initiatives and the Lingering Security Challenges in Sub-Saharan Sahel Region: An appraisal', *African Security Review*, 30 (3), 2021, pp. 338-367.

23 Jonathan Fisher and David M Anderson, 'Authoritarianism and the securitization of development in Africa', *International Affairs,* 91 (1), 2015, pp. 131–151.
24 Hichem Derradji and Ali Madouni, 'The Securitization of Development in Africa: Causes, Mechanism and Consequences', at https://hrcak.srce.hr/file/420743 (Accessed 25 February 2023).
25 Marie Deridder, Lotte Pelckmans and Emilia Ward, 'Reversing the Gaze: West Africa Performing the EU Migration-Development-Security nexus', at https://journals.openedition.org/anthropodev/938#citedby (Accessed 16 March 2023).

2

Development Cooperation: A View from Africa

Sanusha Naidu

Introduction

Development has remained a critical issue in the post-colonial African state in the 60 or more years following independence. The Lagos Plan of Action and the Alternative Framework to Structural Adjustment Programmes (AF-SAP), the signing of the Abuja Treaty in 1990, the establishment of the African Economic Community and more recently the adoption of Agenda 2063 have become significant roadmaps for shaping the continent's development agenda.[1]

But in spite of all these frameworks, Africa's development process has remained muted since independence. Wedged between limited progress and being persistently trapped in a primary commodity export cycle, the continent's development cooperation issues have been informed by two competing trends: *development for Africa* and *development by Africa*.

Mainly because of internal and external factors, development cooperation in the African context has been underpinned by the broader debate on self-reliance and the underlying discussion on how such assistance can improve the material and social status of the continent's poor and economically vulnerable. The construct and paradigm of the development discourse in Africa, as it extends to development cooperation, is underscored by the prevailing assumptions that 'the continent needs to be saved'.[2] But more than that, Africa's development agenda and cooperation need to be assessed in the background of a changing international system that is becoming explicitly fluid and is moving towards greater multilateralism. The latter is the central issue for Africa's resurgence, chiefly in terms of whether the continent can leverage its engagement with new and existing actors in how it articulates a to further its new development agenda. Moreover what this 'new development' narrative will entail, and how will be it framed?

To this end, the paper will focus on how the continent's development vision should be conceptualised in the light of the 'Africa rising' narrative. It argues that the new vision for development will need to be in sync with the broader global processes related to development cooperation effectiveness, such as the Busan outcomes, trilateral engagements and the post 2015 development agenda. Finally, the paper will examine the Africa-India engagement and the prospects for improving the development relationship between the two.

Africa's Experience with Development

As highlighted in the introduction and documented in the scholarship on Africa's development thinking, there has been no shortage of frameworks for advancing the continent's development. These include[3]:

- The "Monrovia Declaration of Commitment of the Heads of State and Government of the OAU on the guidelines and measures for national and collective self-reliance in economic and social development for the establishment of a new international economic order" (1979);
- The Lagos Plan of Action for the Economic Development of Africa, 1980-2000 and the Final Act of Lagos (1980);
- Africa's Priority Programme for Economic Recovery 1986-1990 (APPER) which was later converted into the United Nations Programme of Action for Africa's Economic Recovery and Development (UN–PAAERD) (1986);
- The African Alternative Framework to Structural Adjustment Programme for Socio-Economic Recovery and Transformation (AAF-SAP) (1989);
- The African Charter for Popular Participation for Development (1990);
- The United Nations New Agenda for the Development of Africa in the 1990s (UN-NADAF, 1991);

- The Abuja Treaty adopted by the OAU in 1991, came into force on 12 May 1994; and
- The New Partnership for Development, that came into force in 1994.[4]

Each of these frameworks had the overarching objective of eradicating poverty and the socio-economic upliftment of the continent's growing population. Africa's development experience is based on four main pillars. These are:

- Self-reliance and regional integration promoted in the first phase of the development experience which began in the 1970s;
- The promotion of a 'compact' or 'partnership' with external actors, notably from the North in the 1980s to fulfil the continent's development priorities. This has now been extended to emerging and new actors such as, China, India, Brazil, Turkey, and South Korea;[5]
- The concept of popular participation which gained prominence in the 1990s; and
- The advancement of democracy and respect for human rights after 2000, as central principles that are inseparable from development.[6]

In each of these phases self-reliance, collective ownership and finding a development conducive to Africa's structural conditions became the prevailing catch phrases. But each phase also had its unique structural constraints.

For instance, in the 1980s, during the APPER and UN-PAEERD Phase, the countries that were in dire fiscal straits because of mounting debt crisis and the collapse of trade based revenue were compelled by external agencies like the World Bank to implement Structural Adjustment Programmes (SAPS). The SAPS not only pushed African economies into a parochial framework of trade relations that were primarily hinged on the export of resources, but it also locked African states into a model of development defined by what has become known as the 'Washington Consensus'.[7] The 'Washington Consensus' and later the 'Post Washington Consensus' were prescriptive and rigid policies that allowed little room for manoeuvre.

By the end of 1989, the failure of the SAPs had become apparent. In 1990 the United Nations Economic Commission for African (UNECA) recommended the adoption of the Alternative Framework to Structural Adjustment Programmes for Social and Economic Recovery. Popularly referred to as AF-SAP, the Organisation of African Unity (OAU) adopted the programme and endorsed it as a framework for implementation by member-states.

The efforts to counter SAPs proved ineffective because of the lack of resources for implementing either AF-SAP or APPER. The SAPs and the neoliberal policy of the Washington Consensus in Africa's development trajectory were predicated on getting the fundamentals right in respect of fiscal stability and growth. Unfortunately the focus on growth had broader implications for poverty and inequality that became endemic across most African societies while the role of the state was relegated to that of a bystander.

During the 1990s the development focus shifted towards poverty alleviation. This coincided with the changing geo-strategic architecture that marked the end of the Cold War. The decline of the Soviet Union and as Francis Fukuyama proclaimed, the 'End of History'[8] marked the triumph of the Western development model, marked the beginning of a significant period in Africa's development. The SAPs were transformed into Poverty Reduction Strategy Programmes (PRSPs) in 1999 by the International Monetary Fund (IMF).

According to a United Nations Conference on Trade and Development (UNCTAD) report published in 2002, the PRSPs added two new components to SAPs, namely: "attention to [the] public provision of education and health services [and the inclusion] of safety nets and targeted spending programmes to mitigate [against] adverse consequences for poverty [brought on by stabilisation and structural adjustment policies]".[9]

Civil society groups criticised the PRSPs as being nothing more than a 'sugar-coated structural adjustment"[10] rhetoric. According to the critics even though the PRSPs called for the country ownership of the poverty policy framework and advocated the involvement of civil society organisations in the discussions and consultations on processes, it was the International Financial Institutions (IFIs) that determined how the poverty reduction programmes were to be implemented. The United Kingdom based Bretton Woods Project observed that the idea of country ownership and participation promoted by the IFIs was meant to ensure legitimacy and 'define the content of PRSPs' through Country Assistance Strategies.[11]

By the end of the 1990s the development discourse was beginning to take root in the continental landscape. Led by a group, of people who were seen to be enlightened leaders and included heads of state such as Thabo Mbeki of South Africa, and Olusegun Obanjo of Nigeria, sustained efforts were made to revive the discussion on the African Renaissance and Pan-Africanism as the central features, of the continent's development renewal. This resulted in the adoption of the Constitutive Act of the African Union in 2001, which saw the transformation of the Organisation of the African Unity (OAU) into the Africa Union.[12] Concurrently the continental vision was underpinned by the New Partnership for Africa's Development (NEPAD) framework, which was a pan-African policy agenda for advancing Africa's socio-economic development plans. The NEPAD's priority sectors such as infrastructure, food security, regional integration and climate change were included in Africa's development programmes.

The renewed focus on Africa's development paradigm was predicated on the view that the continent needed to develop a framework that was indigenous and based on the principles of 'development by Africa' and 'African solutions to African problems'.[13]

The Development Cooperation Experience in Africa

The aid agenda in Africa has always been externally driven, guided by the motto of 'development for Africa' rather than 'development of Africa'. As highlighted by Naidu and Herman, there are two sides to the aid picture in Africa: one relating to the donors who remain cautious about increasing or doubling development assistance to African states, because of the deemed misuse of funds; while the other is that of recipient African governments who have voiced their frustrations about the shifting goal posts in aid disbursements.[14]

Samir Amin argues that, "aid politics, the choice of beneficiaries, the forms of intervention, [and] their immediate apparent objectives are inseparable from geo-political objectives".[15] In this respect, the Cold War had certainly ensured that aid to Africa was disbursed on the basis of ideological leanings and the competing interests of capitalism versus communism.

The demise of the Soviet Union towards the end of 1989 saw Western governments becoming the main donors of development assistance to Africa. This enabled them to play a dominant role in the design and articulation of aid programmes. For instance while recipient countries designed the social development programmes, the donors' parallel packages were administered by agencies such as USAID. Not only did this put a squeeze on financial resources but also led to competition between national governments and donors. Towards the end of the 1990s donors moved from programme support to budgetary support for development programmes. This was done to rationalise aid disbursements and make them more viable and in alignment with national frameworks.

But this did not change the politics behind the aid disbursements. Conditionalities became the overarching pre-requisites for countries qualifying for aid packages. Although some recipients considered development assistance and cooperation as an intrusion, it also led to the rise of a development aid industry on the continent. Yash Tandon describes this proliferation of non-governmental organisations (NGOs) as part of the strategy to "recolonise Africa from the grassroots".[16] Furthermore the aid industry became a major employer in Africa's non-profit sector.

On the other hand some commentators like Patrick Bond and Khadija Sharife have highlighted the fallacy that aid for development is nothing more than "diverting aid back" to donor countries. According to them this can take the form of the illicit transfer of capital flows, tax avoidance by companies from donor countries or the stashing of money in off-shore bank accounts, and the insistence that consultants from donor countries be in charge of projects and the procurement of goods and services from donor countries – which is commonly referred to as tied aid.[17]

However development cooperation was also responsible for the weaknesses, capacity constraints, and inertia in Africa's public sector bureaucracy. Damisa Moyo[18] in an opinion piece published in the *Wall Street Journal*, in March 2009, noted that "aid to Africa has made the poor poorer and growth slower".[19]

Clearly, then to ensure that development is sustainable, Africa has to learn from its past experiences with development cooperation.

Challenges to Africa's Development and Development Cooperation Agendas

Africa's experience of development, and development cooperation more specifically, has been mixed. This is partly because they have not been able to either reduce poverty or make any meaningful interventions in the socio-economic development of African countries. In most circumstances – and based on this author's own analysis of the continent's development engagements – despite the various attempts made towards forging frameworks of development, such initiatives have not been institutionalised; or transitioned from the vision to reality. And herein lies the difficulty with Africa's development model.

The more fundamental challenge to Africa's development is that it is often built around a personality, who is often seen as the champion of a particular development vision. Kwame Nkrumah's policy of Pan Africanism and Julius Nyerere's Ujamaa[20] have had little traction after these visionaries passed on. This is not to suggest that the political and economic thoughts and beliefs of these leaders have not made any substantial contribution to the African discourse on development. The challenge, however, is that the values and principles that underpinned such paradigms have often become the subtext for philosophical contestation rather than pragmatic policy implementation.

The second issue is that African development frameworks have always co-existed with external initiatives. This has prevented continental initiatives from achieving their objectives. More often than not, external frameworks were promoted at the expense of African plans of intervention. This, of course, led to the weak operationalisation of home-grown initiatives, with donors playing primary roles instead of being facilitators, and the absence of responsibility, ownership, and disbursement of resources by African governments.[21]

A third challenge in Africa's development context has been the changing global economic architecture and the 'African rising' narrative, which has created a new development aid architecture in the continent. As some African countries graduated to middle-income status because of better growth figures, the debate about whether such economies should qualify for development assistance also intensified. Essentially the issue was whether they should finance their own poverty and social development programmes. The debate was in part fuelled by the 2008 financial crisis when most donor countries suffered from serious resource constraints, "forcing them to re-assess the size of aid budgets."[22] The difficulty with such a reorientation of the development policy of Africa's main partners was that the move into middle income status was not always predictable, especially when countries could easily regress into low income economies, and thereby be unable to allocate resources for programmes that were previously financed by donor assistance. In addition, there was an implicit assumption on the part of the donors that the GDP per capita which informed the middle income status, meant that the proportion of people living in poverty in such countries was lower than that in the low income countries. In fact the GDP numbers calculated following the rise in commodity prices distorted the poverty picture in most African countries.

Fourth, African economies continued to be structurally too weak to become globally competitive and take advantage of opportunities despite the record growth rates during the post 1999 commodity boom cycle. The inherent challenge for most resource rich African economies was that the growth was starting from a low base. Therefore when the commodity boom began to taper off, national development programmes had to be restructured as revenues started to decline and national budgets were adversely affected. As a consequence national development plans had to be reviewed, especially in respect of social spending.

Finally, linked to the structural economic transformation of the African state are the immediate concerns regarding the linkages between development and industrialisation. As trade is becoming a factor in the development discourse, in Africa, the course of the continent's industrial path remains an ongoing subject of debate. Regional integration for increasing intra-African trade has underpinned the continent's industrial strategy and has become a key driver for the continent's Agenda 2063 (discussed later). But the difficulty with Africa's industrial development is its transformation from a resource based economy to a value added production site that will be competitive in the global value chain. For most African economies the scales of production are still underscored by a low economic base that is accentuated because they are primarily the producers of resources and consumers of value added goods.

So how long will it take for African countries to achieve developmental industrialisation, and will the new concept of aid for trade enable African countries to adapt to the new global trading environment? At the fifth Global Review of Aid for Trade held from June 30 – July 2, 2015 in Geneva, it became apparent that trade facilitation has become the new focus area for Africa's multilateral engagements. While it is too soon to determine its implications for Africa's global competitiveness, it does appear that the trade for development agenda is replacing the old global architecture of aid for development. But this new development orientation that is focused on the opening up of markets, raises questions about Africa's ability to do so in view of its structural constraints and the impending limitations of preferential market access frameworks such as the Economic Partnership Agreements. The critical point in this regard is whether duty and quota free access granted by emerging economies like Brazil, China and India will afford African economies the requisite resources to become globally competitive.

Agenda 2063 and the 'Africa Rising' Narrative

In 2013 the African Union celebrated the 50th anniversary of the formation of the OAU. To commemorate this historic occasion the heads of states of the AU adopted the 50th Anniversary Solemn Declaration, which mapped out eight priority areas for the next 50 years. These were:

- African Identity and Renaissance;
- Continuing the struggle against colonialism and the right to self-determination;
- The Integration Agenda;
- Agenda for Economic and Social Development;
- Peace and Security;
- Democratic Governance;
- Determining Africa's Destiny; and
- Africa's place in the world.

The sub-text of what came to be termed the Agenda 2063, was the renewed Pan-African focus. It was defined as a:

> ...strategic framework for the socio-economic transformation of the continent over the next 50 years. It builds on, and seeks to accelerate the implementation of past and existing continental initiatives developed at national, regional and continental levels to ensure growth and sustainable development.[23]

Agenda 2063 appears to have been modelled on the lines of the Millennium Development Goals (MDGs). It has seven broad goals with corresponding targets based on the notion of the 'Africa We Want'.[24] The seven goals are:

- A prosperous Africa based on inclusive growth and sustainable development;

- An integrated continent, politically united based on ideals of Pan Africanism;
- An Africa of good governance, respect for human rights, justice and the rule of law;
- A peaceful and secure Africa;
- An Africa with a strong cultural identity, values, and ethics;
- An Africa whose development is people driven, especially relying on the potential offered by its women and youth; and
- Africa as a strong resilient and influential global player and partner.

The seven goals converge with the eight priority areas of the Solemn declaration. But perhaps what makes Agenda 2063 intriguing is that it also coincides with the 'Africa rising' narrative. This view is shaped by data that suggests that the continent is becoming, or has already become, the next frontier for growth and profit making. In 2014 the consulting company McKinsey issued a report[25] in which it highlighted the following:

- Africa today has a combined GDP of USD 2 trillion;
- Over the next 10 to 12 years, Africa is expected to overtake the Middle East to become the second-fastest growing market globally. More than half of Africa's 55 countries are expected to grow faster than 5% annually till 2025;
- By 2025, Africa's GDP will have more than doubled to about USD 5.3 trillion and its consumer spend is expected to be three times of India's present spend; and
- With its working age population expected to reach 845 million, 23 million more than India's in 2013, businesses generating jobs can expect to be welcomed with open arms.

In addition, the report noted that eight African countries will account for about 70 per cent of Africa's total GDP growth from 2013-2025. These are Algeria, Angola, Nigeria, South Africa, Egypt, Libya, Morocco and Ethiopia. The report goes on to say that 30 cities across Africa will witness consumption growth of more than $2 billion over the next five years; and six of these including Johannesburg and Lagos, are expected to achieve consumption growth of more than $10 billion.

The report bases its analysis on the six drivers of the African growth story, namely:

- The African green revolution;
- Macro and micro political stability;
- The commodity boom;
- Ongoing economic reforms;
- Demographic shifts (positive population growth); and
- Access to international capital/finance.

Both the Agenda 2063 and the 'African Rising' narrative suggest that this millennium belongs to Africa's development path. It also reflects a symbiotic relationship between the aspirations and outcomes entrenched in each platform. But both narratives are also informed by the prevailing view that Africa's developmental challenges can be resolved and overcome through market led approaches that are underpinned by regional, continental and global engagements i.e. opening up the markets for both competitive and comparative advantage. Is this an accurate reflection of Africa's development trajectory over the next fifty years as claimed by Agenda 2063 and the continental growth trajectory? Or is it an overly ambitious plan? This question will be examined in the sections that follow.

Getting the Development-Governance Nexus Right in Africa

At the heart of Agenda 2063 is the notion that a paradigm shift will be needed to achieve the goals set out in the vision and action plan. This is a significant issue because a paradigm shift requires a change of mind-set about development is construed, not only in terms of market fundamentals but also in terms of state governance. It is actually about the balance between development and governance; and herein lies Africa's dilemma.

The challenge for Africa's socio-economic development lies in the very nature of the state and its agenda for both political and economic transformation. This is because the state has become the instrument through which economic wealth and political power is acquired by elite political and economic networks. Africa's cycle of development is trapped in a vicious cycle that is characterised by:

- Poor economic diversification;

- Lack of industrialisation;
- Weak physical and social infrastructure;
- Weak human development capacity;
- Dominant political leadership;
- Poor balance of payments; and
- Currency fluctuations.

Agenda 2063 does little to address the structural transformation of the state especially in terms of a new paradigm that would be necessary to guard against transgressions that include intra-state conflicts caused by ethnic tensions and power struggles that lead to coups and other forms of instability.

The challenge of bringing about such a paradigm transformation also coincides with the broader issue of whether the continent's existing economic architecture has been beneficial and successful. The continent's track record in this regard remains mixed. Agenda 2063 in the economic sense needs to be contextualised around the ways in which Africa can restructure its economic policy space to improve its productive capacities in trade, industrialisation and development. A cross border and trade facilitation mechanism implies that Africa must become competitive in intra-continental trade before entering markets outside the continent. This would require means of domesticating and aligning Agenda 2063 with national and regional development plans. It also entails policymaking that will be geared towards long-term programmes rather than setting ambitious short-term targets.

The difficulty of trying to posit a timeframe on Africa's development agenda is that, if the sequencing is not achieved in the first 15 years of the life span of the 50 year period then achieving the overall goal of the 'Africa We Want' will remain just an aspiration. Perhaps it would be rewarding for the MDG inspired Agenda 2063 to identify not just one champion but a group of champions from across the spectrum of government, business, and civil society, who can realise and institutionalise the objectives of programme at the domestic and regional levels. One of the immediate concerns for Agenda 2063 is the issue of domestic resource mobilisation, which will make Africa financially independent.

As discussions around Agenda 2063 continue to expand, it may be useful to make some recommendations for the consideration of the India-Africa development partnership. This will be the focus of the analysis in the next section.

Towards a Sustainable India-Africa Engagement

In 2011, South Korea hosted the 4th High Level Forum on Aid Effectiveness. One of the key takeaways from the forum, which was known as the Busan Partnership for Effective Development Cooperation, was enhancing public-private partnerships, improving aid for trade mechanisms; and strengthening the role of the private sector in the design and implementation of development policies and the delivery of development cooperation.[26] It is in this context that India can provide much needed support for furthering Africa's development.

The McKinsey report highlights four areas wherein New Delhi and India's private sector can play a critical role to further Agenda 2063 and Africa's broader development programme. These are:

- Promoting low cost innovation that targets a rapidly growing consumer market that can led to efficient distribution in a fragmented market and assist Indian companies to competitively develop Africa's consumer goods sector;
- Training people at scale and formulating innovative delivery models that can allow India to boost Africa's IT services sector and create jobs more broadly;
- Sharing India's expertise in manufacturing and robust distribution networks in agrochemicals, fertilisers, farm equipment, and so forth which can allow Indian companies to support the aspirations of African agriculture; and
- Supporting an entrepreneurial mindset, and engineering talent that has a proven track record in the Indian market can help Indian companies participate in building Africa's infrastructure sector.[27]

Much of this was deliberated and improved upon during the India-Africa Forum Summits of 2008, 2011, and 2015. It can be focused again in the next Summit to align it better with Agenda 2063. Africa needs to develop a coherent strategy along with India and other partners that will be critical to the continent's development agenda. It is for Africa to determine which of its Agenda 2063 goals would be compatible with external partners and how this engagement should be pursued. This needs to be based on the new global agenda for development as per the new working framework of the Sustainable Development Goals while taking into consideration the impact of climate change on development programmes.

Perhaps critical to the Africa-India partnership is the contextualization of the African Continental Free Trade Agreement (AfCFTA). The agreement of the AfCFTA entered into force in May 2019 and remains a strategic economic programme that advances inter and intra continental trade as well as deepen the integration project under Agenda 2063 and the 'African We Want'.

Since its inception, 46 African states have deposited their instruments of ratification to date (February 2023) and the Secretariat which is hosted in Accra, by Ghana has been increasing its operationalization of the key instruments and protocols informing the Agreement. These include:

- The Rules of Origin;
- The Tariff concessions;
- The online mechanism on monitoring;
- The Pan-African payment and settlement system; and
- The African Trade Observatory.

Apart from developing a cohesive African trade regime. The AfCFTA offers India an opportunity in preparation of the pending 4th India-Africa Forum Summit to deepen trade ties. Trade is seen as a significant driver in Africa's development trajectory where India can play a strategic role.

Two way trade is yet to reach that affirming level of USD100 billion that was noted in the 2011 IAFS. According to the Indian External Affairs Minister bilateral trade between the two actors had "reached USD 89 billion in 2021-2022, compared to USD 56 billion in the previous year."[28] What is important is to gauge the quality and dimensions of the trade in respect of India's footprint in agro-processing, the pharmaceutical sector, food security, and opening up vital markets aligned to technological innovation and access to competitive goods and services. What is clear is that trade and investments remain a key driver for both India's state authorities and private sector as noted by the Indian Minister of Commerce and Industry, Piyush Goyal, in his comments to the 17th CII Partnership in July 2022: "It's time we also looked at further deepening and strengthening the trade partnership and possibly look at giving greater trading access to both the African continent and to India so that we can expand this trade faster."[29] At the same time the minister also outlined that the following four pillars will be critical in advancing the trade dynamic with Africa, namely: people, business, trade and government.[30] The Minister's comments at the 17th Conclave Meeting in 2022, is aligned to the objective of more than doubling trade with the Continent to USD 200 billion in the next seven years by 2030.

Trade finance is another area of importance in leveraging and consolidating two-way trade. Also speaking at the 17th CCI Partnership meeting, July 2022, the managing director of India's Exim Bank, Harsha Bangari, noted "that India's merchandise exports have surpassed USD 400 billion mark for the first time in 2021-22 and [the country] recorded a remarkable year-on-year growth of 44 per cent Similarly, Africa's total merchandise exports have increased by over 30 per cent from USD 393 billion in 2020 to USD 514 billion in 2021."[31]

For the same period "Indian export services crossed USD 250 billion [and was estimated] to reach USD 50 billion [in 2022]."[32] The majority of the services in export is in IT and ITES. The nature of exports and imports is clearly seen as a positive sign in terms of Africa leveraging the potential benefits through the African Continental Free Trade Agreement (AfCFTA) in its engagement with India in sectors such as the consultancy services market, strengthening values chains in agriculture and food processing, developing digital infrastructure and enabling infrastructure development in promoting the green economy.

Furthermore, Prime Minister Modi's, 10 point principle summarised below provides the context in informing and guiding India's development partnership and expanding the engagement under the AfCFTA as summarised below:[33]

1) Africa will be at the top of our priorities. We will continue to intensify and deepen our engagement with Africa. As we have shown, it will be sustained and regular.
2) Our development partnership will be guided by your priorities. It will be on terms that will be comfortable for you, that will liberate your potential and not constrain your future. We will rely on African talent and skills. We will build as much local capacity and create as

many local opportunities as possible.

3) We will keep our markets open and make it easier and more attractive to trade with India. We will support our industry to invest in Africa.
4) We will harness India's experience with digital revolution to support Africa's development; improve delivery of public services; extend education and health; spread digital literacy; expand financial inclusion; and mainstream the marginalised. This will not just be our partnership to advance the UN Sustainable Development Goals, but also to equip the youth of Africa for their place in the digital age.
5) Africa has 60 per cent of the world's arable land, but produces just 10 per cent of the global output. We will work with you to improve Africa's agriculture.
6) Our partnership will address the challenges of climate change. We will work with Africa to ensure a just international climate order; to preserve our biodiversity; and, adopt clean and efficient energy sources.
7) We will strengthen our cooperation and mutual capabilities in combating terrorism and extremism; keeping our cyberspace safe and secure; and, supporting the UN in advancing and keeping peace.
8) We will work with African nations to keep the oceans open and free for the benefit of all nations. The world needs cooperation and not competition in the eastern shores of Africa and the eastern Indian Ocean. That is why India's vision of Indian Ocean Security is cooperative and inclusive, rooted in security and growth for all in the region.
9) This is especially important: as global engagement in Africa increases, we must all work together to ensure that Africa does not once again turn into a theatre of rival ambitions, but becomes a nursery for the aspirations of Africa's youth.
10) Just as India and Africa fought colonial rule together, we will work together for a just, representative and democratic global order that has a voice and a role for one-third of humanity that lives in Africa and India. India's own quest for reforms in the global institutions is incomplete without an equal place for Africa. That will be a key purpose of our foreign policy.

The above set of principles, reaffirm India as a strategic partner in instrumentalising and empowering Africa's development pathway. What is interesting to extrapolate from the Prime Minister's speech was the implicit emphasis of mutual agency, respect and benefits based on a relationship of recognising that Africa has a critical role to play in determining the trajectory of the engagement based not on a one size fits all approach. But rather one where Africa has an equal ownership and responsibility in shaping the contours of the kind of development outputs it is seeking. This is where the continental free trade agreement enables for trade and development to intersect with the Prime Minister's vision, thereby creating more of an impetus for deepening the development cooperation partnership. The latter is being realized through the adoption of public-private partnerships as the way New Delhi conceptualises the interplay of its business acumen around commercial ventures in areas where it has a comparative advantage, particularly in Small Medium and Micro Enterprise (SMME) and Medium Scale Micro Enterprise (MSME) development. This can be further supported through the historical lens of the ITEC programme (that is still considered as a critical cornerstone of India's development cooperation framework) where knowledge transfer, peer learning, research and development, science and technology exchanges, skills transfer and capacity building form the core principles of India's South-South Cooperation and complements Africa's development agenda.

Conclusion

The impetus to Africa's long-term development can be given only by Africa itself. While looking to strengthen partnerships with new development partners, Africa cannot afford to view these new actors as panaceas for their development trajectory. Instead African governments need to start recognising that even though strategic players like India with their business acumen can assist Africa in its private sector development and industrialisation programmes, this cannot only be responsibility of India's corporates. The African private sector also needs to invest in Africa's development and learn to be global innovators from India's private sector. And this means that Africa needs to move from its traditional role as a recipient of aid or credit for development cooperation to shaping its development engagement with external partners.

This will require Africa to take ownership of its development relationships in a much more pragmatic manner and ensure that such relationships can be leveraged to meet the continent's development needs under Agenda 2063. Agenda 2063 does not mean that it should be business as usual for the African development process. For India the 4th iteration of the IAFS will be key in understanding that the continent's political, economic and social architecture is changing rapidly. In this context the nexus between India's overall Africa policy and its development cooperation framework has to extend beyond a historical and rhetorical perspective. Both sides have to be measure the quantitative and qualitative impact in terms of the 'Africa that should be'.

NOTES

1 For an overview of Africa's development issues and plans, see Anthony Baah, *History of Africa's Development Initiatives*, at http://www.sarpn.org/documents/d0000407/P373_Baah.pdf, (Accessed 30 May 2015). For more on the Abuja Treaty see http://www.dfa.gov.za/foreign/Multilateral/africa/aec.htm and on Agenda 2063 see http://agenda2063.au.int, (Accessed 30 May 2015).

2 Robert. R Farrell, "Can Africa be Saved?", *The Real Truth*, Vol. 13, No. VI, September 2015 (no page numbers) at http://realtruth.org/articles/090605-002-africa.html, (Accessed 9 September 2015).

3 This section is drawn from Emmanuel Edoun, "The African Development Experience" at http://agenda2063.au.int/en/sites/default/files/Emmanuel%20Edoun%20-%20THE%20AFRICAN%20DEVELOPMENT%20EXPERIENCE.%20edited%20version.docx, (Accessed 20 April 2015).

4 NEPAD is a combination of two plans. A troika of African Presidents led by Thabo Mbeki (South Africa) and included Olsegun Obasanjo (Nigeria) and Abdelaziz Bouteflicka (Algeria) advocated the first plan called the Millennium Action Recovery Plan (MAP). MAP was unveiled at the January 2001 World Economic Forum. The second plan called the Omega Plan was championed by Senegalese President Abdoulaye Wade and presented to the Summit of Francophone Africa in January 2001. Eventually both plans were merged to form a third initiative called the New African Initiative (NAI) in May 2001. In May 2004 after consultations and compromises the NAI evolved into NEPAD. For more on NEPAD see http://www.nepad.org (Accessed 15 May 2015). For an analysis of the NAI and AU see H. Melber, "The New African Initiative and the African Union: A Preliminary Assessment and Documentation", *Critical African Issues*, No. 25, 2001, pp.1-36, at http://www.diva-portal.org/smash/get/diva2:248858/FULLTEXT01.pdf, (Accessed 15 June 2015).

5 The African Union has 21-signed partnerships with external actors.

6 These four pillars are drawn from Africa Institute of South Africa, *Africa's Development Thinking since Independence: A Reader*, AISA Press, Pretoria, June 2002, Pretoria, pp. 6-8.

7 The World Bank adopted structural Adjustments Programmes (SAPS) in the 1980s as policies aimed at restructuring economies towards a growth path of recovery. Countries that implemented SAPS, and hence what came to be known as the Washington Consensus, had to follow a set of prescriptive neo-liberal framework of conditionalities that included austerity measures such as monetary devaluation, liberalisation of trade; banning restrictions on imports and exports; cutting public sector expenditure and disbursements; pushing for private investment; increasing foreign direct investment; opening up of national stock markets where relevant; eliminating

the fixation of prices; and tried to limit the role of the state in economic affairs. In short SAPS was the implementing programme of the Washington Consensus. But perhaps what made the Washington Consensus unpopular was its intervention in domestic affairs of African states applying a set of democratic governance conditionalities as a prerequisite to qualify for financial and non-financial resources. See T Mkandawira and C.S.Soludo (eds.), *African Voices on Structural Adjustment*, CODESRIA, Dakar, Africa World Press, July 2002, p.512.; Also see T. Mkandawira, "Social Policy and the Challenges in the Post Adjustment Era", in Eva Paus (ed.), *Getting Development Right: Structural Transformation, Inclusion, and Sustainability in the Post Crisis Era*, Palgrave Macmillan, New York, 2013, pp. 61-82.

8 Francis Fukuyama, "The End of History", *National Interest*, at https://ps321.community.uaf.edu/files/2012/10/Fukuyama-End-of-history-article.pdf, (Accessed 15 April 2015).

9 UNCTAD, *From Adjustment to Poverty Reduction: What is New?*, Geneva, 2002, p.4, at http://unctad.org/en/Docs/pogdsafricad2.en.pdf, (Accessed 15 April 2015).

10 Atieno Ndomo, "PRSP Rhetoric: Sugar-Coated Structural Adjustment Reality", *Participatory Learning and Action*, 51, April 2005 at http://pubs.iied.org/pdfs/G02116.pdf, (Accessed 15 April 2015).

11 The Brettonwoodsproject, *PRSPs: A Continuation of Structural Adjustment*, 5 April 2004, at http://www.brettonwoodsproject.org/2004/04/art-42231/, (Accessed 15 April 2015).

12 African Union, "Transition from the OAU to the AU", at http://www.au2002.gov.za/docs/background/oau_to_au.htm (Accessed 15 April 2015).

13 See E Maloka and Elizabeth le Roux (eds.), *Africa in the new Millennium*, Africa Institute of South Africa, Pretoria, 2001.

14 Sanusha Naidu and Hayley Herman, "Africa's New Development Partners: China and India: Challenging the Status Quo?" in Hakima Abbas and Yves Niyiragira (eds.), *Aid to Africa: Redeemer or Coloniser?*, Pambazuka Press, Nairobi, 2009, pp.143-144.

15 S. Amin, "Aid for Development" in Ibid, p.64.

16 L. Aubrey, *The Politics of Development Cooperation: NGOs, Gender and Partnership in Kenya*, Routledge Studies in Development and Society, New York, 1997, p. 27.

17 P. Bond and Khadija Sharife, "Africa battles Aid and Development Finance" in Hakima Abbas and Yves Niyiragira, n. 14, pp. 42-58.

18 Damisa Moyo is the author of the famous book entitled *Dead Aid: Why Aid is not working and how there can be a better way for Africa*, Farrar, Strauss & Giroux, New York, 2011.

19 Damisa Moyo, "Why Foreign Aid is Hurting Africa", *Wall Street Journal*, 21 March, 2009, at http://www.wsj.com/articles/SB123758895999200083, (Accessed 20 April, 2015).

20 Z. Poe, *Kwame Nkrumah's contribution to Pan Africanism: An Afrocentric Analysis*, Routledge, London and New York, 2003, pp. 1-187, at https://marxistnkrumaistforum.files.wordpress.com/2013/12/kwame-nkrumahs-contribution-to-pan-african-agency-an-afrocentric-analysis-blackatk.pdf, (Accessed 10 April, 2015), and B. Ibhawoh and J.I. Dibua, "Deconstructing Ujamaa: The Legacy of Julius Nyerere in the Quest for Social and Economic Development in Africa", *African Journal of Political Science*, Vol. 8, No. 1, 2003, pp. 59-83.

21 Africa Institute of South Africa, no. 6, p.16.

22 Jonathan Glennie, "The Role of Aid to Middle-Income Countries: A Contribution to evolving EU Development Policy", *ODI Working Paper 331*, United Kingdom, June 2011, p.1, at http://www.odi.org/sites/odi.org.uk/files/odi-assets/publications-opinion-files/7189.pdf, (Accessed 20 April 2015).

23 Kassim M. Khamis, "Presentation on Agenda 2063 to the Press Attaches", 5 December, 2014 at http://agenda2063.au.int/en/sites/default/files/Presentation%20to%20the%20Press%20Attaches%20by%20Mr%20Kassim%20Khamis%20-%2005Dec2014.doc, (Accessed 20 June

2015), p. 1.

24 African Union, "Agenda 2063: The Africa We Want", Draft Document, Addis Ababa, May 2014, at http://www.nepad.org/system/files/Agenda%202063%20%20English.pdf, (Accessed 20 June 2015).

25 McKinsey Asia Centre," Joining Hands to Unlock Africa's Potential: A New Indian Industry-led Approach to Africa", March 2014, p. 14, at https://www.google.com/url?sa=t&rct=j&q=&esrc= s&source=web&cd=1&ved=0CB0QFjAAah UKEwjZu96wtovIAhWuINs KHZnmBVY &url=http %3A%2F%2Fwww.mckinsey.com%2F-%2Fmedia%2FMcKinsey%2 520Offices%2FIndia%2FPDFs%2FJoining_hands_to_unlock_Africas_ potential.ashx&usg=AFQjCNGmREiCvYlGlnjAQgOXNX-tWO3bGQ, (Accessed 15 February 2015).

26 OECD, *Busan Partnership for Effective Development Cooperation*, Fourth high Level Forum on Aid Effectiveness, Busan, South Korea, November 29– December 1, 2011, at http://www.oecd.org/development/effectiveness/49650173.pdf, (Accessed, 20 April 2015), p. 10.

27 McKinsey Asia Centre, n. 25.

28 Outlook. 2022. "Africa Plays Important Role in India's Foreign Policy: EAM Jaishankar". *Outlook* Web Desk. 20 July. Available at https://www.outlookindia.com/national/africa-plays-important-role-in-india-s-foreign-policy-eam-jaishankar-news-210529 (Accessed 15 March 2023).

29 Confederation of India Industry. 2022. "Background Note". *17th CII-EXIM Bank Conclave on India-Africa Growth Partnership: Creating Shared Futures*. New Delhi. Available at: https://ciieximafricaconclave.com/Document/India%20Africa%20Background%20Note%20for%20web.pdf. (Accessed 15 March 2023), p. 10.

30 *Ibid*, p. 10.

31 *Ibid*, p.19

32 *Ibid*, p.35

33 Ministry of External Affairs. 2018. "Prime Minister's address at Parliament of Uganda during his State Visit to Uganda". *Government of India*. Available at: https://mea.gov.in/Speeches-Statements.htm?dtl/30152/Prime+Ministers+address+at+Parliament+of+Uganda+during+his+State+Visit+to+Uganda (Accessed 15 March 2023).

3

India-Africa Development Cooperation

Ruchita Beri

The foundation of India-Africa relations rests on anti-colonial solidarity and shared development goals. The most important pillar of India-Africa relationship is a development partnership that seeks to create mutually beneficial interdependencies.[1] The dominant discourse on India's development cooperation underscores that India's development cooperation is unique and is guided by the South-South Cooperation Framework. The main characteristics of this development cooperation model are that it is sustainable and inclusive, based on India's own developmental experience, demand-driven, with no conditions and for mutual benefit.[2] Through its proactive initiatives for enabling South-South Cooperation, India has strongly advocated and demonstrated its leadership in establishing a distinctly southern development discourse.[3] It pursues development cooperation based on an equal partnership, moving away from a donor-recipient model. The essence of India's development cooperation policy with countries in the Global South, including Africa, is the emphasis on 'equal partnership and co-ownership'.[4]

In the last decade, India's engagement with Africa has increased considerably. One indicator is the growing high-level visits from India to Africa. India had also hosted leaders from African countries at the third India-Africa Forum Summit (IAFS) in 2015, the inaugural summit of the International Solar Alliance, and during the G20 Leadership Summit hosted by India in 2023. At the same time, bilateral trade between India and the African region has grown from $68 billion in 2011-12 to 98 billion in 2022-23.[5] In recent years, a series of shocks, the COVID-19 pandemic, the Russia-Ukraine conflict and the resultant food and energy crisis, inflation and high indebtedness, climate emergencies and humanitarian disasters, have all had an adverse impact on the global economy at large and Africa in particular. The African countries are on the lookout for global cooperation to bring about collective prosperity.[6] India has often reiterated the close partnership with Africa. In the words of India's Prime Minister Narendra Modi, "Under Agenda 2063, India is a reliable and close partner in Africa's journey to become a global powerhouse of the future."[7] The addition of the African Union as a permanent member of the G20 under India's G20 presidency in 2023, is a stellar example of India's support to African countries. This chapter analyses the key features of India's development cooperation with African countries. It argues that India's development cooperation model is unique. It is based on three key features of consultation, capacity-building and collaboration. The chapter goes on to examine India's development cooperation projects with African countries in select sectors.

Genesis and Key Features

India has a long history of development cooperation. The origin of India's development cooperation programme can be traced back to the country's pre-independence. As early as 1927, India was involved in training and capacity-building at the request of friendly countries in Africa and other regions.[8] The main philosophy guiding India's development cooperation policy in the early years was based on Gandhi's philosophy of "growth for all" and Nehru's vision of one world that called for harmony and peaceful socio-economic development of all countries.[9]

From the 1960s to the turn of the century, India's development cooperation focused on capacity building, human resource development, technical cooperation and extension of lines of credit (government-to-government) in socio-economic development projects on request or demand from the partner country. In 2003, the Indian government announced the "India Development Initiative". The Initiative was announced by the Indian Finance Minister Jaswant Singh as part of his 2003-04 budget speech. It focused on promotion of development cooperation based on India's experience.[10] One of proposals of the initiative was that the Government of India discontinue the practice of extending Lines of Credit directly to fellow developing countries including those in Africa. Subsequently, in the same financial year, India launched the India Development and Economic Assistance Scheme (IDEAS) to provide LoC through the Government-supported Export Import Bank (EXIM) of India. In 2012, in a landmark development, India announced the establishment of Development Partnership Administration. This is housed within the Ministry of External Affairs.

The forgoing discussion suggests that there are three main features of India's development partnership with African countries. First, India's development cooperation with Africa is based on consultation, within the framework of South-South Cooperation. It reflects the African countries' demands and priorities – something that has been reiterated by Indian officials several times. In 2018, Prime Minister Narendra Modi in an address to the Ugandan parliament noted that, "our development partnership will be guided by your priorities. It will be on terms that will be comfortable for you, that will liberate your potential and not constrain your future."[11] In 2015, during the 3rd India-Africa Forum Summit (IAFS) also, India underscored that its development cooperation initiatives in Africa are aimed at supporting African developmental objectives. The *India-Africa Framework for Strategic Cooperation* released during the 3rd IAFS refers to India and African countries working together on their shared priorities "as defined in Africa's Agenda 2063 and its First Ten-Year Implementation Plan, as well as the Sustainable Development Goals under the 2030 Agenda for Sustainable Development."[12]

Second, this partnership focuses on capacity building. Capacity building, particularly human resource development, has been the buzzword for the India-Africa development partnership. India has been involved in educating and training African youth for decades. The African countries have also emphasized the importance of human resource development. The African Union's Africa Agenda 2063 plan refers to "developing Africa's human and social capital through an education and skills revolution."[13] Leaders like the late President Nelson Mandela of South Africa had said: "No country can really develop unless its citizens are educated. Any nation that is progressive is led by people who have had the privilege of studying."[14] India launched the Indian Technical Economic Cooperation (ITEC) Programme in 1964. Under this flagship programme, India has trained officials not only from

Africa, but also Asia, East Europe, Latin America and the Caribbean. The main objective of instituting this programme was "for the development of our relations with the other developing countries on the basis of partnership and cooperation for mutual benefit."[15] It also reflects the ancient Indian philosophy of *Vasudhaiva Kutumbakam* (Whole earth is one family) and calls for sharing India's development experience with other countries in the world.[16] The Pan-Africa e-Network Project (PAENP) launched in 2009, now relaunched as e-VidyaBharati and e-AarogyaBharati (e-VBAB), aimed at providing tele-education and tele-medicine access to Africa countries.[17] During the 3rd IAFS in 2015, India offered 50,000 scholarships for African students in India.[18]

The Indian Council of Cultural Relations, an autonomous body under the Ministry of External Affairs is one of the organizations involved in implementing these scholarships. The Africa Scholarship scheme for nationals of 54 African countries is an important instrument for training at undergraduate, postgraduate and higher levels at various Government-funded Indian universities. Several Indian private universities like Symbiosis, Sharda and Manipal University offer opportunity for higher education to African students.[19] Approximately 25,000 African students are studying in 500 public and private-funded Indian universities.[20] One significant recent development in India-Africa cooperation in capacity building is the opening of the first international campus of the Indian Institute of Technology Madras (IITM) in Zanzibar, Tanzania in November 2023.This innovative step will go a long way in enhancing Tanzania's capacity in higher education,[21] India's development cooperation, particularly, capacity building programmes are not limited to government to government engagement. A small number of Civil Society Organizations (CSOs) from India are involved in development activities abroad.[22] These CSOs have helped in strengthening people-to-people relations with African countries. They include organizations like the Barefoot College based in Tilonia, Rajasthan. This unique organization provides training to rural women in solar engineering. These trained engineers are popularly known as "Solar Mamas" The Barefoot College has trained over 3000 Solar Mamas from 96 countries across the world including Africa.[23] Self-Employed Women's Association (SEWA) is another CSO that provides vocational training to women in Asia and Africa.[24] Similarly, Pratham offers an innovative primary school education model in Asia, Africa and Latin America. At present, it is involved in ten African countries.[25] The creation of the Forum for Indian Development Cooperation (FIDC) in 2013 has helped in showcasing Indian CSOs' activities further. The Forum brings together Indian academics, members of CSOs and officials from the Development Partnership Administration on one platform to discuss various facets of India's development partnerships.[26]

Third, the India-Africa development partnership is collaborative. India has collaborated with several countries in various sectors that are of high priority for the host country. One of the main instruments of India's development cooperation with African countries is through the concessional Lines of Credit (LoC). The nodal agency overlooking India's development cooperation including LoCs is the Development Partnership Administration (DPA), under the Ministry of External Affairs (MEA). The LoCs are extended by the Government of India under the Indian Development and Economic Assistance Scheme (IDEAS) through the EXIM (Export Import) Bank of India.[27] It is important to note that Indian LoCs to Africa are demand-driven. The LoC projects are initiated and identified by the African country. Over the years, India pioneered and completed several crucial projects and even set up the first-ever industrial units in several countries. Some examples include the first milk processing plant of Mauritania, the first cement plant in Djibouti and the first sugar factory in Ghana.[28] One of the important aspects of the IDEAS scheme is the involvement of India's public and private sector companies in the execution of the project. The Indian LoCs have two main requirements, an Indian company should execute the project and that 75 per cent of goods and services should be exported from India.[29] Through the LoC projects India is seen as a trusted development partner by African countries. These projects have provided local employment and helped uplift the life of many Africans.[30]

Sectors: India-Africa Development Cooperation

In recent years, the India-Africa development partnership has shaped into a multi-faceted engagement covering diverse sectors. As of March 2022, 204 LoCs amounting to $12.37 billion have been extended by India to 42 countries in Africa in various sectors.[31] These include agriculture, construction/

infrastructure, solar power, rural electrification and health, among others. All of India's development cooperation projects to Africa are based on the principles of South-South cooperation, and are focused on enhancing capacities.

Agriculture

Agriculture plays a very important role in African economies. It accounts for about one-third of the continent's Gross Domestic Product (GDP) and provides employment to 50 per cent of the region's population.[32] More importantly, Africa has 60 per cent of the world's arable land but generates only 10 per cent of global agricultural production. Therefore, there is huge potential in Africa's agriculture. A recent study suggests that there is immense possibility for African countries to augment their agricultural production.[33] One of the drawbacks towards that is that Africa's agricultural production is highly concentrated. Within sub-Saharan Africa for example, three countries – Ethiopia, Tanzania and Nigeria – account for 30 per cent of the agricultural production.[34] To achieve greater productivity, there is a need for higher investments in the sector, particularly for improved seeds, fertilizers, agricultural equipment, infrastructure, food value chains, the agro-processing industry and services, etc.

India's strides in agricultural production can greatly benefit African countries, enhancing South-South collaboration between the two regions. One of the key areas of cooperation between India and the African countries is in the field of exchange of seeds, fertilizers, pesticides and agricultural equipment. India also has expertise in agricultural value-chain development and watershed management. African countries are keen to access these inputs and expertise to enhance of their agriculture sectors.

As Table 1 indicates, India has extended LoCs to several African countries in the field of agriculture. India had supplied agricultural equipment and set up a tractor assembly plant in Benin through a LoC of $ 15 million.[35] In Cote d'Ivoire, Indian companies have completed LoC projects related to vegetable oil extraction, production of fruits and vegetables, chips, cocoa and coffee development, while those of fisheries processing and rice production are ongoing.[36] Similarly, in Mali, it has helped in setting up agro-food processing projects and agro-machinery and tractor assembly plants.

Table 1: India's Lines of Credit to Africa for Agriculture

S.No.	*Country*	*Project Name*	*Cost of Projects (In US $ Million)*
1	Benin	Purchase of Agricultural Equipment	4.25
2	Benin	Setting up of a Tractor Assembly Plant	15
3	Burkina Faso	Acquisition of Tractors, Harvesters	30
4	Burundi	Farm Mechanization	4.22
5	Burundi	Preparation of Detailed Project for an Integrated Food Processing Complex	0.17
6	Cameroon	Maize Farm Plantation and Rice Farm Plantation Projects	37.65
7	Cameroon	Cassava Plantation Projects	42
8	Cote D'Ivoire	Agricultural Projects: Vegetable Oil, Cocoa, Coffee, Fruits	25
9	Cote D'Ivoire	Fisheries Processing Plant; Coconut Fibre Processing Plant and (Mahatma Gandhi IT and Biotech Park)	25
10	Cote D'Ivoire	Rice Production Programme	30
11	Ethiopia	Development of Sugar Industry	426
12	Ghana	Sugar Plant Project	35
13	Kenya	Agriculture Mechanization Project	100
14	Mali	Agriculture and Food Processing Projects	15
15	Mali	Setting up of Agro Machinery and Tractor Assembly Plant	27

Source: EXIM Bank's Operative Lines of Credit.

Construction/Infrastructure

Lack of infrastructure is one of the main economic challenges facing African countries. A large number of African countries lag behind the rest of the world in terms of development of key infrastructure, such as energy, roads and railways. There is a dire need to increase investment in the infrastructure sector in the continent. A recent study by Mckinsey calls for a hike in infrastructure investment as a share of the Gross Domestic Product (GDP), from the current 3.5 per cent to 4.5 per cent to improve the situation in the region.[37] This would imply doubling the annual investment in infrastructure for the period 2015-2025 to $150 billion by 2025.[38] In recent years, African countries have recognized the urgency for infrastructure development and have increased Government spending in this sector. At the continental level, in 2012, the African Union Commission (AUC) in partnership with the African Development Bank (AfDB), the African Union Development Agency – a new partnership for Africa's Development (AUDA-NEPAD) – and the United Nations Economic Commission for Africa (UNECA), launched the

Programme for Infrastructure Development in Africa (PIDA).[39] This is a multi-sector programme focused on improving regional infrastructure and integration. In the last decade since its launch, PIDA and successfully implemented the first priority action plan. However, Africa has a long way to go and partnership with external partners is extremely important. Africa's external partners have extended their support towards infrastructure development. China has emerged as an important funder for some of Africa's large infrastructure projects.[40]

India has understood the African countries' desire to bridge the infrastructure deficit. It has been involved in infrastructure projects including railways and connectivity projects, water supply mechanisms, construction of prominent government buildings, solar energy and rural electrification. The India-Africa development partnership is includes several infrastructure projects, given their vital role in regional growth, developmental progress and capacity building. Some of the landmark infrastructure projects by India in Africa include the presidential palace constructed in Ghana, the parliament building of Gambia, the Kosti Power project in Sudan which provides one-third of the country's power, and the Nyaborongo Power Project in Rwanda, which provides one-fourth of the country's power.[41] India has also constructed the Upper Ruvu Water Treatment Plant in Tanzania, which provides clean drinking water to over two million people in the Dar-es Salaam area.[42]

As seen in Table 2, several projects under the domain of construction and infrastructure have been developed by India through LoCs, with each project ranging between US$ 15 and 161 million. Some of them include railways' rehabilitation in Angola, construction of parliament buildings and ministerial buildings in Burundi, the national assembly building complex in Gambia at a cost of US$ 26.65 million, and a new water supply system in Malawi. Multiple projects are currently under construction in Mauritius. These include the Mauritius Police Academy building, the Forensic Science Laboratory and a National Library Project. In Mozambique, India has extended LoC for construction of 900 houses as well as bore wells with hand pumps and small water systems. It has also supplied railway equipment such as locomotives and passenger coaches through an LoC worth $95 million.

Table 2: India's Lines of Credit to Africa for Construction/Infrastructure

S.No.	Country	Project Name	Cost of Projects (In US $ Million)
1	Angola	Railway Rehabilitation	40
2	Benin	Purchase of Railway Equipment	15
4	Burundi	Parliament Building in Gitega and Ministerial Building	161.36
5	Gambia	National Assembly Building Complex	26.65
6	Ghana	Construction of Presidential Office	60
7	Malawi	New Water Supply System	23.5
9	Mauritius	Mauritius Police Academy	24
10	Mauritius	Forensic Science Laboratory	7
11	Mauritius	National Archives & National Library Project	13
12	Mozambique	900 Houses	47
13	Mozambique	Borewells with Handpumps and Small Water Systems	38
14	Mozambique	Railway Locomotives, Passenger Cars and Wagons	95

Source: EXIM Bank's Operative Lines of Credit.

Solar Power

India is the third-largest consumer of energy in the world. More importantly, it also is the country with the largest energy demand in this decade.[43] Fossil fuels dominate India's power sector but efforts are on to significantly increase the share of renewable sources. The global push for energy transition, and to meet the Sustainable Development Goals (SDGs), India is rapidly moving towards renewable energy production. It is the world's third-largest producer of renewable energy today.[44] It is also in the forefront of the shift towards solar energy. It has spearheaded the International Solar Alliance (ISA) that calls for increasing use of solar energy globally.

For Africa too, clean energy is equally important for achieving SDGs and to minimize the adverse impact of economic growth on the environment. Here, India's solar energy partnership through the ISA is capable of introducing substantial changes in the region's energy landscape. It will also help in increasing energy access to the people in the continent. At present, only 44 per cent of the population of Sub-Saharan Africa has access to electricity.[45]

With this backdrop, India has extended Lines of Credit for projects related to solar energy development in several African countries. Table 3 shows India's involvement in the construction of three solar energy-related projects in the Democratic Republic of Congo (DRC), a solar photo-voltaic module

Table 3: India's Lines of Credit to Africa for Solar Power

S.No.	*Country*	*Project name*	*Cost of projects (in US$ million)*
1	DRC	15 MW Solar Photovoltaic Power Project in Karawa Province	33.29
2	DRC	10 MW Solar Photovoltaic Power Project at Lusambo Province	25.27
3	DRC	10 MW Solar Photovoltaic Power Project in Mbandaka, Province Equator	24.55
4	Mozambique	Solar Photo Voltaic Module Manufacturing Plant	13
5.	Mauritius	8 MW Solar Power Plant at Henrietta	10
6	Emid	Solar Street Lighting Project in Sierra Leone	20

Source: EXIM Bank's Operative Lines of Credit.

manufacturing plant in Mozambique and a solar street lighting project in Sierra Leone. A 15 MW Solar photo-voltaic power project in the Karawa province costing US$ 33.29 million, a 10 MW Solar photo-voltaic power project in Lusambo province costing US$ 25.27 million, and a US$ 24.55 million worth, 10 MW Solar photo-voltaic power project in Mbandaka province, constitute the three projects under construction in the DRC.

Rural Electrification

African countries are grappling with the challenge of low electrification and access to electricity which is greater compared to the rest of the world. Around 600 million people in Africa are without access to electricity and half of them live in Nigeria, Ethiopia, Tanzania, the Democratic Republic of Congo and Uganda.[46] In contrast, India has taken great strides towards universal energy access.

In 2018, the Government announced 100 per cent electrification in villages. India reached the milestone of achieving near universal household electric connectivity in 2019. Over 900 million people have gained access to electricity in the country.[47] Over the years, India launched several initiatives to provide quality, reliable, and affordable electricity to rural regions to facilitate production and development. India's achievements in the electricity sector have given hope to African countries.

Table 4 provides an overview of rural electrification projects being implemented by India in several African countries. India has extended Lines of Credit for rural electrification projects in Burkina Faso at a cost of US$ 25 million; a US$ 22.5 million electrification expansion project in Gambia; rural

Table 4: India's Lines of Credit to Africa for Rural Electrification

S.No.	Country	Project name	Cost of Projects (in US $ million)
1	Burkina Faso	Rural Electrification	25
2	Gambia	Electrification Expansion Project	22.5
3	Ghana	Rural Electrification	27
4	Mali	Distribution Project from Cote D'Ivoire to Mali	30

Source: Exim Bank's Operative Lines of Credit.

electrification projects in Ghana; and has provided US$ 30 million for electricity transmission and distribution projects from Cote d'Ivoire to Mali.

Health

The African continent like the rest of the world, had to confront with the health challenges due to the onset of the COVID-19 pandemic. The African countries are also combating outbreaks of other communicable diseases like the Ebola, HIV/AIDS, Tuberculosis, Malaria, as well as non-communicable diseases like heart disease, cancer and diabetes. The region shoulders 24 per cent of the global disease burden, but has access to only 3 per cent of the global medical personnel and facilities.[48] This imbalance creates an enormous burden on the regional healthcare system. The countries in the region have to strive hard to achieve quality healthcare for all. Here, it is important to note that the 2030 agenda for sustainable development calls for global cooperation in achieving universal access for healthcare.

India-Africa cooperation in healthcare is not new and has been prevalent for decades. Large Indian private hospital chains like Apollo and Fortis have a presence in the Democratic Republic of Congo, Nigeria, and Tanzania. Similarly, well-known Indian eye hospitals are functional in several African countries including Madagascar, Mauritius, Mozambique, Nigeria, Rwanda, Seychelles, Uganda, and Zambia. Indian pharmaceutical companies have also made their presence felt in the continent; Africa is one of the largest export destinations for Indian pharmaceuticals. According to the United Nations Economic Commission for Africa (UNECA), Africa has a health-financing gap of at least $66 billion annually.[49] India has stepped in to extend support to Africa's health sector. During the third India-Africa Forum Summit in New Delhi in October 2015, Prime Minister Narendra Modi offered concessional credit of $10 billion over the next five years and a $10 million India-Africa

Health Fund.[50] Further, during the COVID-19 pandemic, India stood together with African countries to fight against vaccine inequity. It also transferred medicines and vaccines to several African countries to deal with the onslaught of the pandemic in the region.

As Table 5 shows, India has extended lines of credits for healthcare development in Africa. India extended a LoC of $ 71.4 million for upgradation of some military hospitals in Cote d 'Ivoire. This project is currently being implemented. Similarly, India is involved in development of rural health posts in Zambia, construction of medi-clinics in Mauritius and supply of medical equipment in Senegal.

Table 5: India's Lines of Credit to Africa for Health

S.No.	*Country*	*Project Name*	*Cost of Projects (In US$ Million)*
1	Cote D'Ivoire	Upgradation of Military Hospitals	71.4
2	Mauritius	E-Health Project	16
3	Mauritius	Construction of 3 Mediclinics	7
4	EBID	Procurement of Medical Equipment and Rehabilitation of Health Establishment in Benin	10
5	Zambia	Pre-Fabricated Health Posts	68
6	Senegal	Supply of Medical Equipment, Furniture and Accessories to Four Hospitals	5

Source: EXIM Bank's Operative Lines of Credit.

Conclusion

India's development cooperation with Africa is a practical demonstration of its goodwill and solidarity with the developmental goals of countries in the region. It also reflect India's efforts to provide technology that is Affordable, Adaptable and Appropriate (AAA) to the African countries.[51] India's ITEC scheme and other scholarships have augmented knowledge transfer to African countries. The LoC projects have helped African nations to understand and appreciate Indian development cooperation. India's LoC's have enhanced African capacities in key sectors such as Agriculture, Infrastructure-construction, solar energy, rural electrification and health. The African countries have largely applauded India's initiatives and some have stated that India's LoC projects have made an immense contribution to their country.[52] For example, India's LoCs to Mozambique have led to increase in pulses exports from the country.[53] Another important benefit is that India's development cooperation has led to technology transfer to African countries. African countries also acknowledge that India's development partnership approach does not impose any priorities and respects the African objectives.[54]

However, some challenges remain. There has been criticism within India regarding the implementation process of the LoCs. It was reported that only a handful of Indian companies were awarded these projects in Africa and other regions. As LoCs are perceived to be a tool for enhancing an African country's development, a greater transparency in the implementation mechanism is essential.[55] The revised guidelines of the IDEAS scheme have addressed these concerns.[56] An early review of the implementation and monitoring mechanism of Indian LoC projects will be fruitful. At the same time, the Indian government should make efforts that the African students studying in Indian universities have a conducive environment during their stay in the country. A few incidents of attacks on African students have had an adverse impact on India's image.[57] More awareness about the African region at the civil society level will help in improving people to people relations between India and Africa. Further, to understand African objectives and demands there needs to be a greater exchange of views between African governments, Indian Missions in Africa, the African Missions in India, the Africa desks and the Development Partnership Administration (DPA) in the Ministry of External Affairs. Further, a greater interaction between different stakeholders in India – the Ministry of External Affairs, the Ministry of Trade and Industry, the Chambers of Industry, the EXIM Bank and think tanks and other CSOs will help in greater transparency and coordination in the implementation of India's development cooperation with the African countries.

NOTES

1 Ruchita Beri, "India's evolving blueprint for cooperation with Africa" in Sachin Chaturvedi and Anthea Mulakala, Ed., *India's Approach to Development Cooperation*, Routledge, 2016 at https://www.routledge.com/Indias-Approach-to-Development-Cooperation/Chaturvedi-Mulakala/p/book/9780367874179# (Accessed 20 August 2022);
Manish Chand, "Towards a New Delhi Model: India's Development Partnership with Africa", in Pramit Pal Chaudhuri (ed.), *India & Africa: Towards a New Dawn*, Ananta Aspen Centre (AAC), New Delhi, p. 101. (Accessed 20 August 2022).

2 Sachin Chaturvedi *et. al.*, "Indian Development Cooperation: The State of the Debate", Institute for Development Studies, England, 2014 at https://opendocs.ids.ac.uk/opendocs/handle/20.500.12413/4381bate (Accessed 20 August 2022).

3 Sachin Chaturvedi and Anthea Mulakala, *India's Approach to Development Cooperation*, Routledge, 2016, at https://www.routledge.com/Indias-Approach-to-Development-Cooperation/

Chaturvedi-Mulakala/p/book/9780367874179# (Accessed 20 August 2022).

4 Ibid.

5 Government of India, Ministry of External Affairs, "Remarks made by External Affairs Minister, Dr. S. Jaishankar at the Business Community Interaction" July 8, 2023 at https://www.mea.gov.in/Speeches-Statements.htm?dtl/36766 (Accessed 22 July 2023)

6 United Nations Economic Commission of Africa, *Economic Report on Africa 2023: Building Africa's Resilience to Global Economic Shocks,* 17 November 2023 at https://repository.uneca.org/bitstream/handle/10855/49992/b12040071.pdf?sequence=1&isAllowed=y (Accessed 25 November 2023)

7 "PM's remarks at the BRICS-Africa Outreach and BRICS Plus Dialogue" 24 August 2023 at https://www.pmindia.gov.in/en/news_updates/pms-statement-at-the-brics-africa-outreach-and-brics-plus-dialogue/ (Accessed 30 August 2023)

8 "Introduction" in Sachin Chaturvedi and Anthea Mulakala Ed., *India's Approach to Development Cooperation*, Routledge, 2016, at https://www.routledge.com/Indias-Approach-to-Development-Cooperation/Chaturvedi-Mulakala/p/book/9780367874179# (Accessed 20 August 2022).

9 Shyam Saran, "Nehru and the Concept of One World - Idealistic Fantasy or Practical Necessity?", 2014, at https://www.ris.org.in/sites/default/files/Opinions-Comments/Nehru%20and%20the%20Concept%20of%20One%20World%20_Final_.pdf (Accessed 25 March 2023)

10 Sachin Chaturvedi *et. al.*, "Indian Development Cooperation: The State of the Debate", Institute for Development Studies, England, 2014 at https://opendocs.ids.ac.uk/opendocs/handle/20.500.12413/4381bate (Accessed 20 August 2022).

11 "PM's Address at the parliament of Uganda during his state visit to Uganda", 25 July 2018 at https://mea.gov.in/Speeches-Statements.htm?dtl/30152/Prime_Ministers_address_at_Parliament_ of_ Uganda_during_his_State_Visit_to_Uganda (Accessed 29 August 2022).

12 Ministry of External Affairs, Government of India, 'India-Africa Framework for Strategic Cooperation.' India-Africa Forum Summit, 29 October 2015 at https://www.mea.gov.in/Uploads/PublicationDocs/25981_framework.pdf (Accessed 23 January 2023).

13 Agenda 2063 : Our Aspirations for the Africa We Want at https://au.int/agenda2063/aspirations (Accessed 15 December 2022).

14 'Oprah Talks to Nelson Mandela' at https://www.oprah.com/world/oprah-interviews-nelson-mandela/5 (Accessed 21 December 2022).

15 Ministry Of External Affairs, *50 years of ITEC* at https://www.mea.gov.in/Uploads/PublicationDocs/24148_REVISED_50_yrs_of_ITEC_brochure.pdf (Accessed 20 September 2022).

16 Ibid.

17 Ministry of External Affairs, "Pan African e-Network Project (PAENP)", Government of India, at https://mea.gov.in/Portal/ForeignRelation/Pan_African_e_docx_for_xp.pdf (21 March 2023)

18 "Text of PM's statement at the Inaugural Ceremony of the third India-Africa Forum Summit on 29th October 2015", 29 October 2015 at https://www.pmindia.gov.in/en/news_updates/text-of-pms-statement-at-the-inaugural-ceremony-of-the-third-india-africa-forum-summit-on-29th-october-2015/ (Accessed 27 December 2022).

19 "Indian universities race to attract East African students", *India Today* 13 August 2013 at https://www.indiatoday.in/education-today/news/story/indian-universities-race-to-attract-east-african-students-173648-2013-08-12 (25 March 2023)

20 Ibid

21 "IIT Madras's campus in Zanzibar opens with 45 students" *Times of India* 7 November 2023 at https://timesofindia.indiatimes.com/city/chennai/iit-ms-campus-in-zanzibar-opens-with-45-students/articleshow/105025745.cms (Accessed 10 November 2023)

22 Emma Mawdsley and Supriya Roychoudhury, "Civil Society Organisations and Indian Development Assistance" in Sachin Chaturvedi and Anthea Mulakala, Ed. *India's Approach to Development Cooperation* London, Routledge, 2016. pp.79-93

23 The Barefoot College, Tilonia, 'About us" at https://www.barefootcollegetilonia.org/about-us?lightbox=dataItem-l74bl44j (Accessed 24 March 2023)

24 SEWA, "History" at https://www.sewa.org/about-us/history/ (Accessed 24 March 2023); "Ahmedabad: SEWA to tap trade linkages with five African cooperatives" *Indian Express* 8 December 2016 at https://indianexpress.com/article/india/ahmedabad-sewa-to-tap-trade-linkages-with-5-african-cooperatives-4416040/ (Accessed 24 March 2023)

25 Pratham Education Foundation, "About us," Pratham Education Foundation https://www.pratham.org/about/ (Accessed 24 March 2023); Rukmani Banerji and Mamta Murthi, "Here's how we can turn this learning crisis around" at https://blogs.worldbank.org/voices/heres-how-we-can-turn-learning-crisis-around (Accessed 10 December 2023)

26 FIDC, "About us" at https://fidc.ris.org.in/en/about-fidc (Accessed 24 March 2023)

27 Ministry of External Affairs, Government of India "Lines of Credit for Development Project", Government of India at https://mea.gov.in/Lines-of-Credit-for-Development-Projects.htm (Accessed 23 November 2023).

28 Ibid

29 EXIM Bank, *Lines of credit* https://www.eximbankindia.in/lines-of-credit (Accessed 22 March 2023)

30 Ministry of External affairs, Government of India, "Inaugural Address by EAM, Dr. S. Jaishankar at the 18th CII-EXIM Bank Conclave", 14 June 2023 at https://www.mea.gov.in/Speeches-Statements.htm?dtl/36681

31 Exim Bank, *Building a resilient Africa: Enhanced role of India,* Working Paper No. 110, March 2022 at https://www.imcnet.org/storage/content_gallery/Exim%20Bank%20WP%20110_BUILDING%20A%20RESILIENT%20AFRICA_ROLE%20OF%20INDIA.PDF (Accessed 21 March 2023).

32 Landry Signe and Chido Munyati, "How Africa's new Free Trade Area will turbocharge the continent's agriculture industry", 14 March 2023 at https://www.weforum.org/agenda/2023/03/how-africa-s-free-trade-area-will-turbocharge-the-continent-s-agriculture-industry/ (Accessed 21 March 2023).

33 Lutz Goedde, Amandla Ooko-Ombaka and Gillian Pais, "Winning in Africa's agricultural market", 15 February 2019 at https://www.mckinsey.com/industries/agriculture/our-insights/winning-in-africas-agricultural-market (21March 2023)

34 Ibid.

35 Ministry of External Affairs, Government of India, "India-Benin bilateral relations", 2022 at https://mea.gov.in/Portal/ForeignRelation/Final_India_Benin_bilateral_brief_Nov_2022.pdf (21 March 2023)

36 "India - Cote d'Ivoire bilateral Brief 2022" at https://mea.gov.in/Portal/ForeignRelation/Open_Bilatera_Cote_d_ivoire_brief_Nov2022.pdf (Accessed 23 December 2022).

37 Mckinsey, *Solving Africa's Infrastructure paradox,* 6 March 2020 at https://www.mckinsey.com/capabilities/operations/our-insights/solving-africas-infrastructure-paradox (Accessed 18 September 2023)

38 Ibid

39 African Union, Programme for Infrastructure Development for Africa at https://au.int/en/ie/pida

40 Hannah Marais and Jean-Pierre Labuschagne, *If you want to prosper, consider building roads: China's role in African infrastructure and capital projects at* https://www2.deloitte.com/us/en/insights/industry/public-sector/china-investment-africa-infrastructure-development.html

41 "Ministry of External Affairs, Government of India, "Remarks by Minister of State for External Affairs at Development Cooperation Dialogue, Forum for Indian Development Cooperation organized by RIS" 20 March 2021 at https://www.mea.gov.in/Speeches-Statements.htm?dtl/33691/ (Accessed 10 March 2023)

42 Ministry of External Affairs, Government of India, "Lines of Credit for Development Project", Government of India at https://mea.gov.in/Lines-of-Credit-for-Development-Projects.htm (Accessed 23 November 2023).

43 Press Trust of India, "India to see biggest jump in energy demand globally: IEA" at https://economictimes.indiatimes.com/news/india/india-to-see-biggest-jump-in-energy-demand-globally-iea/articleshow/95124144.cms?utm_source=contentofinterest&utm _medium =text &utm_campaign=cppst (Accessed 23 December 2022).

44 Press Information Bureau (PIB), "Renewable Energy in India", 9 September 2022 at https://pib.gov.in/FeaturesDeatils.aspx?NoteId=151141&ModuleId%20=%202 (Accessed 15 December 2022).

45 IEA, *Africa Energy Outlook 2022* at https://www.iea.org/reports/africa-energy-outlook-2022/key-findings (Accessed 23 December 2022).

46 David Lecoque, 'Close to 600 million people are still without access to electricity in sub-Saharan Africa' at https://www.ruralelec.org/rural-electrification (Accessed 30 January 2023).

47 IEA, *India Energy Outlook 2021* at https://iea.blob.core.windows.net/assets/1de6d91e-e23f-4e02-b1fb-51fdd6283b22/India_Energy_Outlook_2021.pdf (Accessed 20 December 2022).

48 Seth Akumani "Addressing Africa's Healthcare Challenges" athttps://www.movement health 2030.com/en/resources/addressing-africas-healthcare-challenges (21 March 2023)

49 United Nations, Economic Commission for Africa, *Healthcare and Economic Growth in Africa*, Addis Ababa, 2019 at https://repository.uneca.org/handle/10855/43118 (Accessed 18 January 2023).

50 "Text of PM's statement at the Inaugural Ceremony of the third India-Africa Forum Summit on 29th October 2015", 29 October 2015 at https://www.pmindia.gov.in/en/news_updates/text-of-pms-statement-at-the-inaugural-ceremony-of-the-third-india-africa-forum-summit-on-29th-october-2015/ (Accessed 27 December 2022).

51 Confederation of Indian Industry, 'Africa" at https://www.cii.in/InternationalRegions.aspx?enc=6Zpu9+0 MgRzmLc1BDCqTC6Hnaop1iVSIOO5XnW3ESJ70EdhVpVHfcan+AKC6 FqKCU uzBTxB5l4p7T8V46lwHOQ== (Accessed 16 January 2023).

52 Gurjit Singh, *The Harambee Factor : India-Africa Economic Partnership,* Macmillan, New Delhi, 2022.

53 ORF, "Need for further improving LOCs with African countries", 24 March 2014 at https://www.orfonline.org/research/need-for-further-improving-locs-with-african-countries (Accessed 22 June 2022)

54 Ibid

55 P. Vaidyanathan Iyer, 'Exim Bank's red flag: Why most Africa deals go to so few firms?' *Indian Express,* 20 October 2015 at https://indianexpress.com/article/india/india-news-india/exim-banks-red-flag-why-most-africa-deals-go-to-so-few-firms/ (Accessed 20 January 2023).

56 Press Information Bureau, Government of India, "Lines of Credit" 23 December 2015 at https://pib.gov.in/newsite/PrintRelease.aspx?relid=133835 (Accessed 20 March 2023); Department of Economic Affair, Ministry of Finance, Government of India, "Guidelines on Concessional Financing (CF) under IDEAS 2022" 31 March 2022 at https://dea.gov.in/sites/default/files/OM%20on%20Guidelienes%20on%20CFS%20under%20IDEAS% 202022%20-%2031%20March%202022.pdf (Accessed 25 March 2023)

57 BBC, "Attacks on Nigerian students shock India" 28 March 2017, *BBC News* at https://www.bbc.com/news/world-asia-india-39415903 (Accessed 25 March 2023)

4

India-Africa Co-operation: Trade and Investment

Aparajita Biswas

India's relations with the African continent date back to many centuries. These relations, built through trade and commerce, have been strengthened through regular interaction between communities and traders especially from the west coast of Gujarat and parts of south India, with Abyssinia (Ethiopia), Somalia, Mombasa, Zanzibar and even as far south as Mozambique. The role that Indian traders played had widespread ramifications. Not only did they introduce new bazaars, but also helped in initiating changes in their daily livelihood.[1]

Over time, European colonial rule in Asia triggered the largest labour migration across the Indian Ocean. Vast populations moved from Asia to East and South Africa, to work as indentured labour in sugar, cotton and tea plantations, besides rail construction projects in British colonies in East and South Africa. The trade and commerce was dictated by an underlying mission to subordinate colonial interests to the will of Imperial authority. Both India and Africa experienced this exploitative arrangement in their respective colonial eras.

Since independence, India had been looking out for a new basis of relations with the African countries, free from colonial nuances. The first official contact between India and African countries started during the Asia-Africa Conference of Bandung, Indonesia in 1955, co-sponsored by India. The Bandung Conference brought Indian and African leaders to one common platform. It was a precursor to an international fora of Afro-Asian solidarity based on the contention that Asians and Africans shared common political and economic objectives that could be better achieved through cooperation. South-South Cooperation has been adopted by the Non-Aligned Movement, which remained the principal module of India's relations with Africa. A new set of dynamism had emerged that facilitated India-Africa relations to move forward.

In the 1960s and 1970s, India set up joint ventures as a supplementary aspect of bilateral trade to promote South-South Cooperation and expand its economic and trading relations with African countries. For example, it was in 1956 the B.K. Birla Group set up the Indo-Ethiopian Textiles Share Company in Ethiopia. By 1960, the unit began production and subsequently supplied half of Ethiopia's textile market.[2]

These joint ventures had a wider impact on the African economies, helping them diversify their production base. It created jobs for the Ethiopian people and India earned considerable goodwill. The Emperor of Ethiopia, Haile Selassie, was so happy that he awarded B.K. Birla the medal of the Meinelik II', the highest Ethiopian award of that time.

Though in the initial years the cotton textile firms served as an impetus for the first successful joint ventures abroad, the Indian private sector companies soon diversified their capital for foreign investment in Africa. They started to invest more in value-added non-traditional products like light engineering, raw materials-intensive industries, chemicals and pharmaceutical products, electrical and service industries, and gradually expanded to the hospitality industries like hotels and restaurants.

In 1964, India set up the Indian Technical and Economic Cooperation (ITEC) and the Special Commonwealth African Assistance Programme for Africa (SCAAP). These cooperation programmes laid the foundation for the political and economic partnership between India and African countries. Over the years, the scope of India's economic engagements with Africa has increased remarkably. A number of economic developments in India and African countries facilitated the growth.

India's Economic Reforms and Growth of India-Africa Trade and Investment

India-Africa relations flourished significantly after India began to liberalise its economy to trade and foreign investment under economic reforms introduced by the then Finance Minister, Dr. Manmohan Singh, under the leadership of the then Prime Minister P.V. Narasimha Rao in 1991. These reforms led to the liberalisation of the economy and generated significant improvement in its growth rate. In the late 2000s, India's economic growth reached 7.5 per cent, as it progressed towards a free market economy. The country became more conscious of its growing need to secure supplies of food and energy, exploited new export markets, and attracted foreign capital and technological knowhow. The issue of energy security was important in India's scheme of things along with food security and the escalating demand for oil and other natural resources. It was imperative for Indian policy makers and Indian companies to explore new avenues to expand operations into various countries.

India has begun to recognize Africa's vital role for its economic development during this time. Since the first decade of 2000, Africa also witnessed economic success. The continent's buoyant economy, improved political governance and 'Africa Rising narratives' began to attract Indian policy makers and the private sectors as well. To boost India's two-way trade, both the government and the private sector through their multiple agencies, introduced a number of programmes and diplomatic initiatives. On the one hand, the Focus Africa Programme, the triennial India-Africa Forum Summits (IAFS), Duty-Free Tariff Preference Schemes, Buyer's Credit under the National Export Insurance Account (NEIA), are key driving programmes of the Government of India.[3]

On the other hand, the Indian private sector is equally activate with its programmes. For instance, the Confederation of Indian Industry (CII) has organized 14th India-Africa Project Partnership Conclaves since 2005 (CII-Exim Bank: 2020). The Federation of Indian Chambers of Commerce and Industry (FICCI) has promoted trade with its flagship programme, 'Namaskar Africa'. Thus, the combined net flows from India to Africa emerging from governmental efforts and private sector investment, 'form another part of [the] sustainable model of cooperation with Africa, which has in turn given a huge incentive to many Indian companies to seek opportunities in Africa'.[4]

Bilateral Trade

Exports

As a direct impact of these developments, trade flows between India and Sub-Saharan Africa have expanded in absolute terms, from almost nothing in early

2000s to about US$ 78 billion in 2014, before settling to about US$ 89.5 billion in the fiscal year that ended on 31 March 2021.[5] As of 2022. India's exports to Africa grew at a rate of 32 per cent annually and accounted for 9.6 per cent in India's total exports. India's imports from Africa grew at a rate of 23 per cent annually and accounted for 7.8 per cent in India's total imports. In fact, the larger ambitions are to take bilateral trade beyond the level of US$ 200 billion by 2030 with a compound annual growth rate of 12 per cent.[6]

India's trade has also benefited from the various schemes of the Government, the decision to offer duty-free access to Indian markets in all Least Developed Countries (LDCs) in the first India-Africa Forum Summit in 2008 is one example. Around 34 African countries are direct beneficiaries of the scheme as this has increased exports of cotton, cocoa, copper ore, and other commodities from LDCs in Africa to India.[7] Moreover, to assist African countries to reduce their debt burden, India has cancelled 'US $24 million worth of debt of seven Heavily Indebted Poor Countries (HIPCs): Ghana, Mozambique, Tanzania, Uganda, Zambia, [and] Guyana'.[8]

This is an important strategy to boost trade. As a result, between 2010 and 2011 and 2019-20, African exports to India have increased by around $5 billion, establishing a new market for African goods. It is observed that "Even though India is far behind in the actual trade value when compared to China, it has quickly sprinted ahead of other big players from advanced economies like US, Germany, France, etc. to become one of the top actors in trade with SSA."[9]

Compared to its imports, India's exports to Africa have shown more diversity in commodity composition. In 2020, South Africa remained the major destination of India's exports to Africa. Other important destinations include Nigeria, Mozambique, Egypt, Tanzania and Kenya. About 20 per cent of exports comprise fuels including non-crude petroleum oil to Mozambique, Togo, Tanzania, Kenya and South Africa; chemicals (18.5 per cent), including pharmaceutical products to Nigeria, Egypt and Kenya; and machines and electrical goods (12.59 per cent) to Nigeria, South Africa and Egypt.[10]

There is a shift in the pattern India's exports too. The market for rice and manufacturing goods ranging from textiles and pharmaceuticals to light machinery and transport vehicles such as trucks and inexpensive cars, has increased considerably. The export items together accounted for 38.8 per cent of India's exports to Africa by 2019-2020. India has around 50 per cent share in the African rice export market. In 2020-21, India's rice exports (Basmati and non-Basmati) rose by a huge 87 per cent to 17.72 million tonnes (MT) from 9.49 MT achieved in 2019-20. In terms of value realisation, India's rice exports rose by 38 % to USD 8815 million in 2020-21 from US$ 6397 million reported in 2019-20. In terms of Rupees, India's rice export grew by 44 per cent to Rs 65,298 crore in export potential for India, estimated at over US$3 billion, largely due to the deficit of rice production in these countries, given the poor yields and strong consumption. In 2021, India exported 2,000 tonnes of rice to these countries. Countries such as Senegal and Benin depend completely on Indian rice exports.[11]

Moreover, Africa is a growing market for the automobile industry because of rising incomes and improved infrastructure. Two-wheelers from Bajaj and TVS are vastly favoured by the African youth and have become the main means of mobility for middle class Africans. In this sector, India has expanded its exports at a considerably faster pace than other Asian players such as China and Korea. The big differential among these Asian tigers is that while India has focused on the passenger car market in Africa, China's advantage rests on transport equipment. This tells us about India's comparative advantage and the aspirations of the growing African population. India was the first choice for vehicle imports into South Africa despite the lengthy COVID-19 lockdowns and overall decline in vehicle sales in 2020, according to the latest 2021 auto report.[12]

Pharmaceuticals are a major component of India's trade expansion strategy in Africa particularly with the country's stated objective of diversification of exports in terms of both products as well as destinations. According to Pharmexcil, roughly 20 per cent of India's pharma exports of around US$17 billion go to African countries, making these countries a launch pad in international strategies for a significant number of Indian exporters.[13] Cipla and Ranbaxy are providing low-cost anti-retroviral medicine compared to costly Western drugs, and gradually penetrating the African markets. With the expertise and knowledge in producing generic drugs, the Indian pharmaceutical companies offer credible and affordable healthcare solutions. The poor in Africa have benefited immensely from India's generic and low-cost drugs. In fact, pharmaceuticals are a low-hanging fruit that can be exploited by Indian firms and is strengthening the pharmaceutical manufacturing capacity in Africa. India's expertise in producing generic drugs that sell at one-fourth of their previous prices has been a beneficial component of the trade partnership with Africa. In 2017, two Indian generic pharmaceutical companies, Mylan and Aurobindo, disrupted the market by marketing the generic ARV at $75 per patient a year, which will be supplied in 92 countries, most of them in Africa.[14]

Moreover, the COVID-19 pandemic has propelled the rapid growth of the Indian pharma industry. The Indian vaccine industry developed the COVID vaccine with indigenous technology in collaboration with India's research institutions like the Indian Council of Medical Research (ICMR) and the National Institute of Virology (NIV), within the shortest time on par with developed countries like the United States. India supplied more than 25 million doses of Made-in-India vaccines to 41 countries in Africa, including nearly 1 million doses as grant to 16 countries and more than 16 million doses under the COVAX facility, to 33 countries in Africa.[15]

Imports

India's import pattern is highly lopsided over the years, focusing on certain regions in the continent. Despite the growing rate of trade, the point to consider is that trade between India and Africa is still driven by a few products, which go to limited number of countries. Primary commodities like crude oil, gold, coal and other minerals accounts for 75 per cent of India's main imports from Africa. Energy is moving increasingly to the forefront of India's strategic interests and Nigeria has displaced Saudi Arabia as India's top oil supplier and become its top trading partner in Africa. Gold is India's second-largest import from Africa. While India depended solely on South Africa for its gold imports in 2001, the share of South Africa fell to 22.8 per cent, with Ghana (48.4 per cent) and Tanzania (12.3 per cent) emerging as major new exporters of gold to India. Today, gold accounts for nearly 80 per cent of India's total imports from Ghana.[16]

Bilateral trade with Ghana has also grown from US$ 1.2 billion in 2011-12 to over US$ 4.5 billion in 2018-19, with the West African nation enjoying a positive trade balance. Similarly, India's gold imports amounting to US$ 100.6 million in 2018-19 drove bilateral trade between the Republic of Cote d'Ivoire or Ivory Coast to cross the US$ 1 billion for the first time. Other imports include raw cashew nuts, vegetables, metals and minerals that originate from various African countries such as Benin, Sudan, Zambia, South Africa, Morocco, Guinea and Cote d'Ivoire.[17]

Between 2010 and 2018, Mozambique, Zambia, Senegal and Tanzania have seen significant growth in the value of their exports to India. It may be noted that some of these countries were not even among India's top ten trading partners in the recent past. Mozambique's National Statistics Institute recorded that India took 34.3 per cent of the country's exports last year, at $1.6 billion, replacing South Africa, which was the top export market for Mozambique in 2016. Coal, cashew nuts and beans are among the main products that India buys from Mozambique.[18]

Challenges

In spite of growing trade, there are several challenges. Over the last decade, only ten countries account for nearly 60 per cent of India's total trade with Africa. Of them, India enjoys a positive trade balance with Egypt and Mozambique, while having a deficit with the rest of the countries. In 2019-20, India's trade deficit with Africa stood at US$ 8.7 billion (Exim Bank-CII: 2020). The alarming factor relates to Nigeria, with which India had a trade deficit of US $11,002 – the topmost among African countries. An article in *Scroll* quoted the Indian High Commissioner who cautioned that 'India's energy security is important, of course; but too much focus on oil risks stunting the development of the long-term relationship that should be a priority'.[19] To achieve the goal of US$ 200 billion, it is necessary to diversify trade by diplomatically negotiating with African countries. There is a necessity for more geographical diversification of India-Africa trade flows.

India's Initiative to Facilitate Trade

Several Initiatives have been taken by the Indian government to facilitate trade between India and Africa. For instance, to boost trade through multilateral fora, the EXIM Bank of India has extended Lines of Credit (LOCs) to a number of African regional organisations like COMESA, ECOWAS, SADC, EAC, ECCAS and has been implementing sub-regional and national programmes through the framework of the various RECs.[20]

The LOCs lead to asset creation in Africa and help catalyse confidence in the Indian economic partnership. Besides LOC's, the Exim Bank of India also sanctions Buyer's Credit under the National Export Insurance Account (BC-NEIA) to Africa for the protection of Indian exporters. As on 31 March 2022, under the BC-NEIA programme, India Exim Bank has sanctioned an aggregate amount of US$ 2.0 billion under the BC-NEIA for 21 projects in Africa.[21]

At the policy level, India and Africa have been engaging closely on trade policy, with close coordination and synchronisation between the regions on crucial issues like agricultural subsidy and the protection of food and livelihood of the farmers, at the Doha Round of trade negotiations in the World Trade Organization (WTO). With the aim of enabling trade between both the regions, India and Mauritius signed the landmark Comprehensive Economic Cooperation and Partnership Agreement (CECPA) on 22 February 2021, which covers 310 exports items from India. The CECPA is the first trade agreement signed by India with a country in Africa. It will enable enhancement of export competitiveness and enlarging the existing scope for collaboration, inter-alia, in the fields of Investments, Financial Services, Textiles, Small and Medium Enterprises, Information and Communication Technology, Healthcare, Pharmaceuticals and a number of other sectors between India and Mauritius.[22]

Likewise, special rela-tions still exist with states such as South Africa as both the countries are working together under the BRICS format and the India-Brazil-South Africa Dialogue Forum (IBSA) – both advocate reorganizing the international system. Such alliances have 'created a new dynamic in international relations, drawing together the three most powerful economies of the southern hemisphere in a regional axis for the first time'.[23]

At the policy level, India has been engaging closely with leading African countries, at the Doha Round of trade negotiations in the World Trade Organization (WTO) on crucial issues like agricultural subsidy and the protection of food and livelihood of the farmers. The establishment of the BRICS Bank is significant for African countries. It is positioned as a financial institution that will provide African countries with alternative source of development funding and help them enhance trade and investment with BRICS member countries. India and South Africa are also active in the G20 forum. In 2021, on the issue of post-COVID economic recovery, both the countries has ensured extending the Debt Service Suspension Initiative to the world's poorest countries at the G20 Summit.

Furthermore, India has welcomed the African Continental Free Trade Area (AfCFTA), which came into force in 2018 and has made Africa the world's largest free trade area. The FTA has 1.2 billion consumers and a combined GDP of $3.4 trillion. The agreement is not only good for Africa; concomitantly, it will provide a unified continental market that Indian firms can easily access and tap into – potentially increasing the scope and level of India's engagement with Africa. Indian products which will be benefit from AfCFTA reform, are textiles, apparel, leather, wood and paper, vehicle and transport equipment, electronics and metals. India views this development as yet another opportunity to boost trade and economic ties with Africa.[24]

India's Investment in African Countries

The attractiveness of Africa as India's investment destination has increased in recent years on the back of strong economic growth, an improved business environment and better investment regulations, high rates of return on investment and a rising consumer market. According to the Director of the Confederation of Indian Industry (CII), 'The resilience of the Indian and African economies and the many new emerging sectors driven by digital technologies and the green economy create a new set of opportunities between Africa and India that the businesses of both sides must leverage to the optimum'.[25]

Indian FDI in Africa is a unique combination of both private sector and State-driven investment. It is driven by the search for markets, and is pulled despite an adverse business environment. According to the Ministry of External Affairs, Government of India, India has become the fifth-largest investor in Africa with its cumulative investment at US$ 70 billion between April 2010 and March 2022.[26] It is estimated that the Indian investments in Africa can go up to US$ 150 billion by 2030.

So far, as 2022, Indian investment has been concentrated in a few key sectors which tend to deliver more employment and broader economic spill overs. For example, the manufacturing sector occupies 36 per cent of India's Foreign Direct Investment followed by financial, insurance, real estate and business services 22 per cent, agriculture, hunting, forestry and fishing 14 per cent, transport, storage and communication services 11 per cent, wholesale, retail trade, restaurants and hotels 9 per cent, construction 4 per cent, others 4 per cent.[27]

The bulk of Indian FDI is directed to acquiring existing businesses or to making "brownfield" investments, which readily employ locals and procure supplies locally. Indian companies and financial institutions face the risk of investment problems in implementing projects in African countries, where there are unresolved conflicts, issues of governance, and territorial/ ethnic divisions, but lately, these conventional concerns are being offset by the high rate of returns on investment in many of the countries.

Indian private sector companies have been proactive in Africa over the past several years. They have done so 'through mobilising government, institutional as well as private initiatives, forging stronger public-private partnerships (PPPs) and joint venture initiatives between African and Indian firms'. For instance, the Confederation of Indian Industry (CII) and Exim Bank of India have organized 17th India-Africa Project Partnership Conclaves, later rechristened as India-Africa Growth (IAG), since 2005. The IAG has brought together Indian and African companies, aiming to encourage Indian exporters to access African markets and spread their presence there. These events offer opportunities to policymakers, bureaucrats and captains of business and industry to discuss in person, the pros and cons of establishing businesses and industry and deepen ties.

The increasing participation of African countries in the conclaves and the growing relevance of the platform have together given shape to policy dialogues of the Government of India, Exim Bank and the industry. Thus, the combined net flows from India to Africa emerging from governmental efforts and private sector investment, 'form another part of sustainable model of cooperation with Africa, which has in turn given a huge incentive to many Indian companies to seek opportunities in Africa.'[28]

In the beginning, India's business interest and investments in Africa were largely driven by small and medium enterprises and traders. Gradually, the number of FDI projects are becoming more diversified, covering a variety of sectors such as oil and mining, textiles, ICT and agriculture. These sectors have begun to attract bigger Indian companies like Reliance, Varun Beverages, Bharti Airtel, Essar Group and the Tata Group.

Oil and Mining

ONGC Videsh, the overseas arm of State-owned Oil and Natural Gas Corporation (ONGC) has been the most active multinational company in Africa, operating in the hydrocarbon sector So far, the OVL has invested around $8 billion in Africa and aims to double this investment over the next 3-4 years. Totally, the company has five exploration projects in Africa – one in Libya, two in Nigeria, one in Egypt and one in the Joint Development Zone: Nigeria-Sao Tome Principe. In Libya and Sudan, OVL/ONGC accounts for 99 per cent of Indian investments. Presently, the ONGC Videsh Ltd (OVL) and the Indian Oil Corporation Ltd (IOCL) are in talks with Tullow Oil Plc to jointly acquire around 50 per cent participating interest in the latter's US$ 3.4 billion oil project in Kenya.[29]

In Nigeria, the ONGC has "not only carried out exploration and production successfully in very difficult terrains, but has also been responsive to the needs of local population in terms of development of healthcare facilities and education centres etc." [30] (Biswas: 2020). The OVL has framed a Corporate Social Responsibility Policy for achieving the objectives in all its overseas projects. The company provided scholarships to four Sudanese students for pursuing courses in management and engineering. The company also contributed US$ 2 million for the sponsorship of the South Sudan Special Project to create an amicable business atmosphere in South Sudan so that it can pursue its business plans and strategies in the future. (OVL: 2013). However, it seems that India is all set to close one of its flagship investments in the Greater Nile Oil Project in Sudan. This is because the Sudanese government has not paid for oil it is lifting since 2011. In 2019, ONGC, along with China's CNPC and Malaysia's Petronas, formally notified the Sudanese government of their intention to exit from the oilfield.[31]

In the mining sector, India has established itself with the activities of Coal India Limited (CIL) in Mozambique and South Africa, and Vedanta in Zambia. Vedanta Resources and its copper operations in Zambia illustrate the success of the Indian private sector in Africa, where the company bought a majority shares in Konkola, one of Africa's largest integrated copper producers, in 2004. Those moves have been supported by a gradual expansion of Indian financial institutions across Africa, spearheaded by the operations of three State-owned banks: Bank of Baroda, State Bank of India and Bank of India.

Agriculture

Indian multinationals are also enthusiastic to invest in African agricultural sector. So far, about 80 Indian companies have invested US$ 2.3 billion in buying or leasing huge plantations in Ethiopia, Kenya, Madagascar, Senegal and Mozambique to grow foodgrains and other cash crops for the Indian market. The idea that Africa could become a breadbasket for India, as India's domestic demand outstrips the country's capacity to produce the food it needs, has begun to make this region of Africa important for India's plans about long term food security.[32]

Remarkably, in the agriculture sector, the Government of India is operating at two levels – one, it has undertaken a number of programmes and policies to raise agricultural productivity, to ensure food security to these countries, and the other, the Indian private sector companies are allowed to invest and acquire land for cultivation in African countries. Besides, to promote agribusiness in various African countries, the Government of India is working to launch several programmes in various African countries. Food testing laboratories have already been set up in Nigeria and Zimbabwe in collaboration with the International Crops Research Institute for the Semi-Arid Tropics (ICRISAT). The largest LOC approved by Exim Bank in the African continent at the time of writing is with Ethiopia (US$ 640 million) for its Tindaho Sugar Project.[33] The Exim Bank also extended LOC to $27 million to Senegal for export of equipment, and an irrigation project in 2006. All these LOCs have facilitated Indian investments in African countries.

Indian firms are increasingly attracted by the large tracts of fertile land in African countries, offered at almost throwaway rates, duty-free imports of capital goods and zero duty on farm exports facilities. More than 80 Indian companies have invested around $2.4 billion in buying or leasing huge plantations in Ethiopia, Kenya, Madagascar, Senegal and Mozambique to grow foodgrains and other cash crops for the Indian market. The leading Indian investors in African agriculture include Karuturi Global, one of the world's largest producers of cut roses. In 2011, Karuturi Agro Products acquired 1,00,000 hectares of land in the Jikao and Itang Districts of the Gambela region in Ethiopia and bought farmland in Kenya to grow sugarcane, palm oil, rice and vegetables. In Kenya, Karuturi Global invested a total of US$ 150 million (IDE-JETRO). What Karuturi started a few years ago has opened the floodgates for many Indian corporates.[34]

Several Indian companies have already leased land in Africa and many others are looking at opportunities in commercial agriculture in various African countries. Indian corporate houses like Tata, the B.K. Birla Group, Jaipuria, Shapoorji Pallonji, B.M. Khaitan-owned McLeod Russel India and Ruchi Soya have acquired huge tracts of land on lease in various African countries. Many of these corporate houses have taken the acquisition route for their investments. However, at the same time, Indian investors also faced severe criticism from various quarters because of their investments in land.

Notably, the Government of India is encouraging Indian private sector companies to invest in African land to produce food items like vegetable oil and pulses, the present supply of which is insufficient to meet this country's demand. In 2016, India signed a MoU with the Mozambique government to procure pulses since production in India has kept pace with the growing demand.[35] Under the MoU, both parties have agreed to assured import of 200,000 tons of pigeon peas from Mozambique annually.[36]

Besides agriculture, Indian private sector companies are also investing in textile industries. In early 2007, Raymond signed a MoU with the Ethiopian government to set up a garment facility. It invested around Rs. 130 crore in Ethiopia to set up a textile plant with a capacity of two million jackets, while Best Corporation invested Rs. 30 crores as a first phase investment. KPR Mill Limited is another Indian company, which set up a garment unit in Ethiopia. It has also opened its factory at the Mekelle Industrial Park under collaboration with ITC's Supporting Indian Trade and Investment for Africa (SITA) programme.[37]

KPR has invested Rs. 25 crores for a capacity of 10 million units, which will provide employment to nearly a thousand people. Ethiopia is a favourable destination for Indian investors as it offers ready-to-use sheds, income tax breaks, training subsidies, cheaper labour and a tax-free gateway into the US, Europe and China.[38]

Further, the opportunity of 'vertical complementarities along value chains between Africa and India are growing'. For instance, out of among Africa's top 20 items traded with India, 'clear complementarities exist in the cotton-textile-garment value chain. Western African countries supply raw material (cotton) to India, which supplies intermediate materials (fabrics) to apparel producers in Mauritius, Nigeria, South Africa and other African countries.'[39]

Information and Communications Technology (ICT)

Indian companies have a first-mover advantage within Africa's ICT sector as growth of this sector is expected to triple by 2025, to US$ 80-95 billion. The digital journey undertaken by India has helped African countries to promote digital transformation through setting-up of IT Centres, Science & Technology Parks and Entrepreneurship Development Centres (EDC). Further, multiple successful digital tech-driven companies like Bharti Airtel, Essar, Tata and Wipro have managed to gain a strong foothold in the region. Recently, after the Nigerian government banned Twitter, an Indian micro blogging network start-up – Koo – managed to gain a significant following and an active user base in that nation. These educational opportunities have contributed to the development of African human capacity or her human resource, enabling the continent to rise up to the challenges of development in the 21st century. While the big Indian ICT companies like Bharti Airtel, Essar, Tata and Wipro have a significant presence in Africa, there are sufficient possibilities for mid-sized ICT enterprises to enter the industry, preferably by collaborating with local service providers. Indian software companies Tata Consultancy Services (TCS), Infosys and Wipro have all expanded their operations and delivery centres in Africa. They have also collaborated with local universities and institutes to train Africans for skilled jobs in the ICT sector.

Expansion of the ICT sector has benefited African countries since ICT stimulates growth in industries and facilitates enterprise innovation, efficiency and job creation. Bharti Airtel, which acquired Zain Telecommunications' Africa operations in 2010 and currently has 110 million subscribers in 17 African countries, employs 3,300 people across the continent has an extensive presence in Africa. Airtel Africa employs more than 3,300 people across the continent.[40] Over the last few years, the company has taken up locally relevant projects in Education, Youth development, Health and the Environment under its Corporate Responsibility and Sustainability Programme. Its flagship programme in Africa, "Adopt-a-School", currently reaches 27,000 children in 56 schools in the rural corners of 14 African countries and is hugely popular.[41]

Challenges

The key challenges that the Indian industry faces pertain to the lack of infrastructural development of regional markets in Africa coupled with lack of market information and huge transportation costs which, in turn, raise costs for traders and investors alike. There is also no data available for skilled labour. A paper by the Institute of Security Studies South Africa, reveals that although there is a strong interest within the Indian private sector in boosting trade and investment in Africa, it is not expanding fast enough because of lack of a proactive stance matched by the same level of engagement from African partners.

Apex business organizations in most of the African countries have limited interactions with India. Even the African regional economic communities (RECs), such as the East African Business Council and the Economic Community of West African States (ECOWAS) Business Council, remain in their infancy. According to a CII report, many Indian companies have identified poor regional market integration in Africa as a problem. In particular, poor integration has made it difficult to move products across borders. Thus, India supports 'any integration efforts on the African continent, as they would result in various advantages, especially with regards to trade facilitation and the development and upgrading of value chains.[42]

According to a joint study conducted by the CII and the World Trade Organisation (WTO), India's major concern is the lack of proper financing mechanisms for exports – a view supported by African traders.[43] A majority of African exporters also do not know much about export promotion schemes like the Duty-Free Tariff Preference (DFTP), which has been offered by the Indian Government to 26 Least Developed Countries from Africa. In this regard, the role of the commercial wings of the Indian Embassy in African countries is particularly important, to facilitate trade between two regions as they can provide information regarding several opportunities for market expansion to African exporters. India needs proactive Embassy in African countries.

On the other hand, the robust Chinese economic presence in African countries is a major concern for India, as China is allocating massive funds under its Belt and Road Initiative projects to build infrastructural facilities across Africa. China's government, its Exim Bank and its companies have together lent approximately $143 billion between 2000-2017, much of it for large-scale infrastructure projects, as per reports from the China-Africa Research Institute (CARI) at Johns Hopkins University. As a result, China has not only been able to increase its trade and investment but also influence the political and economic decision making of the African governments.

Conclusion

In sum, over the last few years, India-Africa relations have witnessed a revival, with trade and investments growing and gradually intensifying between the two regions. However, the potential to expand them further is substantial. There is a need for India to work further on equitable distribution to diversify exports in Africa by diplomatically negotiating with African countries. India realizes that Africa is one of the fastest growing consumer markets in the world and is projected to have 1.7 billion consumers by 2030.[44] Thus, several new initiatives have been taken to boost trade and investments with African countries. To increase its goodwill, India has funded many popular projects in Africa. For example, India's cooperation incorporates power projects and dams in Sudan and Rwanda; a sugar factory in Ethiopia and a technology park each in Mozambique and Swaziland. India also provided funds to set up the presidential palace in Ghana, the National Assembly building in Gambia and very recently, the Mahatma Gandhi Conventional Centre in Niger. Through these various programmes, India has contributed to the socio-economic impact in the lives of ordinary people in various parts of Africa. Moreover, Africa formed the Africa Continental Free Trade Area (AfCFTA) in 2018, an outcome of Africa's continued efforts towards economic integration. Hence, at present, it is imperative for India to act proactively and give the AfCFTA priority on its foreign policy map.

NOTES

1 Gregory Robert, *India and East Africa: A History of Race Relations within the British Empire, 1890–1939*, Oxford University Press, Oxford, 1971, p. 8.

2 *Joint Ventures Abroad*, Indian Investment Centre, New Delhi, 1976.

3 "Background Paper: Digital Conclave on India Africa Project Partnership, Partners in Development, Building New Synergies", CII-EXIM Bank, at https://www.ciieximafricaconclave.com/Document/Reports/Background%20Paper%20CII%20Exim%20Bank %20Digital%20Conclave.pdf. (Accessed 10 April 2021)

4 Aparajita Biswas (ed.), *India-Africa Enduring Partnership: Emerging Areas of Cooperation*, Gyan Books, New Delhi, 2013, pp. 14.

5 "India-African trades reached a record US$89.5 bln in FY2020/2021" at https://www.ecofinagency.com/public-management/2107-43753-india-african-trades-reached-a-record-us-89-5-bln-in-fy2020/2021. (Accessed 26 September 2022)

6 *Building a Resilient Africa: Enhanced Role of India*, Exim Bank of India, Mumbai, 2022.

7 "Deepening South-South Collaboration: An Analyses of Africa and India's Trade and Investment," at file:///C:/Users/A%20M%20D/Downloads/Deepening-South-South-Collaboration_%20(1).pdf. (Accessed 19 December 2021)

8 "Indian Transition to a Global Donor" at https://www.realityofaid.org/wp-content/uploads/2013/02/ROA-SSDC-Special-Report6.pdf. (Accessed 18 January 2020)

9 "Are Economic Relations with India Helping Africa? Trade, Investment and Development in the Middle-Income South" at https://www.brookings.edu/wp-content/uploads/2019/03/Are-Economic-Relations-with-India-Helping-Africa.pdf. (Accessed 10 August 2020)

10 Exim Bank of India, no. 5.

11 "India's rice exports rose by over 33% to 11.79 MT in first seven months of current FY, likely to surpass last FY's record over 17MT", Ministry of Commerce and Industry, Press Information Bureau, at https://pib.gov.in/PressReleasePage.aspx?PRID=1782368. (Accessed 8 January 2022)

12 "India's cumulative investments in Africa stand at USD 70 billion: MEA", Economic Times, at https://economictimes.indiatimes.com/news/india/indias-cumulative-investments-in-africa-stand-at-usd-70-billion-mea/articleshow/91796693.cms. (Accessed 5 December 2021).

13 "Looming Chinese threat to Indian Pharma Exports in Africa", Express Pharma, at https://www.expresspharma.in/latest-updates/looming-chinese-threat-to-indian-pharma-exports-in-africa/.(Accessed 10 August 2020)

14 No. 8.

15 "India offers vaccines, medical supplies to support African countries hit by Omicron variant", Hindustan Times, athttps://www.hindustantimes.com/india-news/india-offers-vaccines-medical-supplies-to-support-african-countries-hit-by-omicron-variant-101638204689736.html. (Accessed 30 November 2021)

16 Deepening South-South Collaboration: An Analysis of Africa and India's Trade and Investment https://www.eximbankindia.in/Assets/Dynamic/PDF/Publication-Resources/SpecialPublications/Deepening-South-South-Collaboration_An-Analysis-of-Africa-and-Indias-Trade-and-Investment.pdf. (Accessed 10 October 2020)

17 Ibid

18 Mozambique: Trade with India Swells to €1.7bn; Scope to Grow Further. Club of Mozambique" at https://clubofmozambique.com/news/mozambique-trade-with-india-swells-to-e1-7bn-scope-to-grow-further-diplomat (Accessed 18 July 2021)

19 "Beyond oil: India needs to reimagine its ties with Nigeria" at https://scroll.in/article/764442/beyond-oil-. (Accessed 3 May 2022)

20 Exim Bank of India, no. 5.

21 Ibid

22 No. 10.

23 Ian Taylor, 'India's Rise in Africa', *International Affairs*, 88 (4), 2012, pp. 779–98.

24 "Time is ripe for India to explore trade deal with AfCFTA: Commerce Secretary", Business Standard, at https://www.business-standard.com/article/economy-policy/time-is-ripe-for-india-to-explore-trade-deal-with-afcfta-commerce-secy-122072001324_1.html. (Accessed 23 November 2022)

25 "India-Africa economic engagement must expand to new sectors: CII report", CII, at https://www.cii.in/PressreleasesDetail.aspx?enc=e3/8aHedPZvmMC0LHHkZ1cQvGM8/2r4xD/XNhVbDezs=. (Accessed 9 September 2021)

26 "India's cumulative investments in Africa stand at USD 70 billion: MEA", *Economic Times*, at https://economictimes.indiatimes.com/news/india/indias-cumulative-investments-in-africa-stand-at-usd-70-billion-mea/articleshow/91796693.cms. (Accessed 18 December 2022)

27 Exim Bank of India, no. 5.

28 Aparajita Biswas, no. 4.

29 "State Run oil cos Look to acquire Kenya Project" at https://www.livemint.com/companies/news/ovl-ioc-eye-50-in-kenya-project-11665427798801.html. (Accessed 6 August 2021).

30 Aparajita Biswas, "Evolution of India Africa Forum Summit", in Iwata Takuo (ed.), *New Asian Approaches to Africa*, Vernon Press, USA, 2020, pp. 40.

31 "Non-payment of dues forces ONGC to withdraw from Sudan oil fields", *Business Standard*, at https://www.business-standard.com/article/companies/non-payment-of-dues-forces-ongc-to-withdraw-from-sudan-oil-fields-120091700059_1.html. (Accessed 15 April 2021)

32 Aparajita Biswas, no. 4.

33 "Exim Bank to assist Sugar Industry Rehabilitation in Ethiopia", The Economic Times,at https://economictimes.indiatimes.com/industry/banking/finance/banking/exim-bank-to-assist-sugar-industry-rehabilitation-in-ethiopia/articleshow/4066049.cms?from=mdr. (Accessed 30 July 2020)

34 "Karuturi Global Limited" at https://www.ide.go.jp/English/Data/Africa_file/Company/ethiopia03.html#:~:text=Karuturi%20Global%20Limited%20is%20the,500%20million%20rose%20stems%20annually. (Accessed 6 August 2020)

35 "India inks MoU with Mozambique to import 3.75 lakh tonne pulses", *Economic Times*, at https://economictimes.indiatimes.com/news/economy/foreign-trade/india-inks-mou-with-mozambique-to-import-3-75-lakh-tonne-pulses/articleshow/53522441.cms?from=mdr. (Accessed 27 January 2019)

36 "Memorandum of Understanding between the Government of the Republic of Mozambique and Government of India on Production and Marketing on Pigeon Peas" at https://www.tralac.org/images/Discussions/MoU%20Between%20GOI%20and%20Mozambique%20on%20 Cooperation%20in%20Production%20and%20Marketing. (Accessed 23 July 2021)

37 "Exim Bank's Financing Initiatives and Activities in Africa", EXIM Blogs, at https://www.eximbankindia.in/blog/blogcontent.aspx?BlogID=14&BlogTitle=Exim%20Bank. (Accessed 3 November 2022)

38 "Why Indian Textile Mills find Ethiopia Attractive" at https://www.rediff.com/business/report/why-indian-textile-mills-find-ethiopia-attractive/20190123.htm. (Accessed 4 August 2020)

39 "Deepening South-South Collaboration: An Analyses of Africa and India's Trade and Investment" at https://www.eximbankindia.in/Assets/Dynamic/PDF/Publication-Resources/SpecialPublications/Deepening-South-South-Collaboration_An-Analysis-of-Africa-and-Indias-Trade-and-Investment.pdf. (Accessed 12 January 2023)

40 "Airtel Africa completes 10 years of operations", The Hindu BusinessLine, at https://www.thehindubusinessline.com/info-tech/airtel-africa-completes-10-years-of-operations/article31785376.ece. (Accessed 15 February 2021)

41 "Airtel Annual Report 2015–2016", at https://www.airtel.in/airtel-annual-report-2015-16/download-center.html. (Accessed 23 November 2022)

42 "Deepening Africa-India trade and investment partnership, Addis Ababa, Ethiopia" United Nations Economic Commission for Africa (UNECA), at https://www.uneca.org/sites/default/files/PublicationFiles/africa-india_trade_and_investment_study_fin.pdf. (Accessed 19 August 2020).

43 "India Africa: South South Trade and Investment for Development", WTO, at https://www.wto.org/english/tratop_e/devel_e/a4t_e/global_review13prog_e/india_africa_report.pdf. (Accessed 26 April 2022)

44 UNCTAD, *Economic Development of Africa Report 2023: The Potential of Africa to Capture Technology-Intensive Global Supply Chains*. 2023 at https://unctad.org/system/files/official-document/aldcafrica2023_en.pdf (Accessed 20 September 2023)

5

UN Peacekeeping Operations in Africa: India's Expanding Contributions and Rationales

Yeshi Choedon

According to the UN Charter, the Great Powers were expected to play a major role in maintaining international peace and security through the collective security system. However, this could not materialise because of the Cold War between the Eastern and Western blocs. Instead of standing by helplessly because of the deadlock in the Security Council, the member states at large felt the moral responsibility to do something to deal with conflicts in various parts of the world. They devised an innovative mechanism of peacekeeping operation wherein military personnel were used not for fighting but to maintain peace. Instead of the Great Powers, the small and medium powers became active in managing conflicts through the peacekeeping mechanism.

India played a pioneering role in conceptualising and operationalising this mechanism. India could play a leading role at the initial stage not because of its material power but because of its credentials as a non-aligned country. Despite the significant challenges that India confronted domestically and in its neighbourhood, it made substantive contributions in terms of material and personnel to UN peacekeeping operations. Till now, 2, 50,000 Indians have served in 49 of the 71 UN Peacekeeping missions established around the world since 1948. One hundred seventy-seven of its peacekeepers laid down their lives in these operations. Due to its immense contribution and active engagement over time, some scholars refer to India as the backbone of UN peacekeeping operations.[1] The first peacekeeping operation in Africa was the UN Congo Operation (ONUC) of the 1960s, in which India played the leading role. It was a unique operation and assigned very challenging tasks to the Indian peacekeepers. However, those challenges proved minor compared to the challenges the Indian peacekeepers faced in the post-Cold War era in Africa, wherein the scale and scope of India's participation in UN operations increased dramatically.

As the UN Operation in Congo of 1960–64 was the first operation in Africa, this chapter starts by tracing how India took part in it. Then it discusses India's contribution to the UN peacekeeping operations in Africa in terms of the number of operations in which Indian peacekeepers deployed in the past and current operations. The scale of India's participation in the on-going operations is also highlighted, along with the fatalities Indian peacekeepers suffered in the operations in Africa. As the contribution in quantity does not reflect the full scale of India's participation, this chapter also highlights the quality of Indian involvement in terms of unique characteristics such as professionalism, a humane approach, reliable peacekeepers, and varied contributions. As the State does not engage in activities purely out of altruism, this chapter examines the motivating factors that made India participate in UN peacekeeping operations in Africa. It shows how the rationale of its participation in operations in Africa changed according to the changing contextual situation.

India's Participation in Terms of Quantity

The deadlock among the major powers in the Security Council during the Cold War paralysed the UN Security Council as it could not operationalise the collective security provisions of the UN Charter. This deadlock provided an opportune moment for Middle Powers like India to play significant roles in maintaining international peace and security through a new mechanism of peacekeeping operation. India made a substantial ideational contribution towards the conceptualisation of peacekeeping and its guiding principles. It also gave support in terms of materials and military personnel for the peacekeeping mechanism. India's involvement was acceptable to the warring States because of its non-aligned credentials. It participated in seven of the 13 peacekeeping operations during 1948–87.[2]

The only peacekeeping operation in Africa during the Cold War was the UN Operation in Congo of 1960–64, in which India played a pivotal role. The crisis erupted because Congo was ill prepared for independence, and Belgium was reluctant to relinquish its territorial control. On 30 June 1960, a few days after independence, the new Congolese leaders made an urgent appeal for UN military support to deal with the unauthorised actions of Belgian troops stationed in Congo, who had clashed with the Congolese military, and declaration of secession by the mineral-rich province of Katanga. The UN Security Council authorised the Secretary General "to provide the Government with such military assistance".[3] This authorisation differed in various ways from all other operations in this era. At one level, this Resolution called for traditional peacekeeping in a conflict between Belgium and Congo. It was also expected the UN military force to assist the Congolese government in dealing with the various factions within the country to ensure its territorial integrity. Although the Secretary General could deploy some 3,500 troops in the Congo in less than a week, the situation deteriorated further because by then, Congo had become the hotbed of Cold War politics. Eventually, in February 1961, the Security Council gave the peacekeeping forces the unprecedented mandate to "take immediately all appropriate measures to prevent the occurrence of civil war in the Congo, including arrangements for cease-fires, the halting of all military operations, the prevention of clashes, and the use of force, if necessary, in the last resort."[4]

Initially, India's participation in the UN Operation in Congo (ONUC) was limited to providing logistic support, but after the robust mandate of February 1961, India contributed a significant number of combat troops and played a pivotal role until June 1964. Besides bringing the situation under control, the Indian peacekeepers also provided humanitarian assistance to the local Congolese population through such activities as providing medical treatment to many local people by Indian doctors in UN hospitals in the Congo, building new bridges over a 200-kilometre stretch of highway and so on.[5] The Indian troops had to operate in risky situations under several constraints. India lost 39 soldiers in the Congo operation, the first major loss in a UN operation.[6] Besides troops, India also provided substantial financial aid and humanitarian assistance to the Congolese, despite its domestic economic challenges.

With the end of the Cold War and the collapse of the Soviet Union in the late 1980s, there was greater consensus among the permanent members of the Security Council, which led to the launching of many new peacekeeping operations with multi-dimensional tasks. Unlike the Cold War era, most of the conflicts that required UN intervention in the post-Cold War era have been intra-State conflicts. Internal rivalries have been triggered by struggle over natural resources or challenges posed to the existing regime by various groups that have been labelled as ethnic and religious conflicts for easy mobilisation and justification.[7] The neighbouring countries and major powers are involved in these internal conflicts, which are termed 'internationalised internal conflicts' that result in failed or weak States. In Figure 1 below, the orange-marked section shows the trend of 'internationalised internal conflicts' and the green-marked section shows the intra-State conflicts. The Figure shows the drastic increase in 'internationalised internal conflicts' and intra-State conflicts in the post-Cold War era.

Fig. 1: Armed Conflict by Type from 1946 to 2021

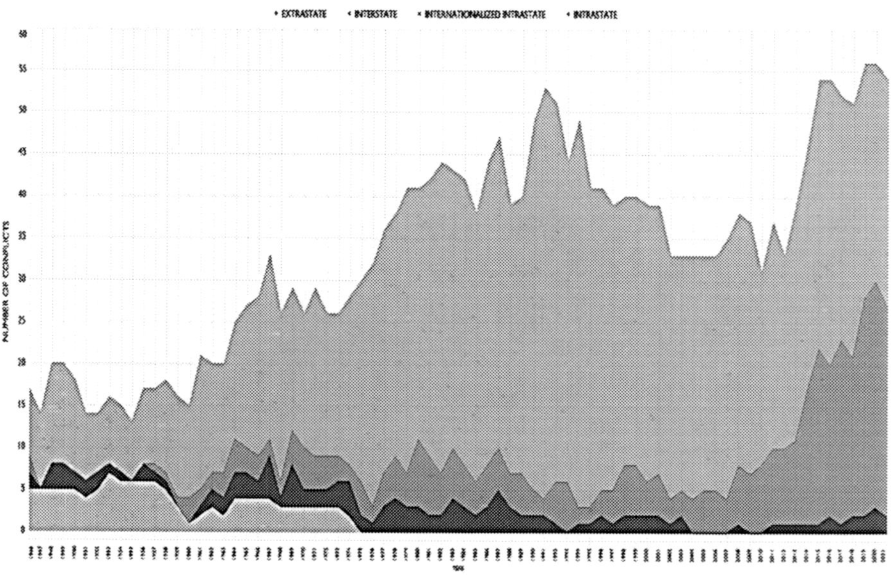

Source: Department of Peace and Conflict Research (n), "Uppsala Conflict Data Program," at https://ucdp.uu.se/downloads/index.html#armedconflict (Accessed on 15 December 2022).

Although intra-State conflicts have broken out in various continents in the post-Cold War era, most have occurred in Africa. As of now, out of 71 peacekeeping operations, 53 have been deployed in Africa, and India participated in 21 of them, as reflected in Table 1. Many of these operations have been authorised to 'use of force' under Chapter VII of the UN Charter.

Table 1: India's Participation in UN Peacekeeping in Africa

S. No.	*UN Operation*	*Country*	*Duration*	*Chapter VII mandate*
1	ONUC	Republic of the Congo	July 1960 – June 1964	Yes
2	UNTAG	Namibia	May 89 to May 91	No
3	ONUMOZ	Mozambique	Dec 92 to December 94	No
4	UNOSOM	Somalia II	Mar 93 to Dec 94	Yes
5	UNOMIL	Liberia	Sep 93 to Sep 97	No
6	UNAMIR	Rwanda	Oct 93 to Mar 96	Yes
7	UNOMSIL	Sierra Leone	Jul 98 to Oct 99	No
8	UNAMSIL	Sierra Leone	Nov 99 to Feb 01	Yes
9	UNAVEM I	Angola	Jan 89 to May 91	No
10	UNAVEM II	Angola	May 91 to Feb 95	No
11	MONUA	Angola	June 1997 to February 1999	No
12	UNAVEM III	Angola	Feb 95 to Jun 97	No
13	MONUC	Republic of the Congo	Nov 1999 to June 2010	No
14	MONUSCO	Republic of the Congo	July 2010 till date	Yes
15	UNMEE	Ethiopia and Eritrea	Mar 2001 to July 2008	No
16	UNMIL	Liberia	September 2003 –till date	Yes
17	ONUB	Burundi	June 2004 to 31 December 2006	Yes
18	UNOCI	Côte d'Ivoire	April 2004 till date	Yes
19	UMMIS	Sudan	March 2005 to 9 July 2011	Yes
20	UNISFA	Abyei	June 2011 till date	Yes
21	UNMISS	South Sudan	May 2014 till date	Yes

Source: United Nations Peacekeeping (n), "Troops and Police Contributors," at https://peacekeeping.un.org/en/troop-and-police-contributors (Accessed on 12 December 2022).

India is currently participating in three of the five on-going peacekeeping operations in Africa and has contributed large numbers of personnel and materials for these operations, with 4771 personnel. India has made a substantial contribution to the operations in terms of the number of peacekeepers in the Democratic Republic of Congo (MONUSCO) and South Sudan (UNMISS), as reflected in Table 2.

Table 2: India's Participation in On-going Operations

Peacekeeping Mission	*Police*	*Experts on the Mission*	*Troops*	*Staff*	*Total*
MONUSCO	138	17	1853	26	2034
UNISFA	0	8	307	10	325
UNMISS	16	17	2327	52	2412
Grand Total	154	42	4487		4771

Source: UN Peacekeeping (n), "Contribution of Uniformed Personnel to UN by country, Mission, and Personnel Type" at https://peacekeeping.un.org/sites/default/files/03_country_and_mission_ 54_september_2022.pdf (Accessed on 12 December 2022).

In terms of fatalities, India has lost around 177 personnel in UN operations, out of which 125 were in Africa, as reflected in Table 3. These numbers indicate the significant Indian contribution to UN peacekeeping operations in Africa.

Table 3: Number of Indian Fatalities in the UN Peacekeeping Operations in Africa (as of 31 October 2022)

Missions	*Country*	*Number of Fatalities*
ONUC	Republic of the Congo	39
MONUC	Democratic Republic of the Congo (DRC)	13
MONUSCO	Democratic Republic of the Congo (DRC)	19
ONUMOZ	Mozambique	02
UNAMSIL	Sierra Leone	05
UNAVEM	Angola	02
UNMEE	Ethiopia and Eritrea	04
UNMIL	Liberia	04
UNMIS	Sudan	04
UNMISS	South Sudan	15
UNOCI	Côte d'Ivoire	01
UNOSOM II	Somalia	15
UNSOS	Somalia	01
UNTAG	Namibia	01
	Total	125

Source: UN Peacekeeping (n), "Fatalities by Nationality and Mission" at https://peacekeeping.un.org/sites/default/files/stats_by_nationality_mission_2_80_october_2022.pdf (Accessed on 14 December 2022).

India's Participation in Terms of Quality

India is known not only for its contribution in terms of numbers, but also for the quality services provided in the field. The quality services of the Indian peacekeepers are attributed to the long tradition of Indian forces, continuous battle experiences, and the nature of tasks they are engaged in, domestically.

Professionalism

One of the significant qualities of the Indian peacekeepers applauded by the civilians in the conflict areas, some of the host States, the UN and other international agencies is their high competence and professionalism. Keeping in view the sensitivity of the Indian government on the authorisation of the 'use of force,' the Indian peacekeepers have been cautious in operations with the mandate under Chapter VII of the UN Charter. India has no objections to the UN's intervention in intra-State conflicts, but it has strong apprehension regarding interference in internal affairs on 'humanitarian grounds.' Despite the concern and opposition voiced by developing countries including India, the UN Security Council has frequently authorised the UN peacekeepers to 'use force' to protect civilians and international personnel, restore stability in the conflict-affected States, and carry out their other mandated tasks. However, India's apprehension of the use of force and intervention on humanitarian grounds did not lead to a confrontation with those who favoured it.[8]

Instead, India contributed troops in the UN peacekeeping operations with such mandates to make a difference in the actual operations in the field. Table 1 shows that out of 21 peacekeeping operations in Africa in which India participated, 11 had been authorised to use force under Chapter VII. Despite the robust mandate in these operations, the Indian peacekeepers have stuck to the position that the final solution to internal conflicts cannot be arrived at by military force but through political negotiation. This principle is ingrained in the psyche of Indian soldiers because of their experience with counter-insurgency operations within India. They have been sensitised to the principles of the minimum use of force and respect for human rights because they are constantly subjected to media spotlight and scrutiny by civil society in India. They believe that a military role in counter-insurgency operations should be limited to 'restoring normalcy' to enable a political solution.[9] Indian military personnel and diplomats thus emphasised the need for finding political solutions to intra-State conflicts while they engaged in peacekeeping operations in Africa. Indian peacekeepers followed the 'hold the fire' approach rather than the 'pull the trigger' policy. Western troops have most commonly followed the latter approach in the operations.[10] The conflict-affected African countries generally welcomed Indian troops because of their professionalism, expertise, and competence.[11]

Humane Approach

Another distinctive characteristic of Indian peacekeepers in Africa has been their humane approach through provision of basic services to conflict-affected people. The Indian contingents to the UN peacekeeping operations invariably include Indian military engineers, medical teams, and logistic experts. These components play crucial roles in carrying out various social and developmental activities in their deployment areas beyond the call of duty. The Indian UN peacekeepers have volunteered medical services, veterinary support and engineering services to the local population, "which has contributed to sustaining the livelihood of conflict-impacted local communities."[12] For instance, Indian veterinarians serving with the UN Mission in South Sudan (UNMISS) assisted cattle herders as they were losing much of their stock to malnutrition and disease. They also provided vocational training, life-saving medical assistance, and significant road repair work.[13] Similarly, the Indian contingent also set up vocational training camps and laboratories for IT training to provide the capacity for alternative livelihoods for the local population in the Democratic Republic of Congo.[14]

This humane ethos among the Indian peacekeepers is due to their experience back home, where they are frequently called upon to provide humanitarian assistance during man-made and natural disasters. This kind of assistance has now become 'part of the normal duty' of Indian soldiers.[15] Further, these soldiers have the tradition of carrying out developmental activities and providing various facilities to the local community while being posted in the border areas of India, which are less developed than the rest of the country. These domestic experiences have stood the Indian peacekeepers in good stead during their tenures in UN missions. Thus, the Indian peacekeepers have handled the 'multifarious challenges of peacekeeping with a judicious combination of military professionalism, human understanding and compassion.[16]

Reliable Peacekeepers

India does not participate in the UN operation at every available opportunity. India did not participate in the UN operations in Mali and Central Africa as these were deployed in the aftermath of the French operations in 2013. Non-participation in these operations might have been because India did not want to deploy its military personnel to clean up the mess left behind after the French operations. Similarly, India did not participate in the hybrid operation in Darfur, nor did it participate in any of the non-UN operations, even though some of them were authorised by the UN Security Council.

When it participates in the UN-commanded peacekeeping operation, India has displayed the unique capacity to sustain large troop commitments over prolonged periods with 'staying power' even in the most challenging situations. Indian peacekeepers have exhibited their risk-taking ability and staying power in several operations in Africa, such as in Somalia, Rwanda and DRC.[17] Despite the challenging security environment in Somalia, for instance, India was one of the few troop-contributing countries (TCCs) that retained its original strength and stayed on until the mission exited in November 1994. Similarly, India was among the few countries that maintained its peacekeeping troops in Rwanda throughout the crisis while many other TCCs withdrew their troops in the face of the deteriorating situation in 1994.[18]

Even when Indian personnel were forced to withdraw, they did so on the basis of certain principles—for instance, the Indian Major General V.K. Jetley, as the UN Force Commander of the UNAMSIL, exposed the involvement of political figures and military commanders of African countries in the diamond trade and smuggling in Sierra Leone. He was dismissed under pressure from African States. India decided to withdraw the entire Indian contingent from Sierra Leone as a mark of protest.[19]

Another notable occasion was when India threatened to withdraw all its troops and 23 transport and attack helicopters from the operations in the DRC in 2008. India made a substantial contribution in terms of military personnel and utility as well as attack helicopters for the operation when most countries were reluctant to send their troops because of the volatile situation. However, the Indian peacekeepers were accused of corruption, sexual exploitation, non-fulfilment of their obligation to protect civilians, and favouring some anti-government rebels. Above all, the DRC government informed the UN that it did not want any more Indian peacekeepers. India threatened to withdraw all its troops and helicopters in the wake of this humiliation, which would have crippled the UN mission.[20] This threat was not due to the lack of staying power but to demand that peacekeeping is kept above petty politics. India is known to be a reliable peacekeeper, having one of the longest and most consistent records of participation in UN peacekeeping operations in Africa.

Varied Contributions and Training

India is one of the troop-contributing countries with the unique ability to deploy standalone capabilities in terms of organisational structure, assets, equipment, and logistics. The Indian contingents do not depend on the UN or other countries for support to carry out their tasks. This standalone capacity has been displayed in Somalia, DRC and Sudan.[21] India's contribution to UN peacekeeping operations in Africa is also remarkable because of its ability to deploy varied personnel, not just military troops. India has the tradition of deploying air force and navy personnel in UN operations. The association of the Indian Air Force with UN missions started with the Congo operation in 1961. Since then, the Indian Air Force has participated in the Somalia, Sierra Leone, DRC, and Sudan operations. In recent years, the Indian Air Force contingent comprising attack and utility helicopters has also played a useful role, for instance, in the UN peacekeeping operation in DRC and Sudan.[22]

The Indian Navy participated for the first time in a UN mission in Somalia. Indian ships and navy personnel were involved in patrol duties off the Somali coast, in humanitarian assistance on shore, and in transporting men and material for the UN.[23] In fact, in some of the operations in Africa, India has demonstrated its capacity to provide an integrated force comprising land and naval forces with requisite air support.[24] Apart from personnel from the three defence forces, India has contributed police personnel who are required to monitor and mentor the local police personnel and assist in developing local police capacity.

India also has a long tradition of deploying women in UN peacekeeping operations. As early as 1960, India sent women to the Armed Forces Medical Services to serve in the UN Peacekeeping Mission in Congo. In the post-Cold War period, apart from women forming a part of medical units, the Indian

Army has also contributed lady military officers and Staff Officers to UN missions. When the UN started deploying the police to deal with law and order issues in conflict-affected countries, India began to contribute women police officers also. Since the adoption of Resolution 1325 in 2000 by the UN Security Council, India has pledged to increase its share of uniformed women peacekeepers for UN missions. Various Indian uniformed women peacekeepers have played an exemplary role in peacekeeping operations. For instance, Major Shobha Nair, commissioned into the Indian Army in 2006, served as a Military Officer in the United Nations Organization Stabilization Mission in the Democratic Republic of the Congo (MONUC). Major Suman Gawani is another example of an Indian woman military officer who served in the UN Mission in South Sudan (UNMISS) from November 2018 to December 2019. She was the focal point of contact for gender issues in the Mission. She encouraged the participation of women in joint military patrols to maintain gender balance. She also visited various sites across South Sudan in an attempt towards gender integration in planning and military activities. India's most creative and innovative deployment was the All-Female Formed Police Unit (FFPU) to the United Nations Mission in Liberia (UNMIL) in 2007. It was the first-ever all-women team in UN peacekeeping history. Despite Liberia being one of the most challenging operational environments, the Indian FFPU continued to serve until the end of the Mission. It was the most distinctive and practical way of sensitising the public about gender issues and promoting gender mainstreaming.[25] The Indian female police unit not only carried out their mandated tasks effectively but also served as a role model as more Liberian women came forward to join the police force.

Due to its high quality and vast experience of serving for decades in UN Peacekeeping Operations, India could establish the Centre for United Nations Peacekeeping (CUNPK) in New Delhi, which trains the peacekeepers of other countries as well. It has taken the lead in hosting specialised training courses for peacekeepers on sexual violence in armed conflict situations. CUNPK commenced the first United Nations Peacekeeping Course for African Partners for three weeks commencing on 25 July 2016, in New Delhi.[26] The latest exercise was a two-week training module of 41 peacekeepers from 19 African countries conducted jointly by Indian and US trainers at the CUNPK in May 2018. India has also contributed a large number of combat and utility helicopters for UN peacekeeping operations in Africa. In 2022 India agreed to deploy a utility helicopter unit to the UN mission in Mali to provide much-needed support to the UN peacekeeping operation. Thus, India made a unique contribution in the UN operations in Africa both quantitatively and in terms of the quality of services and variety of personnel.

Rationale for Participation

Various factors motivated India to participate in UN peacekeeping operations in general and Africa in particular. Initially, India's active engagement with peacekeeping operations was hinged on its commitment to liberal democracy. India's participation in UN peacekeeping operations was projected as an obligation to maintain international peace and preserving international norms and values.

India also protects and promotes its national interests by blending its national and larger interests with its participation in UN peacekeeping operations. During the Cold War era, India's participation in the UN peacekeeping operations in developing countries, specifically in Africa, was characterised as an expression of its solidarity with the developing countries who shared historical experiences of colonial subjugation and freedom struggle. Some of the intra-State conflicts in the post-Cold War era were even viewed as a legacy of the colonial era, and India continued to adopt a committed anti-colonial posture.[27] One of the major driving forces of India's involvement in peacekeeping operations was to express its solidarity with the African countries.

In addition to the expression of solidarity, the economic factor is another motivation for India's engagement with UN peacekeeping in Africa in the globalised era. India is motivated to ensure the unimpeded flow of oil and gas supplies from Africa for its energy security and to gain access to the raw materials required for its rapid industrial development. The Indian peacekeepers served its national interest by generating goodwill among African countries towards India. The goodwill strengthened the economic and trade relationships between India and the African countries.[28]

Another reason for India's participation in UN peacekeeping operations in Africa is to gain experience and exposure for the Indian peacekeepers. They get on-the-job training in diverse military traditions and technologies.[29] India's armed forces also get invaluable exposure to various scenarios and of working in coordination with multinational military forces in Africa.

The much-talked-about rationale for India's participation in UN peacekeeping operations has been its desire to be recognised as a great power. This desire is not of recent origin. Nehru's support for the United Nations was also partly because it provided India with a forum to project its global role and status. He wanted India to attain its rightful place in the international community, which it was entitled to "by virtue of its geography, population and contribution."[30] India's participation in UN peacekeeping operations enabled it to gain visibility and recognition as a responsible power contributing to maintaining international peace and security. India has cited this contribution since the 1990s for bolstering its claim for a permanent seat in the UN Security Council.[31] Its contribution to the UN peacekeeping operations in Africa may constitute a means of cultivating goodwill as there are 53 African States whose support is essential for India's attempt to acquire permanent membership to the UN Security Council. Their support is also crucial for any major positions India takes at the United Nations. The above discussion shows that motivational factors for India for participation in UN peacekeeping operations in Africa have changed according to the changing contextual situation.

Conclusion

India has played a pioneering role in the UN peacekeeping operations since its inception. Its contribution to managing inter-State and intra-State conflicts through UN peacekeeping operations has been substantial. Among all the regions, India has participated in the maximum number of UN peacekeeping operations in Africa. Out of 53 UN peacekeeping operations deployed in Africa, India participated in 21 of them, with many mandated under chapter VII of the UN Charter. Today, India has been contributing 4771 peacekeepers in three on-going operations in Africa. Out of 177 fatalities of Indian peacekeepers, India has lost 125 peacekeepers in the UN operations in Africa. These numbers indicate the substantial Indian contribution to managing the conflict in Africa through its participation in UN peacekeeping operations.

India is also known for providing quality services while participating in UN peacekeeping operations. The various stakeholders have applauded the

Indian peacekeepers for their high competence and professionalism. They have been cautious in operations with the mandate under Chapter VII of the UN Charter. Through their experience of dealing with counter-insurgency operations within India, the Indian peacekeepers are conscious of their view that the final solution to internal conflicts cannot be arrived at by military force but through political negotiation. Therefore, the Indian peacekeepers follow the 'hold the fire' approach rather than the 'pull the trigger' policy even in UN operations. Due to their professionalism, expertise, and competence, the conflict-affected states in Africa generally welcome Indian peacekeepers.

Another distinctive characteristic of Indian peacekeepers in Africa is their humane approach. They provide basic services to the conflict-affected people in Africa, such as medical services, veterinary support to protect their livelihood, engineering services, vocational training, repairing the road, and so on. This humane ethos among the Indian peacekeepers has been inculcated by their domestic experience of assisting the people of less developed border regions of India where the Indian troops are deployed to safeguard the Indian border regions.

Among the troop-contributing countries to the UN operations, India has displayed the unique capacity of making large troop commitments over prolonged periods with 'staying power' even in the most challenging situations, such as Somalia, Rwanda and DRC. Even in instances where Indian personnel were forced to withdraw or threatened to withdraw, they were on the basis of certain principles, as discussed above in the case of Sierra Leone and DRC.

India is one of the few troop-contributing countries with the unique ability to deploy stand-alone capability and varied personnel, not just military troops. India has the tradition of deploying air force, navy and police personnel in UN peacekeeping operations in Africa. India is also one of the few countries that could contribute a large number of combat and utility helicopters to support peacekeeping operations in Africa.

India also has a tradition of deploying women in operations in Africa, starting with women in the Armed Medical Service in Congo operation in the 1960s. In the post-Cold War, apart from women forming a part of Medical Units, the Indian Army has also contributed lady military officers and Staff Officers to UN operations in Africa. India also contributes women police officers to maintain law and order in conflict-affected African countries. India's most creative and innovative deployment was the All-Female Formed Police Unit (FFPU) to the United Nations Mission in Liberia (UNMIL) in 2007. The Indian female police unit not only carried out their mandated tasks effectively but also served as a role model for the African women. Its contribution of the uniformed women peacekeepers in Africa is a part of the effort to implement the UN Security Council Resolution 1325 of 2000, which focuses on the need for gender mainstreaming in UN peacekeeping operations.

Due to its high quality and vast experience of serving for decades in UN Peace Keeping Operations, India could establish a well-known Centre for United Nations Peacekeeping (CUNPK) in New Delhi, which also trains the peacekeepers of other countries as well. It has carried out various special training for the peacekeepers of African countries to contribute to developing peacekeeping capacities among the African countries.

As the state does not engage in activities purely out of altruism, various factors motivated India to participate in UN peacekeeping operations in Africa. The rationale for its participation in UN operations in Africa changed according to the changing contextual situation. Initially, India was motivated by its commitment to liberal internationalism. Its involvement in UN operations was projected as an obligation to maintain international peace and preserve international norms and values. Another rationale for participation in UN operations during the Cold War was to express its solidarity with the developing countries, including African countries, who shared historical experiences of colonial subjugation and freedom struggle. In the globalised era, the economic factor has been the driving force for its participation in UN operations in Africa to ensure energy security, facilitate the opening up of the African market, and enhance trade and investment opportunities for India. Through India's participation in the UN operations in Africa, it could garner the goodwill of African countries towards India.

The other rationales for India's participation in UN peacekeeping operations in Africa seem to be to gain on-the-job training in diverse military traditions and technologies, gain invaluable exposure to various scenarios, and chance to work in coordination with multinational military forces. Another much-talked-about rationale for India's participation in UN peacekeeping operations has been its desire to be recognised as a great power. It seems particularly relevant in the context of its engagement in Africa as there are 53

African states in the United Nations whose support is crucial for its attempt to gain a permanent seat in the UN Security Council. Their support is also essential to gain acceptance of major positions India takes at the United Nations. Thus, the UN peacekeeping mechanism serves as a useful means to expand India's influence in Africa and gain recognition as a responsible power. In the process, it serves India's various national interests.

NOTES

1 Sharon Wiharta, Neil Melvin and Xenia Avezov, *The New Geopolitics of Peace Operations: Mapping the Emerging Landscape*, Stockholm International Peace Research Institute, September 2012, pp. 14–15.
2 Yeshi Choedon, "India and the Current Concerns of UN Peacekeeping: Issues and Prospects", *India Quarterly*, 62(2), April–June 2007, p. 3.
3 UN Document, S/4387, 14 July 1960.
4 UN Security Council Resolution No. 161, 21 February 1961.
5 Satish Nambiar, *For the Honour of India: A History of Indian Peacekeeping*, United Service Institution of India, New Delhi, 2009, pp. 205, 221.
6 F. Parakatil, *India and the United Nations Peace-Keeping Operations*, S. Chand & Co., New Delhi, 1975, p. 124.
7 Paul Collier, "Doing Well Out of War: An Economic Perspective", in Mats Berdal and David M. Malone (Eds.), *Greed and Grievance: Economic Agendas in Civil Wars*, Lynne Rienner, New York, Delhi, 2000, p. 92.
8 Yeshi Choedon, "India's UN Peacekeeping Operations Involvement in Africa: Change in Nature of Participation and Driving Factors," *International Studies*, 51 (1-4), 2017, p. 23.
9 Ibid., pp. 23-24.
10 Kabilan Krishnasamy, "A Case for India's 'Leadership' in United Nations Peacekeeping," *International Studies*, 47 (2-4), 2007, p. 236.
11 Sushant K. Singh, "Peacekeeping in Africa: A Global Strategy," *South African Journal of International Affairs*, 14 (2), 2007, p.77.
12 Asoke Kumar Mukerji, "UN Peacekeeping: India's Contributions", at https://cgivancouver.gov.in/pdf/Final_UN_Peacekeeping_India_Contributions.pdf (Accessed on 12 December 2022).
13 "Explained: India's role in UN Peacekeeping Missions over the years", *The Indian Express*, 28 July 2022 at https://indianexpress.com/article/explained/india-role-un-peacekeeping-missions-over-the-years-explained-8055483/ (Accessed on 11 December 2022).
14 Hardeep Singh Puri, "The UN Security Council Debate on the Democratic Republic of Congo", 18 May 2011 at https://www.pminewyork.org/adminpart/uploadpdf/91782ind1864.pdf (Accessed on 10 December 2022).
15 Satish Nambiar, "India and United Nations Peacekeeping Operations", 2014 at http://mea.gov.in/articles-in-indian-media.htm?dtl/22776/India+and+United+Nations+ Peace keeping+Operations (Accessed on December 2022).
16 Sushant K. Singh, no. 11, pp. 78-79.
17 Satish Nambiar, no. 5, pp. 234-249; 261-269; 286-289.
18 Yeshi Choedon, no. 8, p. 25.

19 Yeshi Choedon, "India and the Current Concerns of UN Peacekeeping: Issues and Prospects", *India Quarterly*, 63 (2), 2007, p. 159.
20 Yeshi Choedon, no.8, p. 26.
21 Ruchita Beri, "India's Role in Keeping Peace in Africa", *Strategic Analysis*, 32 (2), 2008, p. 209.
22 Vinay Bhatnagar, "India's PKOs: A Historic Perspective and the Way Forward, "*Strategic Analysis*, 35 (6), 2011, pp. 927-28.
23 Yeshi Choedon, no. 8, p. 21.
24 Sushant K. Singh, no. 11, p. 74.
25 Yeshi Choedon, ""Uniformed Women in UN Peacekeeping Operations: An Assessment of India's Contribution", *Journal of Defence Studies*, 16 (3), July–September 2022, pp. 240-242.
26 Yeshi Choedon, no.8, p. 24.
27 Yeshi Choedon, no.2, p. 171.
28 Yeshi Choedon, no.8, p.27.
29 C. Raja Mohan, "India and International Peace Operations", *SIPRI Insights on Peace and Security*, 3, April 2013.
30 Indian Council of World Affairs, *India and the United Nations: Report of a Study Group*, Manhattan Publishing, 1957, New York, p. 28.
31 Yeshi Choedon, "India's Perspective on the UN Security Council Reform", *India Quarterly*, 43(4), October–December 2007, p. 24.

6

Confronting the Rise of Radicalization and Terrorism in Africa

Hussein Solomon

Introduction

That terrorism constitutes a serious threat to Africa's citizens is without doubt. According to the Mo Ibrahim Foundation, there has been more than a 1000 per cent increase in terrorism since 2006.[1] What is disconcerting is that while terror attacks are growing in their intensity in traditional terror hotspots like the Sahel, they are also spreading to other areas where they were hitherto non-existent – such as northern Mozambique. While African States and organizations have attempted to confront the threat, the fresh terror attacks on innocent civilians and the African armed forces suggest that current strategies are simply not working. The increasing geographic spread and severity of attacks also suggest that international efforts at supporting counter-terrorism have thus far failed.

This chapter seeks to provide a brief overview of the reasons for terrorism, examine some of the challenges confronting the African Union and its Regional Economic Communities (RECs) and provide some ways in which the international community can assist their African partners in confronting the threat posed. The international community also needs to take cognizance of what happens in Africa will increasingly have a global impact elsewhere. The existence of various franchises of Al Qaeda and the Islamic State on the continent illustrates the point well as does the expanded footprint of Lebanese

Hezbollah across the continent. We live in a global village where insecurity anywhere threatens security everywhere.

Accounting for the Rise of Extremism in Africa

When attempting to understand the spread of extremism in Africa, we need to acknowledge that this is not a recent phenomenon. Large swathes of West Africa, for instance, were conquered in the name of Islam during the 18th and 19th centuries. These include Ibrahim Mousa who led militant Islam in Vota Kalon, the westernmost tip of Africa, Suleiman Bal who carried the Islamic flag into battle in Senegal, and perhaps the most famous of them all, Sheikh Uthan dan Foudy, who greatly expanded the Sokoto Caliphate throughout much of northern Nigeria beginning in 1804.[2] At the same time, it needs to be acknowledged that radicalization and attendant terrorism has increased in recent years – jettisoning more moderate Islamic practices. The reason for this increase relates to both external and internal factors.

Twenty per cent of the world's Muslims live in Africa and given the recent demographic trends, this blighted continent will host a larger share of the globe's Muslim population. For the past few decades African Muslims have been the target of extremist interpretation of Islam – the result of proselytization activities by various Gulf countries. Saudi Arabia has been for years propagating its austere Wahhabi brand of Islam across the continent. For instance, 16 of Saudi Arabia's Muslim World League's offices as well as 36 offices of the International Islamic Relief Organization and several offices of the World Assembly of the Muslim Youth are located in Sub-Saharan Africa. The latter two are subsidiary organizations of the League.[3] It is hoped that the changes occurring inside Saudi Arabia will also positively impact its approach to its proselytization activities in Africa. Of course, Riyadh is not alone in this endeavor. Tehran's support for the militant Islamic Movement of Nigeria[4] and Qatar's support for Malian extremists like Ansar al-Dine (Defenders of the Faith) and the Movement for Unity and Jihad in West Africa (MUJAO) further illustrate the point made.[5]

Radicalization of Africa's Muslims are not only the result of external actors but also the governance failures of Africa's leadership. Consider the following statistics from the African Development Bank:

- Sixty per cent of Africans are engaged in low-paid, unpredictable and informal jobs;
- Half of Africa's population subsists on less than US $1.25 a day; and
- Only half of Africa's youth is economically active.[6]

Here, an important caveat is needed: not all people within States are similarly affected by distressing economic conditions. In Mali, for instance, the average poverty rate is 64 per cent. In the Tuareg-dominated and Muslim north, the corresponding figures are much higher. In Timbuktu, the poverty rate is 77 per cent, for Gao it is 78.7 per cent and for Kidal, it is a staggering 92 per cent.[7] Should we then be surprised that Tuaregs responded to the call of the Islamists of Ansar Dine in 2012 to declare jihad on Bamako? A similar dynamic is also at play in Nigeria. While 27 per cent of the population in the largely Christian south lives in poverty, the figure for the overwhelming Muslim north is an astounding 72 per cent. Should we be surprised that Boko Haram's labeling of the Nigerian State as *taghut* (evil) finds such resonance amongst young men in northern Nigeria.[8] The reinforcing divides: geographical, ethnic, and religious within the context of political alienation as a result of the dearth of democracy has made framing a comprehensive counter-terrorism policy challenging in the extreme.

These cleavages in society and the inability of Africa's political leadership to create inclusive societies are also reflected in the counter-productive counter-terrorism policies pursued by African countries. In the Sahel region, the counter-terrorism tactics and instruments employed by states have served to undermine human security, harden the region's ethnic, racial and religious fault lines and have thus made reconciliation almost impossible. The Malian armed forces have made use of Songhai ethnic militias in northern Mali as a force multiplier. However, these Ganda Koy (Masters of the Land) and Ganda Iso (Sons of the Land) militias engaged in human rights atrocities which further incensed Tuareg and Arab populations in the north, preventing the emergence of a truly inclusive Malian State.[9] To illustrate the point, one Ganda Iso recruit, spoke of what he learnt at his training camp: *"Lets' face it! Tuaregs do not want to share a country with us. They feel that we are inferior. Before the 2012 crisis, we did not understand that this is our land that they want. Before they invented Azawad [Tuareg desire for an independent homeland called Azawad], this was the Songhai Empire, the Ghana Empire, and the Mali Empire. They would have to understand that we Black sedentary people, we are the owners of the land. The time when we are divided and controlled by enslavers [reference to Tuaregs historically enslaving Africans] is over. Before, we did not realize this. This is what I have learned here, as well as making good friends. And we are ready to die to defend our land against these narco-terrorists".*[10]

A similar dynamic is at play in the Lake Chad Basin. Concerned about the infiltration of Boko Haram in the area, N'Djamena has armed local ethnic militias. However, given the tensions over the fertile region whose territory supports agriculture, pastoralism and fishing, this has served to cause these tensions to escalate into armed violence. Some of these armed ethnic militias accused the Buduma ethnic group inhabiting the Basin of colluding with Boko Haram and promptly attacked them.[11] This was clearly a case of local groups appropriating the discourse of global jihad to increase control of fertile territory. The cases of Mali and Chad remind us that governments in the Sahel need to think of the long-term consequences of arming local ethnic militias in the fight against jihadists.

Identity theorists whose work examines the manifold roles that identity plays in generating popular support for terrorist organizations, assist with the recruitment of new members and the types of attacks undertaken also support critical terrorist scholars' position on the central importance of identity.[12] Research conducted by Schwartz, Dunkel and Waterman emphasizes how terrorist groups could emerge where there is a confluence of different identities.[13] Cultural identities which stress the collective over the individual coupled with a fundamentalist and literal interpretation of religious texts as well as a social identity based on sharp contrasts between the in and out group, all contribute to terrorism. Consider here the case of the 4,000-strong Macina Liberation Front (MLF) which instrumentalizes Islam for reasons of ethno-centric nationalism. This is an ethnic Fulani (also called Peul) movement which seeks to revive the 19th century Macina Empire. There are 20 million Fulani spread across the Sahel who form the recruits for the MLF.[14] The same could be said of the Kanuri-dominated Boko Haram[15] who recruit not only from the 7 million Kanuri in Nigeria, but also amongst the 1.1 million Kanuri in Chad, the 850,000 Kanuri in Niger and the 56,000 Kanuri in Cameroon.[16] In an effort to broaden their appeal, Boko Haram has also reached out to Hausa-Fulani people across the region, but the upper echelons of the movement remains Kanuri-dominated. Far from having global jihadi organizations facilitating cooperation amongst the region's disparate Islamists, it is the local kinship networks driving such cooperation. Moreover, far from forming some united Islamic front, the cooperation amongst Islamists sharing different ethnicities are often "*short-term, opportunistic alliances to ensure the continuation of the respective groups' activities rather than more substantive long-term bonds of affiliation.*"[17]

Operational Challenges Confronting African Counter-Terrorism Efforts

Having briefly explored some of the reasons fueling extremism in Africa, we now briefly examine some African responses. It needs to be acknowledged that some very good continental legislation exists to confront the challenge of terrorism. These include the Algeris Convention on the Prevention and Combating of Terrorism of July 1999 and the AU Plan of Action on the Prevention and Combating of Terrorism of September 2002. The enactment of legislative frameworks at continental, sub-regional and domestic levels, however, does not necessarily translate into successful counter-terror strategies on the ground as the emergence of Islamic State franchises on the African continent, the violent resurgence of Boko Haram, the strengthening of Al Qaeda in the Islamic Maghreb (AQIM), or the tenacity of Al Shabaab would attest to. Indeed, Martin Ewi and Kwesi Aning sadly write that, "*... the AU is yet to overcome a legacy of the OAU, namely a tendency to adopt landmark decisions and make pronouncements without ensuring effective and appropriate follow-up.*"[18]

The discrepancy between promise and performance is best illustrated in the decision of the African Union to also focus its Regional Economic Communities (RECs) on security issues and the desire to create regional standby brigades; in reality, this has been very much a paper tiger exercise – with the actual realization of the ASF being constantly postponed. Finally, in December 2017, the ASF was declared to have reached "full operational capability". However, this seems to be more a political decision as opposed to reflecting an incontestable fact. Thomas Mandrup in his assessment of the ASF notes,

> "*Several of the regions have not validated their pledged capabilities for several years, if ever, and a number of the regional forces are only in the planning phase, or in the process of being established; there is also still uncertainty in*

the decision-making process framework around deployment, where the regions regularly express concerns; and finally the funding of operations remains a challenge."[19]

The moribund nature of the RECs became all too apparent in 2012 when Islamists captured northern Mali. The UN Security Council passed a Resolution – the UNSC Resolution 2071 – on 12 October 2012 calling on ECOWAS to prepare an international intervention force and giving them 45 days to lay out detailed plans.[20] On 7 November 2012, West African army chiefs adopted a plan to expel Islamists from northern Mali. The plan was that 3,000 West African troops would target the main population centres in northern Mali. Nigerian soldiers were to make up the bulk of the force while Senegal, Burkina Faso and Niger contributed 500 troops each.[21] This military blueprint was subsequently passed by the ECOWAS regional heads of state. On 26 November 2012, this blueprint was formally presented to, and adopted by, the UN Security Council.[22] France, meanwhile, undertook to provide 'logistical aid' to the ECOWAS force and began training the Malian armed forces with a view to retaking the north.[23]

While cumbersome diplomatic processes for authorizations and other necessities were taking place, the Islamists of Ansar Dine, Al Qaeda in the Islamic Maghreb (AQIM) and the Movement for Unity and Jihad in West Africa (MUJAO) moved rapidly southwards from their northern strongholds to capture the town of Konna – only a few hundred kilometres north of the capital, Bamako. Worse was the fact that Islamists, having consolidated their position in Konna, began their advance on Mopti, the last major town before reaching the capital. Clearly, processes need to be streamlined for sub-regional, regional and international responses to effectively respond to the jihadist threats sooner than later. Commenting on this issue, Bill Roggio noted that "*...any delay in taking action in northern Mali has given the jihadists an opportunity to indoctrinate, train, and organize recruits from West African nations, and then send them home to establish networks there.*"[24]

On realizing that if Mopti fell Bamako would be next, former French President Francois Hollande decided to act by launching Operation Serval in January 2013. This began with aerial strikes of the Islamists' positions in Konna by French helicopter gunships and Mirage jets of the French 4th Helicopter Combat Regiment of Pau, which were based in Burkina Faso.[25] Meanwhile,

French soldiers based in neighbouring Chad and the Ivory Coast moved rapidly to protect Mopti while dislodging the Islamists from Konna and eventually, Gao, Kidal and Timbuktu.[26]

The pace of events clearly wrong-footed ECOWAS and the 15-member West African bloc had to scramble to send in a force to join the French. Eventually, with other countries like Benin pledging 300 soldiers, the ECOWAS force reached 4,000 and was deployed in northern Mali.[27] As ECOWAS did not have proper airlift capability, the British sent two military transport aircraft to transport the ECOWAS troops and equipment into Mali.[28] If anything proves that the AU's much vaunted peace and security architecture, based on the RECs, is little more than a paper tiger, it is this Malian debacle. Under the circumstances, it is no surprise that African States are attempting to find solutions outside of the current AU structures. As a result, the African Mission in Somalia (AMISOM) as well as the G-5 Sahel initiatives were established outside formal AU structures and are extra-regional in form. In the case of the G-5 Sahel initiative, there was an international dimension to it in that, they worked closely with the 4,000 French troops in the region under Operation Barkhane.[29]

The African Union, ultimately, is an inter-State body and its efforts at counter-terrorism are frustrated by national political elites and weaknesses of the African State. There have been instances where political elites have made use of counter-terror legislation to consolidate their draconian rule thereby undermining the democratic aspirations of their citizens. The resultant popular alienation then renders these hapless citizens vulnerable to the propaganda of extremist elements and renders genuine counter-terror efforts illegitimate. In other instances, States either over-state or under-state the magnitude of terrorism in their countries for their own reasons.

Uganda's President Yoweri Museveni, for instance, attempted to accentuate the linkages between Al Qaeda and domestic terror groups like the West Nile Bank Front and the Lord's Resistance Army, with a view to solicit international support. The point being made is that if the AU or the RECs are reliant upon information being supplied by State actors and if this information is deliberately tainted by narrower political considerations, then strategy formulated on such flawed information is bound to be ineffective, if not counter-productive.[30]

There is however something even more worrisome and that is the growing criminalization of the African State and the fact that terrorists are exploiting this to expand their influence into State structures.[31] Former Nigerian President Goodluck Jonathan noted that Boko Haram sympathizers are located within the Executive and Legislative arms of government, in the Judiciary, as well as in the armed forces, police and other security agencies.[32] In South Africa, meanwhile, terror suspects have been tipped-off before police raids; State witnesses in terrorist cases under witness protection have been killed, resulting in terror suspects walking free.[33] In Somalia, meanwhile, arms meant for the Somali National Army miraculously found their way into the hands of Al Shabaab fighters. The problem with the AU is the implicit assumption that the good State is taking the fight to the bad terrorists and with a bit of help (training, assistance with legislative frameworks, etc.) it can win this fight. At no point is the truism considered that the bad terrorists are both out there and inside State structures. While the issue of corruption is certainly dealt with in the AU's Plan of Action, what is occurring are not isolated incidents of corrupt officials working for the terrorists in exchange of some financial reward but systemic and institutionalized corruption where senior government officials do not have any loyalty to the State or its citizens. Several scholars have examined this growing criminalization of the African State. William Reno termed this phenomenon "Shadow States".[34]

The foregoing also raises the question as to why would countries share information with other countries, if those countries security services are leaking. In other words, it is one thing to foster regional and continental counter-terror regimes through the adoption of various plans and conventions as the AU has been attempting, it is quite another thing for such co-operation to take place in this context.

The Way Forward

The challenge of terrorism is multi-dimensional and needs a comprehensive approach from the level of the State to the RECs and onto the AU itself. Foreign partners who seek to assist Africa to overcome these challenges need to understand the nature and specificity of the African terrain. If they do not, they merely become part of the problem – exacerbating as opposed to ameliorating the terrorist threat posed. The United States' overly militarized responses to the terror threat and its uncritical support to incumbent governments responsible for the oppression of their own people speaks of Washington's ignorance of local cultures, ignorance of the State in the African context, ignorance of history and ignorance of African militaries. Donovan Chau argued: "*Understanding unique foreign histories and cultures better enables formulation of sound US military policy. The defence approach lacks substantial depth and breadth of knowledge of foreign peoples and lands, especially SSA... The US military does not possess institutional knowledge of SSA. Institutional means sustained, indepth and diverse knowledge, as opposed to narrow, temporary and cursory. It also means possessing immediately-available subject matter expertise; this could be within the military or through the military's connections with academia and the private sector.*"[35] In similar vein, Smith rhetorically asks his American audience: "*Do we see what the Africans see? In a lots of cases, we misinterpret; we don't understand, we don't get to the heart of the issue.*"[36] Ignorance of the local context is fueling such misperceptions within the US administration. Writing on Nigeria in *Foreign Affairs*, Ambassador Prince Lyman and J. Stephen Morrison noted "*...the US embassy lacks a single American speaker of Hausa, the main language of northern Nigeria, has no consulate or permanent representation in the north.*"[37]

There are four areas in which the international community, armed with knowledge of local context, can assist African countries. The international community's support for Africa's countering radical ideologies could include legal assistance for the enactment of legislation that would ban ideologies that discriminate within societies, divide society into war and peace zones and legitimize violence.[38] Of course, such counter-radicalization legislation would not be effective if governments themselves are helping to divide communities by promoting sectarianism and are not responsive to the community's needs.

A second area where assistance is needed relates to the retraining of African armed forces with greater emphasis being placed on the development of highly mobile 600-troop battalions as opposed to bigger and more rigid brigades of 3,000 troops or a corps of 10,000 troops. But training itself will not be of any use if military professionalism is non-existent. In Mali, under President Toure for instance, recruitment into the armed forces required a relative at the level of a Colonel or a General. Skill sets or professionalism did not seem to matter. Under the circumstances, should we then be surprised that the Malian armed forces crumbled so spectacularly in 2012 at the beginning of the Tuareg/Islamist insurgency?[39]

A third area is providing assistance in specialized technical areas. Counter-terrorism efforts on the part of Nigeria's police are hobbled by the incapacity of the National Police Force to gather intelligence and undertake scientific investigations. According to Amnesty International, most police stations do not document their work because there is no database for fingerprints, no systematic forensic investigation methodology; only two forensic laboratories, a few trained forensic staff and insufficient budgets for investigations. Under the circumstances, police tend to rely on confessions which form 60 per cent of all prosecutions. However, it often appears that such confessions are extracted under duress. In the process, the guilty often escape punishment while the innocent suffer. In terrorism-related cases, it means that despite the multitude of arrests of alleged Boko Haram members and sympathizers, it hardly affects the sect's endurance and capacity to carry out fresh atrocities.[40]

Fourth, there are economic dimensions of radicalization and recruitment into terrorist organizations alluded to earlier. The United Nations Development Programme's study on extremism in Africa demonstrates without doubt that if an individual was either educated or a working professional, such a person was less likely to join a jihadist group. Indeed, employment, the UNDP study stressed, was the single most frequently cited 'immediate need' at the time of joining.[41] International partners seeking to assist African countries fighting the scourge of terrorism should assist in opening up economic opportunities in African countries, helping small and medium enterprises and providing access to their markets at preferential rates. Research has indicated that the bulwark of liberal democratic values, such as pluralism, tolerance and secularism is a vibrant middle class. Where such a middle class does not exist, extremism will take root in whatever form – be it religious fundamentalism or vile ethnocentric nationalism.[42]

NOTES

1 M. Cochi, "Terrorism in Africa", *Sub-Saharan Monitor*, 19 May 2017 at https://www.eastwest.eu/en/opinion/sub-saharan-monitor/terrorism-since-2006-attacks-in-africa-increased-by-1000. (Accessed 23 February 2022)

2 Y.F. Hasan, "The Historical Roots of Afro-Arab Relations," in Khair El-Din Haseeb (ed.). *The Arabs and Africa*, Croom Helm and Centre for Arab Unity Studies, London, 1985, pp. 39-40.

3 D. McCormack, “An African Vortex: Islamism in Sub-Saharan Africa,” Occasional Paper Series No. 4. The Centre for Security Policy, Washington DC, 2005, p. 6.

4 John Campbell and Jack McCaslin “Death of Iranian General Soleimani Provokes Muted Reaction in Africa's Giants,” Council on Foreign Relations, 7 January 2020 at https://www.cfr.org/blog/death-iranian-general-soleimani-provokes-muted-reaction-africas-giants (Accessed 23 February 2020).

5 S. Allemandou, “Is Qatar fueling the crisis in north Mali?,” France 24,23 January 2013 at www.france24.com/en/20130121-qatar-mali-france-ansar-dine-mnla-al-qaeda-sunni-islam-doha (Accessed 21 February 2020).

6 African Development Bank, *African Statistical Yearbook 2013*, Tunis, 2013, pp. 30-36.

7 H. Solomon, “Critical terrorism studies and its implications for Africa,” *Politikon: South African Journal of Political Studies,* 42 (2), 2015, p. 230.

8 Ibid., p. 228.

9 M.A. Boisvert, “Failing at Violence: The Long-Lasting Impact of Pro-Government Militias in northern Mali since 2012”, *African Security,* 8 (4), 2015, pp. 272-298.

10 Ibid., p. 285.

11 “Chad: Fighting Boko Haram in Chad: Beyond Military Measures”. *ReliefWeb*. 8 March 2017 at<http://reliefweb.int/report/fighting-boko-haram-chad-beyond-military-measures> (Accessed 9 March 2017).

12 S.J. Schwartz, C.S. Dunkel, and A.S. Waterman, ‘Terrorism: An Identity Theory Perspective’, *Studies in Conflict and Terrorism,* 32, 2009, p. 539.

13 Ibid., pp. 537-559.

14 C. Gaffey, “Mali Hotel Attack: What is the Macina Liberation Front, Mali's Boko Haram”, *Newsweek,* 24 November 2015 at <http://europe.newsweek.com/mali-hotel-attack-who-are-macina-liberation-front-malis-boko-haram-397727> (Accessed 9 March 2017).

15 Z.P. Pieri, and J. Zenn, “The Boko Haram paradox: Ethnicity, religion and historical memory in pursuit of a Caliphate”, in J.J. Hentz, and H. Solomon, (eds.), *Understanding Boko Haram: Terrorism and Insurgency in Africa,* Routledge. London. 2017, p. 42.

16 “Kanuri People”, Wikipedia, 2013 at < https://en.wikipedia.org/wiki/Kanuri_people> (Accessed 25 October 2017).

17 C. Barrios, and T. Koepf, “Introduction and Summary”, in C. Barrios, and Koepf, (eds), *Re-mapping the Sahel: Transnational Security Challenges and International Responses,* Issue Report No. 19, European Union Institute for Security Studies, Paris, June 2014, p. 6.

18 M. Ewi and K. Aning, “Assessing the Role of the African Union in Preventing and Combating Terrorism in Africa,” *African Security Review,* 15 (3), 2006, p. 42.

19 T. Mandrup, “The African Peace and Security Architecture – A System of the Past or Adapting to the Future?” *DefenceWeb*. 12 April 2018 at www.defenceweb.co.za/index.php?option=com.content&view=article&id=51339 (Accessed 16 January 2019).

20 “Malians Protest Foreign Intervention Plans”, *News24,* 18 October 2012 at http://www.news24.com/malians-protest-foreign-intervention-plans> (Accessed 29 August 2017).

21 J. Cole, “France, ECOWAS Intervene in Mali to Halt Advance of Radical Fundamentalists”, Informed Comment, 13 January 2013 at < http://www.juan-cole.com/2013/01/intervene-advance-fundamentalists.html> (Accessed 20 August 2017).

22 S. Daniel, “Mali Military Intervention Strategy Adopted,” Middle East Online, 7 November 2012 at http://www.middle-east-online.com/english/?id=55438 (Accessed 21 August 2017).

23 “Mali Crisis: France to Give Logistical Aid”, News24, 16 October 2012 at http://www.news24.com/mali-crisis-france-to-give-logistical-aid (Accessed 24 August 2017).

24 B. Roggio, “US, UN Add Ansar Dine to List of Terror Groups,” *The Long War Journal,* 21

March 2013 at http://www.longwarjournal.org/archives/2013/03/us_adds_ansar_dine_t.phph#xzz2tr56oE2c (Accessed 25 August 2017).

25 J. Cole, no. 21.

26 "Africa, French Forces Target Ansar Al-Din", *Maghrebia*. 13 January 2013 at <http://maghrebia.com/en_GB/articles/awi/newsbriefs/general/2013/01/13/newsbrief-01> (Accessed 28 August 2017).

27 Ibid.

28 Ibid.

29 "Mali: Sahel Coalition Formed", Strategy Page, 16 February 2017 at<https://www.strategypage.com/qnd/mali/articles/20170216.aspx> (Accessed 9 March 2017).

30 J. Cilliers "Africa: Root Causes and the `War on Terror'", *Africa Security Review*, 15 (3), 2006, p. 64.

31 J. Cilliers, "Terrorism and Africa", *Africa Security Review*, 12 (4), 2003, p. 100.

32 H. Solomon, "Carnage Continues in Nigeria", 11 January 2012 at <www.icsr.info/blog/Carnage-Continues-in-Nigeria> (Accessed 4 January 2017).

33 H. Solomon, "Jihad: A South African Perspective". Sun Media, Bloemfontein, 2013; D.W. Potgieter, *White Widow, Black Widow: Is Al Qaeda Operating in South Africa?* Penguin Books, Johannesburg, 2014.

34 W. Reno, *Warlord Politics and African States*, Lynne Rienner Publishers, Boulder, Colorado, 1999.

35 C.C. Chau, *US Counter-Terrorism in Sub-Saharan Africa: Understanding Costs, Cultures and Conflicts*, Strategic Studies Institute, p. 19, 31 May 2008 at https://www.StrategicStudiesInstitute.arm.mil (Accessed 31 January 2020). .

36 Quoted in N. Turse, "The US Diaspora of Terror in Africa: The US Military Involvement in the Unravelling of a Continent," *The Nation*, 18 June 2013 at http://www.thenation.com/article/174847/us-diaspora-terror-africa (Accessed 3 February 2020).

37 P.N. Lyman and J. Stephen Morrison, "The Terrorist Threat in Africa," *Foreign Affairs*, 83 (1), January/February 2004, p. 81.

38 W. Phares, *The War of Ideas: Jihadism Against Democracy*, Palgrave Macmillan, 2007, p. 78.

39 H. Solomon, *Terrorism and Counter-Terrorism in Africa: Fighting Insurgency from Al Shabaab, Ansar Dine and Boko Haram*, Palgrave Macmillan, London, 2015, p. 71.

40 Ibid.

41 *Journey to Extremism in Africa: Drivers, Incentives and Tipping Point for Recruitment*, United Nations Development Programme, New York, 2017, pp. 4-5.

42 H. Solomon, and I. Liebenberg, *Consolidation of Democracy in Africa: A View from the South*, Ashgate Publishing, London, 2000; H. Solomon and A. Tausch, *Islamism, Crisis and Democratization: Implications of the World Values Survey for the Muslim World*, Springer, Switzerland, 2020.

7

India-Africa Engagement in Counter-Terrorism: An African Perspective

Sallie Simba Kayunga

Terrorism in its broadest sense refers to attempts to further political ends by using violence to create a climate of fear, apprehension and uncertainty. Since the colonial period, Africa has experienced five major forms of terrorism, namely: insurrectionary terrorism; loner issue terrorism; nationalist terrorism; state terrorism; and global or new terrorism. Whereas various strategies have been put in place to combat terrorism, this paper argues that India has played, and can play a bigger role in combating terrorism on the African continent. India is contributing towards mitigating a variety of socio-economic and political conditions in Africa, which produce grievances that have been used by militant groups to justify their recourse to violent actions through trade. Secondly, India's military engagement with Africa plays a major role in mitigating terrorism. Thirdly, India contribution in peacekeeping operations is facilitating the process of state-building on the continent. Lastly, India's role in securing the Indian Ocean is strategically important for dealing with some aspects of terrorism in Africa.

Meaning of Terrorism: There is no precise definition of "terrorism". In November 2004, the UN Secretary General's report defined terrorism as any act "intended to cause death or serious bodily harm to civilians or non-combatants with the purpose of intimidating a population or compelling a government or an international organization to do or to abstain from doing any act."[1] Others define terrorism as political violence in an asymmetrical conflict that is designed to induce terror and indiscriminate psychological fear through the violent victimisation and destruction of non-combatant targets.[2] According to Heywood terrorism in its broadest sense refers to attempts to further political ends by using violence to create a climate of fear, apprehension and uncertainty.[3] Whatever the definition, terrorism is characterised by three things: the act itself, its victims and its perpetrators. Its actions involve clandestine violence that has a seemingly indiscriminate character. Its victims are normally innocent civilians, and its perpetrators are non-state bodies, that are intent on influencing the actions of government or international organisations.[4]

According to Andrew Heywood, there are five major forms of terrorism: insurrectionary terrorism; loner issue terrorism; nationalist terrorism; state terrorism; and global or new terrorism. Insurrectionary terrorism aims at the revolutionary overthrow of a state. Loner or issue terrorism aims to promote a single cause. State terrorism on the other hand can be defined as terrorism carried out by government agencies, such as the police, military or intelligence agencies to create fear in the population. Nationalist terrorism or separatist movements have the aim of ending colonial rule or occupation, often with the purpose of gaining independence for an ethnic, religious or national group. Nationalist terrorism is of particular interest. It is instigated by insurgent groups fighting the government within a particular state. These groups either aim at gaining control of government, influencing the policy of government or they seek autonomy. Even though the causes of these movements may be genuine, they are often characterised by one element i.e.: to foster insecurity among the population and drive them to seek protection from the insurgents.

Lastly, International, global or "new terrorism" aims inflicting damage and humiliation on a global power, or to transform global civilisation relations. Unlike nationalist terrorism which has a secular motivation, religious motivation is its most defining feature. Because terrorism has become a religious imperative, even a sacred duty, rather than a pragmatically selected political strategy, the terrorist groups and the functions of political violence have changed critically.[5] Instead of the violence having a strategic character, that is, a means to an end, it is now becoming increasingly symbolic.

Theoretical Perspectives on Terrorism: At the theoretical level, terrorism can be understood from three perspectives: realism, liberalism, and the critical perspective. Realist thinking about terrorism tends to place a strong emphasis on the state/non-state actor dichotomy. Terrorism is usually viewed as a violent challenge to the established order, often as a bid for power.[6] According to realism the motivations behind terrorism are largely strategic in character. Terrorist groups usually use clandestine violence and focus on civilian targets mainly because they are too weak to challenge the state openly through conventional means. They attempt to weaken the resolve of a government, they cannot destroy.[7] Since the objective of terrorism is to subvert civil order and overthrow the political system, the counter-terrorism strategy as per realism should be uncompromising. The state should be prepared to contravene political morality in order to protect a political community that is under threat. Realism, therefore, tends to be unconcerned about whether counter-terrorist strategies infringe on civil liberties. The important issue is whether the counter terrorism strategy works.

From a liberal perspective, it is primarily non-state actors who engage in terrorism. According to them, terrorism is motivated by ideology rather than power seeking. According to liberals terrorism is the manifestation of a political and religious ideology that promotes an exaggerated sense of injustice and hostility, and so blinds the terrorists to the moral and human costs of their actions.[8] From this perspective, terrorism is an attack on the very principles of all liberal-democratic values – openness, choice, debate, tolerance, etc. The counter-terrorist strategies should therefore be consistent with liberal democratic values and should not infringe on human rights and civil liberties.

There are two main critical perspectives on terrorism. The first reflects the views of radical theorists such as Chomsky and Falk. According them, both state and non-state actors are at times involved in terrorism, because both at times are involved in the killings of unarmed civilians. State terrorism is much more significant than non-state terrorism because states have a greater coercive capacity than non-state actors. According to Chomsky and Falk, terrorism is largely a state mechanism of violence against civilians, either to maintain themselves in power or to extend their political and economic influence over other states.[9]

The second critical perspective on terrorism is shaped by constructivism and post-structuralist thinking. It is based on the belief that most of the commonly accepted views of terrorism foster stereotypes and misconceptions. In their view terrorism is a social or political construct, which is often used to define certain groups and political causes as non-legitimate, by associating them with images of immorality and violence.[10] By implication, institutions and political structures that are against terrorism are seen as legitimate.[11] The terrorists are seen as the perpetrators and these political institutions and structures as the victims.

This paper will largely be informed by the realist perspective on terrorism, though in some instances it will argue that at times terrorism is socially and politically constructed to ensure political legitimacy for those in power and to characterise certain groups and political causes as non-legitimate, by associating them with images of immorality and violence.

Terrorism in Africa: Africa as a continent has experienced numerous forms of terrorism. Armed uprisings were inevitable in some countries during their struggle for independence. This was particularly true of countries under Portuguese colonialism i.e. Angola, Mozambique and Guinea Bissau. Other African countries, particularly those developed as settler colonies, such as Kenya, South Africa, Namibia and Zimbabwe also had to be liberated through armed struggles. As mentioned earlier, the reasons for these liberation movements were genuine, though some of their strategies and tactics often involved fostering insecurity among the people. The second phase of terrorism was associated with Cold War politics. During this period several African leaders and intellectuals were assassinated in order to dissuade the population from adopting certain ideologies, particularly, leftist ideologies.

The third phase, which was a characteristic of the 1970s, 1980s, and 1990s, saw the emergence of armed struggles in independent Africa states, particular due to·the failure of democratisation, their failure to deliver, and also because of the rise of identity based groups, struggling for autonomy and independence. In this context, armed struggles have been a characteristic of post-independence politics in Uganda, Ethiopia, Chad, Sudan, Central African Republic, and the Democratic Republic of the Congo, among others. The fourth phase can be characterised as Africa's experience with international terrorism. Due to the fragility of some of the African states and also its geo-strategic location, the African continent has been a victim of acts of terrorism perpetrated by organisations from outside the continent. Examples of such terrorist attacks include: the 1973, attempted assassination of the US ambassador in Khartoum (Sudan); the Entebbe hijack;[12] the 1998 bombing by Al Qaeda of the USA embassies in Dar es Salam (the United Republic of Tanzania) and, Nairobi (Kenya); and the 2002 Al Qaeda simultaneous bombing of an Israel airliner and an Israel owned hotel, popular with Israeli tourists in Mombasa, Kenya. In July 2010 suicide bombings were carried out against crowds watching the screening of the 2010 FIFA World Cup final match at two locations in Kampala, Uganda. The bombing left 74 dead and 70 injured. Al-Shabaab claimed responsibility for the attacks as a retaliation for Ugandan support for AMISOM.

The fifth phase consists of the emergence of terrorist groups with territorial ambitions, that is, the desire to capture and create states with defined boundaries, or to redefine African boundaries by creating new states, outside the current framework. Such groups include among others: Al Shabab in Somalia; the Boko Haram in Nigeria and Al-Qaeda in the Islamic Maghreb (AQIM), a militant organisation which aims to overthrow the Algerian government and institute an Islamic state; the Ansar al-Shari'a in Tunisia (AAS-T) and Ansar al-Shari'a (AAS) Benghazi, Libya.

Numerous factors contribute to growth of terrorist organisations in some countries in Africa. These include central governments with weak institutions and with only a tenuous control over expansive territories; the ubiquity of uncontrolled weapons and ammunition; porous and inaccessible borders; heavily armed militias and tribes with conflicting loyalties and agendas; high unemployment among young males along with slow-moving economic development; divisions between the country's regions, towns, and tribes; political paralysis due to infighting and distrust among and between political actors; and the absence of a functioning police force or national army.

Combating Terrorism in Africa: The "Soft" Approach: Combating terrorism requires multifaceted approaches. These include what is increasing being referred to as "soft approaches". Soft approaches are based on the assumption that terrorism is a result of structural inequalities and injustices in society, such as poverty, economic inequality, unemployment and the marginalisation of communities in the social, economic and political sphere. The soft approach would, therefore, focus on dealing with the structural issues that give rise to terrorism. In the African context, the New Partnership for African Development (NEPAD) is expected to address these structural issues. Under the NEPAD framework, African states have committed themselves to eradicate poverty and to put the continent on the path to sustainable growth. The NEPAD recognises that peace, security, democracy, good governance and human rights are a perquisite for sustainable development and that long-term solutions for ensuring peace and security in Africa require policy measures for addressing political and social vulnerabilities on which conflict is premised.[13] In order to deal with issues of governance, the African Union adopted the African Charter of Democracy, Elections and Governance on July 30, 2007. It entered into force on February 15, 2012. Amongst other the key issues African states resolved to adhere to the universal values and principles of democracy and human rights. They also committed themselves to the promotion of sustainable development and human security. The framework also lays emphasis on gender equality as well as the effective participation of citizens in the democratic and development processes.[14]

Combating Terrorism in Africa: The "Hard" Approach: The military approach to combating terrorism has been based on two complementary strategies. The first strategy has been the destruction of states perceived to be offering succour to terrorists. The second strategy has been to launch direct attacks on terrorist training camps and terrorist leaders and terrorist organisations. Some examples of the military approaches to combating terrorism in Africa are as follows: In 1998, US air strikes were launched against perceived terrorist targets in Sudan in retaliation for the bombing of US embassies in Kenya and the United Republic of Tanzania; In 1992, the Islamic Salvation Front (FIS), a political party with a perceived extremist bias won the election in Algeria. It was overthrown by the military; likewise, when, in 2012, the Moslem Brotherhood won a democratic election in Egypt, its government was overthrown in a controversial revolution backed by the military. Military approaches were also used to regain the territory in Mali that had been captured by the Ansar Dine. Similar military engagements against the Boko Haram, by the combined forces of Nigeria, Chad and Cameroon are underway in Nigeria.

The military approach as a strategy to counter terrorism however has two major limitations. First, it focuses on the manifestations of the problem rather than its underlying causes. Secondly, the application of massive counter-terrorism activities has often resulted in the violation of human rights.

Combating Terrorism in Africa: Political Approaches: From a diplomatic point of view most countries claim they cannot negotiate with terrorists. The practical reality, however, is that there have always been open or behind the scene negotiations, some of which have yielded good results. At the global level some negotiations which have led to the end of terrorist activities include the Belfast Agreement in 1998 when an agreement was reached on the status and future of the Northern Ireland, thus effectively ending the IRA terrorist activities. The OSLO Accord also resulted in the partial resolution of the Palestinian Question. In Africa, the African National Congress (ANC) in South Africa had been branded by sections of the international community as a "terrorist organisation". The bold steps taken by de Klerk and the ANC towards a negotiated settlement helped to end apartheid in South Africa. Over 30 insurgency organisations have existed in Uganda since the capture of state power by the National Resistance Movement/Army in 1986. Even though the Uganda People's Defence Force have often adopted a military approach, there have always been behind the scenes negotiations, leading to the inclusion of some of the terrorists into the mainstream politics of the country, thus effectively ending their terrorist activities. In spite of the fact that at times terrorism has been resolved through political means, this approach has two major limitations. It is a form of appeasement and marks a moral retreat in the face of intimidation and violence. Secondly, political approaches, quite often strengthen terrorist organisations by legitimising them and their cause.

African Union Frameworks for Combating Terrorism: Africa is part of the global framework to fight terrorism. There are frameworks at global, continental, regional and individual country levels, for fighting terrorism. African countries as members of the United Nations are bound by its protocols and resolutions. Kofi Annan developed a five pillar ant-terrorism strategy, enunciated in the celebrated report entitled "In larger freedom: towards development, security and human rights for all" (A/59/2005), which was duly endorsed by the United Nations 2005 Summit of Heads of State. The strategy seeks to dissuade people from resorting to terrorism or supporting it by: denying terrorist groups funds and materials; deterring states from sponsoring terrorism; developing state capacity to defeat terrorism; and defending human rights

In addition, to the above, the Security Council Resolutions 1267 (1999) and 1373 (2001) among other things, require states to freeze without delay, funds and other financial assets or economic resources of persons who commit or attempt to commit terrorist acts or participate in, or facilitate the commission of terrorist acts or entities owned or controlled by such persons; and prevent the movement of terrorist or terrorist groups by effective border controls and control of issuance of identity papers and travel documents, and by taking measures to prevent counterfeiting, forgery, or fraudulent use of identity papers and travel documents.

Since terrorism is not new to Africa, frameworks have been developed to deal with the problem right from the time of the formation of the Organisation for African Union in 1963. Article 3 (5) of the Charter of the Organization for African Unity condemned in all its forms, political assassinations as well as subversive activities on the part of a neighbouring state or any other state.[15] On the other hand, Article (4) of the African Union, the successor to the OAU, calls for respect for the sanctity of human life, condemnation and rejection of impunity and political assassinations, acts of terrorism and subversive activities.[16] The African Union Peace and Security architecture, particularly the AU Non-Aggression and Common Defence Pact and the Common Defence and Security Policy (CADSP), have identified terrorism as one of the common threats to Africa.

Continental efforts for preventing and combating terrorism have a long history. In 1992, the Organisation of African Unity (OAU), at its 28th Ordinary Session, held in Dakar, Senegal, adopted a Resolution on the Strengthening of Cooperation and Coordination among African States. At this meeting, OAU pledged to fight the phenomenon of extremism and terrorism.[17] It should be noted that this was before 9/11. In June 1994, OAU held its 30th Ordinary Session in Tunis, Tunisia. At this summit, OAU adopted the Declaration on the Code of Conduct for Inter-African Relations.[18] The Declaration rejected all forms of extremism and terrorism, whether under the pretext of sectarianism, tribalism, ethnicity or religion. It also condemned, as criminal, all terrorist acts, methods and practices. The African states expressed their resolve to enhance cooperation to combat such acts. These efforts culminated in the adoption of the OAU Convention on the Prevention and Combating of Terrorism by the 35th Ordinary Session of the OAU Summit, held in Algiers, Algeria, in July 1999. The Convention requires African states to criminalise terrorist acts as defined in the Convention under their national laws. It defines areas of cooperation among states, establishes state jurisdiction over terrorist acts, and provides a legal framework for extradition as well as extra-territorial investigations and mutual legal assistance. The Convention entered into force in December 2002 and to date, 40 Member States have ratified it.

Of significant importance at the AU High-Level Inter-Governmental meeting held in Algiers, Algeria 2002, was the adoption of the AU Plan of Action on the Prevention and Combating of Terrorism. The objective of this Plan of Action was to give concrete expression to the commitments and obligations of member states under the 1999 Convention and the other international counter-terrorism instruments. The Plan of Action seeks to deal with the problem of terrorism from four perspectives:

First, Police and Border control: Among other things African states were expected to enhance border control and surveillance; they were to develop and upgrade the regulations governing border control and security procedures, including land, sea, and air exit points so as to curb infiltration; they were to promote cooperation among police agencies. Second, Legislative and Judicial Mechanisms: African states were expected to harmonise their legal frameworks pertaining to the prevention and combating of terrorism; they were also expected to develop the capacity of the Judiciary to deal with terrorism related cases. Thirdly, Suppressing the Financing of Terrorism: African states were expected to make operational the International Convention for the Suppression and Financing of Terrorism (1999), which criminalises the act of financing terrorism and makes it mandatory for all states to take measures to detect identity or freeze any funds used or allocated for the purpose of committing acts of terrorism. Lastly, Exchange of Information: African states were expected to exchange information and intelligence on activities and criminal acts of terrorist groups. They were expected to coordinate at regional, continental and international level on matters relating to the fight against terrorism. They were also expected to report, all activities undertaken to combat terrorism to the chairperson of the African Commission.

In 2004, as part of the strategy to implement the 2002 Plan of Acton, the African Centre for the Study and Research on Terrorism (ACSRT) was established in Algiers, Algeria. The Centre is not only for centralising information, but it also undertakes studies and analyses of terrorism and terrorist groups. It is also mandated to develop counter-terrorism capacity building programmes for the African continent and coordinate counter-terrorism efforts on the African continent. In addition to the setting up of ACSRT, at its 3rd Ordinary Session of the Assembly of the African Union, held in Addis Ababa in July 2004 an additional Protocol to the 1999 Convention on the Prevention and Combating of Terrorism was also adopted. The Protocol among other things recognises the growing threat of terrorism in the continent and the growing linkages between terrorism, drug trafficking, transnational organised crime, money laundering, and the illicit proliferation of small arms and light weapons.

In October 2010, an AU Special Representative for Counter-Terrorism Cooperation was appointed by the chairperson of the African Union. Among the responsibilities of the Special Representative is to serve as the Director of the ACRST; to mobilise support for the African continent for fighting terrorism; to assess the situation in various member states and to identify and prioritise the security issues to be addressed. In July 2011 at the 17th Ordinary Session of the Assembly of the African Union held in Malabo, Equatorial Guinea an African Model Law in counter-terrorism was adopted for guiding African states in developing counter-terrorism legislations. In addition, the Post-Conflict Regional Cooperative Initiative for the Elimination of the LRA (RCI-LRA) was launched by the AU Peace and Security in March 2012. With support from both the UN and the European Union, this Initiative is aimed at mobilising countries affected by the LRA to eradicate LRA from the region and mitigate its effects.

Regional Counter-Terrorism Frameworks: The AU Action Plan adopted in 2002 provided a framework and a road map for Regional Economic Community (RECs) to implement International Counter-Terrorism Measures as provided in the OAU Convention as well as measures mandated by the UN Security Council Resolution 1373 (2001). As a result all the eight regional economic groups on the African Continent started developing peace and security strategies. Of all the regional groupings, the IGAD, the Economic Community for West African States (ECOWAS) and the International Conference on the Great Lakes Region (ICGLR) have the most advanced frameworks.

In 2003, an Implementation Plan to Counter Terrorism was adopted by IGAD in Kampala. It called upon member states to work towards a common legal framework and to develop extradition and Mutual Legal Assistance (MLA) treaties. It encouraged the ratification of the relevant continental and international instruments to counter terrorism. It called for increased information exchange in the struggle against terrorism. More significant the Plan highlighted the importance of respecting human rights while fighting terrorism. IGAD has also been instrumental in the fight against extremist and radical groups in Somalia, apart from supporting peace efforts in the Sudan.

In West Africa, the Inter-Governmental Action Group against Money Laundering (GIABA) was established by (ECOWAS). The mandate of GIABA is to strengthen the capacity of member states for the prevention and control of money laundering. In addition, ECOWAS coordinated joint efforts to deal with Ansar Dine when it captured a significant size of territory in Mali. It is also currently coordinating regional efforts against Boko Haram in Nigeria.

Within the Great Lakes region the International Conference on the Great Lakes Region (ICGLR) is leading the efforts in the struggle against terrorism. ICGLR was created to deal with issues of insurgency in the region. The Great Lakes region has been the scene of numerous conflicts on the African continent. These conflicts include the 1994 Genocide in Rwanda, the civil war in Burundi, the Lord Resistance armed insurrection in Uganda, the civil war in Sudan and the aggression against DRC by some of its neighbours. As a result of these conflicts DRC has become home to numerous rebel groups, including the Allied Democratic Front, a rebel group allied to Al Qaeda and fighting to overthrow the government in Uganda. It also includes FDLR, a rebel group constituted largely of people who had perpetuated the 1994 genocide in Rwanda, and which aims to recapture power in that country. Other rebel groups include the Mai Mai and M23, which seek either enhanced regional autonomy or capturing power within the DRC.

As a result of the conflicts within the Great Lakes region, a Peace and Security Cooperative Framework for DRC and the region was signed on

February 24, 2013. The framework was aimed at ending the war between DRC and M23 and to pave way for improved peace and security in the Eastern DRC and the broader region. ICGL, AU and UN Security Council also established the Force Intervention Brigade (FIB) to deal with insurgency groups in the region. The mandate of MONUSCO was also strengthened to deal with these insurgency groups.

Limitations of the Counter-Terrorism Efforts in Africa: There are several problems associated with the strategies adopted at continental and regional level to counter terrorism in Africa. These problems include among others: weaknesses within the AU Counter-Terrorism Framework itself; the democratic deficit on the African continent; inter-state conflicts; increasing economic and social inequality; porous borders; collapsed states; and other geo-political interests.

The AU Counter-Terrorism Framework too has numerous weaknesses. The AU, like its predecessor the Organisation for African Unity, has made landmark decisions and pronouncements, but without effective mechanisms to follow them up. Most of the counter-terrorism instruments need to be made operational. The AU lacks the capacity to develop a list of the perpetrators of terrorist acts as provided for in the Plan of Action. It is also unable to verify which member state is complying with, or implementing both the AU and the global counter-terrorism instruments. Whereas member states are required to report to the chairperson of the AU Commission on the activities they have undertaken to combat terrorism, many of them are still reluctant to do so, complaining of reporting fatigue[19] The African Union also lacks adequate human and financial resources to deal with the various aspects of the Plan of Action on the Prevention and Combating of Terrorism.

Democratic Deficit: While most African Countries are signatories to the African Charter on Democracy, Elections and Governance, there is a democratic deficit on the African continent. Africa is the only continent where you still have leaders who can win an election with over 90 per cent of the votes. Regime change through an election can be expected in less than 10 countries. For historical reasons, a number of African countries have dominant party systems with a very limited possibility of the opposition parties ever coming to power. In countries where political power was acquired through armed struggles, democratic processes are less likely to regime change. This creates an environment for people who believe that regime change is only possible through extra-constitutional means. These extra-constitutional means often include terroristic tactics. Because of the democratic deficit, some African leaders are taking advantage of terrorist threats, to brand any member of a legitimate opposition as a terrorist. Terrorism is thus being used in the power games of some political elites on the continent. In Uganda, the war against Al Shabab in Somalia is critical for regime survival. It is being used as a bargaining chip with the Western world. Any attempt to pressurise Uganda to undertake democratic reforms will be countered by threats to withdraw from Somalia, which is likely to make the international community back off.

Social-Economic Inequality: Though most African countries have been registering high rates of economic growth, the gap between the poor and the rich is increasing.[20] The unemployment rates on the African continent are also extremely high. High levels of poverty and unemployment impact significantly on the continent's ability to fight terrorism. Moreover, the porous borders between most African states exacerbate the proliferation of small arms and light weapons and illicit trafficking across borders. In addition, state collapse makes it easy for terrorist groups to organise. Whereas efforts are being made by the International Conference on the Great Lakes Region to eliminate negative forces from the DRC, that country still has a long way go before it can establish its authority over a large part of its territory. In North Africa, the collapse of Libya as a state is partly responsible for the proliferation of extremist groups, not only in North Africa but now in West Africa as well. Besides the issue of weak states, inter-state conflicts make the survival of terrorist groups possible. The conflict in Somalia is partly associated with the rivalry between Ethiopia and Eritrea. To a certain extent the war in Somalia is partly a proxy war between these two regional powers. Within the Great Lakes region, the conflict between Rwanda and the DRC has often undermined efforts to bring stability to the region.

Lastly, one can argue that terrorist groups in Africa are, by and large, a spill over from the Middle East. It can also be argued that political Islam in the Middle East has a lot to do with the US foreign policy in that region. Islam had to be mobilised in order to fight communism in Afghanistan. Islam was also mobilised to bring about regime change in Middle Eastern countries such as Libya, Syria, and Iraq that were perceived to be "pariah" states. The consequence of this foreign policy 'gone wrong' has been the emergence of Al Qaeda, and now the ISIL. The struggle for hegemony between the Shias and the Sunnis, significantly impacts any efforts aimed at defeating terrorist groups in the Middle East. It can also be argued that political Islam is also associated with the failure to resolve the Palestinian question. African counter terrorism strategies are oblivious of these global dynamics. When the Libyan crisis occurred in 2011, the position of the African Union on the issue was entirely ignored. Now the African continent has to deal with the consequences of the decisions of the Western powers with regard to Libya. While a number of problems facing Africa, particularly those associated with terrorism, have global dimensions, the new catchword is "African Solutions to African Problems".

What Role can India play in enhancing counter-terrorism efforts in Africa?

India has been an active participant in developing strategies that are critical for the fight against terrorism at the global level, and Africa in particular, though it can play an even bigger role. Firstly, India is contributing towards the mitigation of a variety of socio-economic and political conditions in Africa, that give rise to grievances that have been used by militant groups to justify their recourse to violence. Trade between India and Africa has grown exponentially during the past decade. The Indo-African trade volume reached $ 53.3 billion in 2010-11; and $ 62 billion in 2011-12. It has risen to $ 89 billion in 2021-22.[21] As of 2022, India has emerged as Africa's fourth largest trade partner after China, the EU and the US; whilst Africa has emerged as India's fourth largest trading partner after the US, China and the UAE. It should be noted that this figure was a meagre $ 3 billion in 2001. At the 2nd India-Africa Forum Summit in 2011, India committed $5 billion for three years, under lines of credit to help Africa achieve its development goals.[22] India also committed an additional $700 million to establish new institutions and training programmes in consultation with the African Union and its institutions.[23] During the 3rd India-Africa Forum Summit, India offered an additional $10 billion under lines of credit and 600 million in grant assistance.[24] According to Simeon Adekanye, the best way to help Africa acquire the capacity to fight terrorism is to help fulfil the noble aims and objects of NEPAD.[25]

Secondly, African can learn a lot from India about the management of diversity and the establishment of inclusive political systems. Instead of following Western models, whose historical, social and economic contexts are very different, the African continent can learn a lot from India about dealing with social and political minorities. The argument here is that political exclusion can fuel extremism. Africa can therefore draw many lessons from India's system of democracy and federal structure.

Thirdly, India can help Africa fight terrorism through technical assistance. Africa can get assistance from India for handling cyber-terrorism and other aspects relating to the plan of action for combating terrorism, particularly in the sphere of counter-terrorism legislation and the capacity of the judiciary to deal with terrorism related cases.

Fourthly, India's military engagement with Africa can play a big role in mitigating terrorism on the continent. India has been training a large number of Africa's military officers at its various military institutions. Currently India has military-to-military cooperation with a third of the 54 African states. Besides, Indian peace-keeping operations in Africa have been remarkably successful. One of the reasons for the rise in terrorist activities in Africa is the fragility of some states. India's contribution to peace-keeping operations is facilitating the process of state-building on the continent.[26]

Lastly, cooperation between India and Africa on strategic issues relating to the Indian Ocean is extremely important for combating terrorism. Recently the Indian Ocean, has been used by terrorists to carry out terrorist activities not only in Africa in particular and the entire world in general. India's role in securing the Indian Ocean is strategically important, for dealing with some aspects of terrorism in Africa.

NOTES

1 Quoted in Memar Ayalew Demeke and Solomon Gebreyohans Genru, "The Role of Regional Economic Communities in Fighting Terrorism in Africa: The Case of the Inter-Governmental Authority of Development (IGAD)", *European Scientific Journal*, Vol. 2, September 2014.

2 Ibid.

3 Heywood, Andrew (2019), Politics (London: Palgrave Macmillan), p. 714.

4 Heywood Andrew (2011), Global Politics (London: Palgrave Foundations), p. 284.

5 Ibid, p. 288.

6 Heywood, 2011: 287.

7 Ibid.

8 Ibid.
9 Ibid.
10 Ibid.
11 Dedeoglu, B., "Bermuda Triangle: Comparing Official Definitions of Terrorist Activity," *Terrorism and Political Violence* (15) 3, 2003.
12 On June 27, 1976 an Air France plane with 248 passengers was hijacked by a member of the Popular Front for the Liberation of Palestine – External Operations (PFLP-EO) under orders of Wadie Haddad, who had earlier broken away from the mainstream PFLP of George Habash. The hijackers had the stated objective to free 40 Palestinian and pro-Palestinian militants imprisoned in Israel and 13 prisoners in four other countries in exchange for the hostages. The flight that had originated in Tel Aviv and was going to Paris was diverted after a stopover in Athens, via Tripoli to Entebbe, the main airport of Uganda. The Uganda government under the leadership of Idi Amin supported the hijackers.
13 African Union (AU), The New Partnership for African Development (NEPAD), 2002.
14 African Union (AU), African Charter on Democracy, Elections and Governance, 2007.
15 The Charter of the Organisation for African Unity.
16 Constitutive Act of the African Union.
17 AHG/Res.213 (XXVIII).
18 AHG/Del.2 (XXX).
19 Martin Ewi and Kwesi Aning, "Assessing the Role of the African Union in Preventing and Combating Terrorism in Africa," *Africa Security Review*, (15) 3 2006, p. 35.
20 Africa Development Bank, "Brief Notes 5: Income Inequality in Africa", March 2012, p. 6.
21 Ministry of Commerce & Industry, "Union Minister Shri Piyush Goyal addresses the inaugural session of CII-EXIM Bank Conclave on India-Africa Growth Partnership", 19 July 2022 at https://www.pib.gov.in/PressReleasePage.aspx?PRID=1842662#:~:text=Speaking%20at%20 the%20 inaugural %20session,years%20is%20based%20on%20shared (Accessed 10 December 2022)
22 Statement by the Minister of State Mrs. Preneet Kaur on "The New Partnership for Africa's Development: Causes of Conflict and the Promotion of Durable Peace and Sustainable Development in Africa" at the joint debate in UNGA, New York October 17, 2012.
23 Ibid.
24 Speech by Indian Prime Minister Narendra Modi at the Inaugural Ceremony of the Third India-Africa Forum Summit, October 26, 2015, New Delhi at http://www.iafs.in/speeches-detail.php?speeches_id=276 (Accessed 10 December 2022).
25 Statement by H.E. Mr. Simeon Adekanye, Deputy Permanent Representative of Nigeria to the United Nations on "Africa's Challenges and Capacity in Countering Terrorism", The Africa-American Institute, New York, 17 February 2006.
26 India has participated in all UN peace-keeping missions in Africa.

REFERENCES

African Union (AU), The African Charter on Democracy, Elections and Governance 2007.

Anneli Botha, "Challenges in Understanding Terrorism in Africa: A Human Rights Perspective," *Africa Security Review* 17 (2) 2010.

Arvind Dutta, "Indo-Africa Defence Cooperation: Need for Enhanced Thrust", *Journal of Defense Studies,* Winter 2008.

Chomsky, N., *Hegemony or Survival: American Quest for Global Dominance*, New York: Henry Holt & Company, 2003.

Constitutive Act of the African Union.

Dedeoglu, B., "Bermuda Triangle: Comparing Official Definitions of Terrorist Activity," *Terrorism and Political Violence* (15) 3, 2003.

Eric Rosand, Alistar Millar, and Jason Ipe, *Implementing the UN Global Counter-Terrorism Strategy in East Africa,* Centre on Global Counterterrorism Cooperation, 2010.

Falk, R., "The Terrorist Foundations of Recent US Foreign Policy" in A. George (ed.) *Western State Terrorism*, Cambridge: Polity Press, 1991.

Fate Report, *Terrorist Financing in Africa*, The GIABA Secretariat, 2013.

Forest J. F. and Jennifer Giroux, "Terrorism and Political violence in Africa: Contemporary Trends in a Shifting Terrorism," *Perspectives on Terrorism,* Vol 5, Nos. 3-4, 2011.

Heywood Andrew, *Global Politics,* London: Palgrave Foundations, MacMillan 2011.

Ignatief M., *The Lesser Evil: Political Ethics on the Age of Terror,* Edinburgh: Edinburgh University Press, 2004.

Martin Ewi and Kwesi Aning, "Assessing the Role of the African Union in Preventing and Combating Terrorism in Africa," *Africa Security Review*, 15 (3), 2006.

Memar Ayalew Demeke and Solomon Gebreyohans Genru, "The Role of Regional Economic Communities in Fighting Terrorism in Africa: The Case of the Inter-Governmental Authority of Development (IGAD)", *European Scientific Journal,* Vol. 2, September 2014.

Walzer, M., "Political Action: The Problem of Dirty Hands" in D Miller (ed.) *Thinking Politically: Essays in Political Theory,* Newhaven: Yale University Press, 2007.

8

India and Africa: The Scope for Cooperation in Counter Terrorism

Sanjukta Banerji Bhattacharya

Terrorist acts are not committed in a social vacuum. Terrorists are emergent of the social process.

—Ajay Gondane

Introduction

If terrorists are emergent of the social process as noted by Ajay Gondane,[1] acts of terror vary across countries, regions and continents, because 'social processes' are not the same in all countries. In the context of the vast continent of Africa, tribe, ethnicity, religion, colonial legacy, post-colonial social and political formations, poverty, political and social conflicts and the impact of structural adjustment programmes have shaped social processes, to name just a few. These are not the same across regions, as there is wide variance across countries, ethnicities, religious groups and regions. Colonial partitions had been arbitrary, creating irredentist groups, and borders have never been well controlled in Africa – with the result that conflicts and wars flow across boundaries and conflict resolution often involves more than one country or one region. Further, in the broad context of Africa's colonial and post-colonial history, politics and economics may be added to social processes as triggers for conflicts, which in extreme cases, can and do lead to terrorist acts. Wide income and power gaps between the rulers and the ruled, long periods of authoritarian rule when human rights violations were committed with impunity, 'clientalist' kleptocracies which marginalised tribal, ethnic, religious and regional groups and reduced their importance in society, politics and the economy, created the objective conditions for socio-political conflict and in some cases, produced sympathetic audiences for extremist ideologies, be they religious or political. Given the right mix of discontent and desperation, State weaknesses, public support and international apathy, charismatic leadership and an ideology that promises a better world/livelihood, some people in the sympathetic audiences can be persuaded to become perpetrators of terrorist acts. In some parts of contemporary Africa, terrorism has become a scourge, more so because the States concerned do not demonstrate the ability to undertake successful counter-terrorism efforts.

The international community, while watchful, interferes only when its particular interests, like keeping sea-lanes open and free from piracy, are affected. India, too, so far, has largely been involved in this activity, and is not committing itself or even officially commenting on other forms of terror. But piracy, more often than not, is part of what may be termed organised crime rather than terrorism.

The main objective of this chapter is to identify areas of counter-terrorism cooperation between India, the country, and Africa, the continent. Africa has a continental organisation the African Union (AU) which is holistic and makes regional or country-specific issues its concern, especially in the context of conflicts, wars and terrorism – one of its aims being to promote the rule of law in the continent. India has excellent relations with it. Moreover, there are regional and sub-regional organisations like the Economic Community of West African States (ECOWAS), the Common Market for Eastern and Southern Africa (COMESA), the Southern African Development Community (SADC), the East African Community (EAC) and the Intergovernmental Authority for Development (IGAD) that are recognised by the AU and with whom India is developing cooperation that will go well beyond the 'economic' component for promotion of regional security, human rights and conflict resolution. After all, economic integration and development require an environment of peace and security and the rule of law to flourish. India also has good bilateral relations with many African States, including those that have become the targets of terrorists, like Nigeria, and is strengthening relations with others. While the major component of these relationships – especially at the bilateral and regional levels – has been economic, it is time to go beyond trade, development and financial issues and include issues of security, particularly counter-terrorism cooperation.

Both the continent and the sub-continent have long histories of terrorism and terror attacks, and it is in the interests of both to find grounds for mutual cooperation. In order to find convergences in the area of counter-terrorism, it is essential to first understand what is meant by the term 'terrorism' and identify common denominators, because terrorism means different things to different people. We are all conversant with the saying: "One man's terrorist is another man's freedom fighter". This is because of varying perspectives, depending on which side of the table one is. There is also a debate as to the root causes of terrorism, and here too, the perspective depends on who or what are the targets, who are involved in the terror acts and what are the drivers (ideology, poverty/lucrative rewards/financial benefits, feeling of deprivation/being wrongly treated, hatred of a society/community etc.) of an act of terror. It is, at the same time, necessary to determine the various causes of terror and contextualise them in the African scenario, in order to find common grounds for counter-terrorism cooperation between Africa and India.

This chapter will first attempt a viable definition of terrorism, without delving into the debate surrounding it. In the second part of the chapter, the possible causes and nature of terrorism in Africa and India will be identified to determine whether there are any similarities, which can provide a basis for cooperation. In the final part, the possible convergences in counter-terrorism cooperation between India and Africa will be explored.

I

A Common Understanding of Terrorism

A definition of terrorism acceptable to both India and the AU countries is essential to set some common denominators for effective cooperation. As per the UN General Assembly Resolution 54/110 of 9 December 1999,[2] terrorism is the use or threatened use of violence against individuals or property to coerce or intimidate governments or societies for *political* objectives. More often than not, the political objectives are couched in social, economic and religious terms, but ultimately, the aim is political. Terrorism is distinguished from common law crimes and other offences in that the motivation is not financial gain, a distinction that is critical in distinguishing terrorism from other organised criminal behaviour.

The physical targets for a terrorist attack may vary from State to State, from time to time and from attack to attack, taking into consideration the level of vigilance or relaxation of anti-terrorist measures, as well as specific grievances or political demands. Sometimes targets are chosen for their propaganda impact as well as their symbolic value. The 11 September 2001 terror strikes on the United States (US) may be placed in this category. Apart from the World Trade Center and the Pentagon, the White House, the bastion of American power had also been a projected target. While terror attacks have been directed at people and property, the aim in more recent times has been to cause maximum damage. However, focusing on targets is to miss the point. The motive of terrorism is to terrorise.

Terrorism by its very nature is an organised and planned event (or policy). The common denominator remains the intimidation of a particular target community or the destruction of a specific politico-economic system. While terror attacks are frequently directed at individuals, groups and symbols, the real target is often a government, a system, a practice or an ideology. By attacking an important symbol (be it a property or persons or both), terrorism seeks to induce retaliation, that is, to start a spiral of action and reaction that could actually further the cause of the terrorists. The attacks on the World Trade Center are a case in point. They fuelled American retaliation in the form of the 'War on Terror', which included the war on Afghanistan and was later used to justify the Iraq War (2003) and drone attacks on Pakistan's North-western region. Many groups of Islamic extremists, on the other hand, saw these attacks as further examples of Western perfidy, fuelling anti-West sentiments and the proliferation and growth of new Islamic militant groups with extreme ideologies that fed on the instability in the aftermath of war, regime changes and government collapses. This is not to suggest that the current spurt in groups that use terror tactics is an indirect consequence of the cycle of action and reaction unleashed by the 9/11 incidents. It would be too simplistic to suggest any such thing in the face of centuries-long ideological rifts based on religion, chronically unstable regions with wide economic and other divides, authoritarian regimes that were exclusive rather than inclusive of the population, and a volatile religion that combined the political with the spiritual. It cannot be denied however, that extremist religious ideology as a justification for terrorist acts gained ground following the World Trade Center attacks and groups, which use terror tactics, have multiplied since then, particularly in certain parts of the world.

It is interesting that the international community has not been able to come up with a commonly accepted legal definition of terrorism, although it has been able to reach a legal consensus on the narrowly defined aspects of what constitutes an act of terror, as for example, hijackings. The problem with not having a single binding definition of terrorism, but setting out what constitutes acts of terror, is that specific acts can be considered as being terrorist acts without also implying that the group associated with such acts is a terrorist group. Moreover, the nature of terrorism differs from country to country. The United Nations Security Council (UNSC) Resolution 1373 of 2001 restricts the description of 'terrorist acts' to international acts to avoid the complexities attached to various national legal systems as well as the issue of sub-State terrorism, whereby a specific country terms a sub-State group as a terror group, but it is not recognised as such in other states. To go by the Palermo Convention (which does not deal with terrorism but organised crime), an offence is transnational if it is committed in more than one State; if it is committed in one State but a substantial part of its planning and preparation takes place in another State; it is committed in one State but has substantial repercussions for other States; or it is committed in one State but involves groups that engage in such acts in more than one State.[3] In contrast, sub-State terrorism is confined to domestic actors.

In Africa, it may be noted, many terrorist actions are perpetrated by sub-State actors; and the same is largely true of India. There is no international instrument as yet that defines or condemns this kind of terror. Here, one may mention the UN General Assembly Resolution 54/110 of 9 December 1999, which states that terrorism comprises "criminal acts intended or calculated to provoke a state of terror in the general public, a group of persons or particular persons for political reasons".[4] While this definition makes mention of "criminal acts", which can provide a broader scope, there are many gaps in this definition, not the least being that it does not say what comprises a sufficient state of "public fear" to designate the perpetrators of the "fear" a terrorist group. The international community has long been debating a Comprehensive Convention on International Terrorism, but has not been able to arrive at any consensus. Further, even if such a Convention was passed, it would still be confined to 'international' terrorism, which has its own definitions, while domestic terrorism will not have any universally accepted definition. In the absence of such a definition, perpetrators of domestic terror may find safe havens in other countries where they will be treated as mere foreigners. This has happened in the case of Khalistani terrorists who took refuge outside India and who have not yet been extradited to India for trial in cases involving overt terrorist acts. The only international consensus seems to be that terrorism is a tactic, a strategy, a *modus operandi,* while there is a serious lack of agreement on who can be called a terrorist or how terrorist goals and objectives can be defined.

II

Terrorism and the Responses to it in India and Africa

There is no social theory or model (so far) that can predict with certainty the factors that will culminate in a particular action or what prompts a group to undertake terrorist action. Only hindsight seems to make for perfect social science in this context. There is wide variance in terrorist activity in Africa and India, in both the past and the present, but while causes for terrorist action may differ widely, it is possible to find some similarities in social processes and backgrounds that can be compared, particularly those which involve social inclusion or exclusion. Both India and Africa faced the brunt of colonialism, which meant that State structures evolved in a nationalist vacuum, with the State and power structures being imposed from above and ultimate control being exercised from a foreign metropolis. The colonial State was the antithesis of the nation-state with power being used to subjugate the nation. In some cases, particularly in Africa, it resulted in whole nations being dispersed across boundary lines. In India, the colonial State believed in dividing and ruling, which aggravated not only religious divisions, but also caste and other divides. Further, it also meant a strong centralised government, which resulted in peripheries and marginalised people – perhaps unintended – but with grave future consequences all the same.

At independence, in the absence of any new concept of Statehood and the unwillingness to embrace the feudal-monarchical or tribal past, the colonial structures of government and governance and the new idea of an impersonal sovereign State were accepted almost *in toto* by the post-colonial State. But in hindsight, the African and Indian narratives began to diverge from this point onwards. While almost every African State went through periods of military/ authoritarian rule (South Africa being marked by white racial rule), the Indian experience was marked by only a brief period of what has been termed the 'Emergency', but democratic norms were never suspended. However, in the background of inequalities between areas and people, it is not surprising that sub-State actors emerged in both India and Africa, with different agendas for challenging or subverting the State, sometimes leading to prolonged insurgencies (and civil wars or even cross-border attacks in the case of some African States) and civil conflict. It is therefore interesting to note the differences in the responses to such conflicts and challenges in the African continent and India. Many African States facing political turmoil or instability, responded with military takeovers and the use of State power – even State terror – to subjugate opposing forces. This fuelled greater discontent and the rise of more extreme political dissidents, united by commonalities of region, ethnicity or religion. India, on the other hand, remained steadfast in its democratic and constitutional commitment, opening spaces for dialogue whenever possible (as borne out by the various accords with insurgent groups), sometimes co-opting the opposition, and persuading dissidents to participate in the democratic processes of governance. At other times, it used force, even the military, to quell an insurgency or when a group resorted to terror tactics, but always within broad constitutional limits (even though the Armed Forces (Special Powers) Act (AFSPA) has been opposed as being draconian, in areas where it has been applied). The rule of law implies the taking of various legal measures to control terrorism or criminal activities. India has passed several acts like the Terrorist and Disruptive Activities (Prevention) Act (TADA), which was in place between 1985 and 1995. It was replaced by the Prevention of Terrorist Activities Act (POTA) in 2002 following the criticism that the TADA had draconian features. The POTA too, was replaced by the Prevention of Terrorism (Repeal) Act, 2004, following allegations that it had been used against political opponents. What is in place today is the Unlawful Activities (Prevention) Amendment Act, 2004, amended again in 2008 and 2012 and then again in 2019, in addition to the National Investigation Agency Act (2008), amended as the National Investigation Agency (Amendment) Act 2019. It must be emphasised that legal provisions are very much in place, and if laws are judged to be too harsh, they are changed by constitutional methods.

Africa's Terror Experience

The nature of terrorist acts has changed over time in Africa, and a rough line dividing two phases in terms of types of terrorism, can be drawn around the 1990s. Before the 1990s, terrorism in Africa was mainly sub-State, affecting millions across the continent. Organisations indulging in acts of terror included the National Union for the Total Independence of Africa (UNITA), the Resistência Nacional Moçambicana (RENAMO), the Mai Mai, the Lord's Resistance Army, the Liberians United for Reconciliation and Democracy (LURD) etc., but only Angola (2861 deaths) figured in the top 20 countries in terms of fatalities due to terror attacks between 1970 and 2007. South Africa (1650) and Algeria (1921) were among the top 20 countries most frequently attacked in the same period. In contrast, India ranked fourth among the most frequently attacked countries with 4318 attacks in the same period, and third in terms of casualties (13434).[5] However, event databases have their limitations particularly because they record actual events and not failed plots or situations where methods other than terror tactics were used to achieve a set goal. These databases also do not mention State terrorism.

In Africa, several political groupings / or persons in the pre-1990s period can be accused of using terrorist methods to come to power or intimidate opponents, as for instance, Charles Taylor in Liberia or Idi Amin in Uganda. Some analysts suggest that while State terror was used to achieve and hold on to power, these same motives were drivers of terror acts among opposition groups as well, particularly because of the extreme centralisation in African States, and because the in-fighting among 'in' and 'out' groups was often a matter of survival. Others suggest that the political behaviour of people in many African States stemmed from the State's material poverty. Where resources are scarce, the object of political contestation often is to secure economic consumption, which in turn is best ensured by capturing State power. In such circumstances, politics can degenerate into a life and death struggle over private access to (sometimes limited) public resources, a zero-sum game of power politics. Like organised crime, terrorism requires opportunity and a favourable environment apart from the practical means to translate radical intent into the actual deed. State instability, rampant corruption, inefficacy of police forces, clientalism, absence of the rule of law etc. provided the opportunity and the space for terror acts. As far as the actual means were concerned, the vast majority of sub-State terror acts required little by way of arms, with the actors resorting to shootings and killings, rather than highly organised hijackings, or the use of sophisticated explosives for blowing up public buildings or installations. Small arms, the result of proxy wars, in which both the US and the Soviet Union participated led to an inflow of money and light weapons, which continue to be easily available in Africa, with an estimated 30 million still in circulation.[6] A conducive environment was often provided by the rivalry between States; insurgent groups in one State indulging in terror acts in that State could find a safe haven and support in a rival State as in the case of Sudan and Ethiopia, Sudan and Chad; the frontline States and South Africa during the apartheid era; the frontline States and Northern Rhodesia during the Smith regime; and several other regions. Interestingly, Prime Minister Benjamin Netanyahu, whose State, Israel, has been both a victim and a perpetrator of terror, once noted that "there is no international terrorism without the support of sovereign states."[7]

If one looks at the supply side of terrorism, one realises that the mismatch between individual needs and the social provision of those needs can lead to frustration. Relative deprivation enhances the perception of inequality in the distributive process, which can lead to social resentment, disillusion and a sense of marginalisation *vis-à-vis* the State. Inadequate socialisation into the mainstream community and intense competition for limited wealth and the coming together of persons with similar perceptions of marginalisation, can have a disastrous effect, particularly if there is a charismatic leadership or ideology or an ethnic or tribal bond to bind them together. The Front for the Liberation of the Enclave of Cabinda (FLEC) in Angola is a case in point. The FLEC wants political autonomy, secession and access to the oil resources of the region. Historically, it was a Portuguese protectorate separate from the Portuguese colony of Angola and had gained a quasi-independent status in 1956, but was later incorporated into Angola, without being consulted. Although rich in oil, the province, from the beginning of its Angolan sojourn, was marginalised and its inhabitants did not reap the benefits of its oil wealth. The FLEC wants separation and has resorted to terror tactics against the Angolan State in its quest for a better status, although a ceasefire was signed in 2006 between the Angolan government and the Cabinda Forum for Dialogue (FCD) and FLEC-Renovada.

In the 1990s however, the nature of terrorism began to change in Africa (as in many parts of the world) following the emergence of Islamic militancy in the continent. Previously, Islamic militant attacks had been largely confined to northern Africa; with the growth and spread of new ideologies, identity based, religiously motivated terror attacks began to take place in sub-Saharan Africa as well. Today, even as African 'wars' for political survival and the capture of resources continue, mobilisation can also increasingly be traced to ethnicity, religion, ideology, and to some extent, political geography, which can ultimately be explained in terms of identity. In the absence of constitutional or other outlets, people belonging to communal identity groups based on race, religion, culture and language, having a common perception of deprivation and marginalisation, can and do combine for militant action, some of whom utilise terrorist methods. While economic survival in the face of climate change is a motivating factor for armed action against other groups and sometimes the State, the religious dynamic is often used as an ideological rationale to rally marginalised people. This has to be seen in the background of the wider narrative being played out in the Maghreb, the Mashreq, as well as in Afghanistan in the wake of the creation of the *mujahideen* following the Soviet occupation of Afghanistan. The very name, 'holy warriors', is suggestive of a primal war between the righteous forces of Islam and the infidel Soviets who had occupied parts of the Dar-ul-Islam, the land of Islam. The subsequent Soviet withdrawal and the abandonment of the Islamic militants by Western interests once the cause of the 'infidel' West was served, led to the return of many of the *mujahideen* to northern Africa, that is, Algeria, Egypt, Sudan, Yemen etc., from where they had responded to the call for a 'holy war' in Afghanistan. They subsequently dispersed to other parts of Africa where they spread their ideology and gathered supporters. The rise of the Al Qaeda and its anti-Western ideology found resonance in the Muslim populations of many African States, common people who struggled for their livelihoods as they watched Western multinationals and their African bourgeois cronies reap the benefits of their resources. There were other reasons for the attraction to extremist ideologies. Some of them were bread and butter issues, but these could be exploited by charismatic religious leaders, promising a better world here and in the hereafter. The bombings of the American embassies in Nairobi and Dar-es-Salaam on 7 August 1998 opened a new chapter in the history of terrorism in Africa; that is, they highlighted a new external focus instead of the domestically oriented terrorism of earlier times. Globalisation was an important factor in the spread of international terrorism, easing the quick movement of ideas, people, money and even arms. The most important facilitating factor was the fast growing international communications network that supports a vast digital knowledge base, quick communication of news, connectivity and access to financial resources from different continents at the click of a mouse. In addition, with increased migration from Africa for economic and other reasons (some legal, some illegal), large diaspora communities with their own unintegrated sub-cultures in the European and American continents, provided a sufficiently resentful base for the recruitment of future terrorists. From the 1990s, the ideological, ideational and financial links between home-grown extremist groups and organisations marked for international terrorism began to spread, and today there are many Islamic militant groups in Africa that although tenuously connected, are all driven by militant ideology. The more commonly known among these are the al-Ittihad al-Islamiya, the Ansar Dine, the Boko Haram, the Jabbatal Islamiya, the Muaskar Anole, the Ras Kambani Brigades, the Islamic State of Greater Sahara (ISGS), the Islamic State of West African province (ISWAP) and the al-Shabaab.

In Africa, the Organisation of African Unity (OAU) had responded to the attacks on American embassies in Kenya and Tanzania in 1998 by adopting a largely unimplemented regional Convention on the Prevention and Combating of Terrorism in 1999, followed by a Plan of Action in 2002, and a Protocol to the OAU Convention (2004). By this time, the OAU had become the African Union (AU), which has the will but continues to lack the capacity to enforce anti-terrorism measures. Some of the regional economic communities (RECs) also have some counter-terrorism programmes, as for instance, the ECOWAS Warning and Response Network (ECOWARN), IGAD's Capacity-Building Programme against Terrorism (ICPAT, 2006), the Eastern and Southern Africa Anti-Money Laundering Group (ESAAMLG), but there is little cooperation between these groups, and in any case, all these are fledgling programmes and largely ineffective. There are country-specific anti-terror laws as well, but not only do they leave much to be desired, they have often been misused to commit human rights violations. For example, Uganda, which was identified in the mid-2000s as a transit point for extreme militants moving to and from the Horn of Africa to North Africa and Europe,[8] had a draconian anti-terrorist legislation which imposed mandatory death penalty for an act of terror that resulted in fatalities, but was used for other lesser offences (the mandatory death penalty was subsequently declared unconstitutional by the Ugandan Supreme Court). On the one hand, the Anti-Terrorist Act was used to suppress dissent from politicians, journalists, etc.[9] while on the other, Uganda has done little to stop money laundering or terror financing. It does not maintain statistics on suspicious foreign exchange transactions nor does it have any kind of a central financial agency to oversee such matters, even though the al-Shabaab and the Allied Democratic Forces operate within and outside Uganda and their activities are reportedly on the rise.[10] In a similar vein, Swaziland's Suppression of Terrorism Act was used to suppress political opposition against the rule of King Mswati III. South Africa's anti-terror legislation is worth mentioning in this context: its Protection of Constitutional Democracy against Terrorism and Related Activities Act (Act 33 of 2004), which came into force in 2005, was challenged by civil society and human rights organisations throughout its deliberative stage and as a result, the South African law is perhaps the least restrictive among African anti-terrorist legislations. Having emerged from decades of apartheid rule, South Africans are mindful about any law restricting human rights. This, it may be mentioned, is an exception. In many States, pressures from opponents unnecessarily delayed the passage of anti-terrorist legislation and it is only because of the efforts of the United Nations (UN) and the US that any laws were passed; but they have not yet had the desired effect. Despite terror incidents in Nigeria over a long period of time, an anti-terror law was finally debated over five years from 2006 to 2011 before the passage of the Terrorism (Prevention) Act. 2011, and the Money Laundering (Prohibition) Act, 2011. However, the enactment of a comprehensive anti-terror law in Nigeria did not significantly address Nigeria's vulnerability to terrorism and violent extremism because some of the governance and security deficits – poverty, youth unemployment, corruption, porous borders, small arms proliferation, and ineffectual national security agencies – were not addressed in a comprehensive and sustainable manner. Nigeria's counter-terrorism efforts can only be effective in addressing violent extremism and other acts of terror, if there is a robust combination of legislative interventions with governance reforms that address some of the acute human security challenges confronting a vast majority of its population.[11] It is, in fact, these and other factors, that have provided a fertile ground for the growth of terrorism for a number of decades, but till the 9/11 terror attacks in the US, there was not much need felt domestically in any African country, or cause for UN pressure on them, to enact domestic legislation or pass regional conventions criminalising terrorism and taking pre-emptive action for its prevention.

Cooperation in anti-terrorism strategies will become even more important in the coming days and years as cooperation between international terrorist groups attains new heights. It is in this context that a few points need to be noted: first, what were essentially national and sub-national terror groups appear to have been incorporated into regional and even global networks of terrorists, that is, there seems to be a perceptible convergence of collective action frames and strategic goals. To cite an example, Boko Haram (the full name is Jama'atu Ahlis Sunna Lidda'awati wal-Jihad, which in Arabic means "People Committed to the Propagation of the Prophet's Teachings and Jihad") was seemingly linked to the Al Qaeda from the beginning with Osama bin Laden (reportedly) sending $3 million as seed money to Nigeria, to help spread his ideology. Correspondence between him and Boko Haram leaders to this effect was found in the Abbottabad compound after the raid in which he was killed.[12] However, Al Qaeda'scentral leadership has never claimed Boko Haram as an affiliate. Instead, Boko Haram's leader, Abubakar Shekau (who died in mid-2021), formally pledged allegiance to the Islamic State in the Levant (ISIL) in March 2015. To quote: "We announce our allegiance to the Caliph of the Muslims, Ibrahim ibn Awad ibn Ibrahim al-Husseini al-Qurashi", referring to Islamic State (IS) leader Abu Bakr al-Baghdadi, and this was accepted formally by an ISIL spokesperson, Mohammed al-Adnani, within a few days.[13] Secondly, the international dimension is not limited to links with other terror organisations but includes attacks beyond boundaries, targeting of foreign nationals, recruitment from the diaspora, international financial flows, etc. Third, there are myriad competing interests, ideas, strategic priorities and tactics across the so-called 'jihadist' groups. While there may be some degree of collaboration between groups, they have different strategic priorities and their tactics too, may vary. For instance, the Boko Haram seeks an Islamic State – a Caliphate (like the ISIL). while another group, the Ansar Dine, is Islamist by intent and even though it has a strict interpretation of Sharia law, it appears to only use Islamist ideology in its quest to establish a State, with the help of money and weapons from Islamic militant sources. Belmokhtar's 'Masked Ones', show no interest in creating a State but use terrorism to exercise influence over regional and Western governments.[14] Last but not the least, it may be noted that while earlier terror groups were interested in capturing State power mainly for self-aggrandisement, now, increasingly, Islamic religious ideology is being used as an excuse for gaining territory across Africa to set up what is being touted as an ideologically conceived Islamic State. In fact, ideologically, Islam must have territory to exercise the *Sharia;* the basis of the Dar-ul-Islam, the 'land of Islam', which in the early history of Islam was ruled by the Caliph, the religious and temporal head, is the *Sharia.* Therefore, capture of territory is necessary-according to some contemporary Islamist ideologues, for true Islam (where the rule of law is seen as rule by the strictures of the *Sharia)* to reign again. While the motives of the earlier groups and the current ones can be seen as political, many of the more recent groups use Islam to justify their political quest for territory. However, this too may be changing particularly in the so-called post-COVID period, the pandemic itself having added to the suffering of common citizens. In addition to an influx of foreign terrorist fighters as the Islamic State and other organizations suffered setbacks in the West Asian region, there has been a resurgence of unconstitutional changes in government, especially between 2020 and 2022, causing political instability, an increase in joblessness and poverty, resulting in further economic hardship, and weak law enforcement capacities.

The fact that terror tactics in the name of Islam or for that matter terror tactics *per se,* continues to plague the African continent can be gauged from a recent statement by UN Deputy Secretary General Amina Mohammed (on behalf of the Secretary General, Antonio Guterres) at the Security Council High-Level Debate on 'Counter-Terrorism in Africa: An Imperative for Peace, Security and Development', on 10 November 2022:

> Terrorists and violent extremists including Da'esh, Al-Qaida and their affiliates have exploited instability and conflict to increase their activities

> and intensify attacks across the continent...In the last two years, these groups have expanded across large areas of the Sahel, increasing their presence in Mali while penetrating further into Burkina Faso and Niger. They have also expanded southward into countries of the Gulf of Guinea that have so far largely avoided terrorist attacks or have recently emerged from armed conflict. Terrorist and violent extremist groups aggravate instability and human suffering. And they can plunge a country emerging from war back into the depths of conflict. Climate disruptions make matters worse, inducing inter-communal tensions and food insecurity that are exploited by terrorists and other criminal groups. And digital tools make spreading hate and disinformation easier than ever.[15]

It may be noted that while new laws and other counter-terrorism efforts have been made, these have not proved effective. The African Union established joint forces to fight terrorism, such as the AMISOM/ATMIS in Somalia, the African Union Mission in Somalia/African Transition Mission in Somalia, the Joint Multinational Force in the Lake Chad Basin, the G5 Sahel Joint Force, the SADC mission in Mozambique (SAMIM), and other bilateral initiatives in Mozambique. The AU also reactivated old legal instruments like the Plan of Action on the Prevention and Combating of Terrorism (2002), the operational framework of the OAU Convention on Combating Terrorism (1999) and its Protocol (2004), the AU Roadmap to Silence the Guns in Africa by 2030 and passed new Resolutions like the Declaration on Terrorism and Unconstitutional Changes of Government in Africa (28 May 2022)[16] to strengthen counter-terrorism efforts, but none of these have had much effect in reducing terror attacks. UN efforts too, like the UN Multidimensional Integrated Stabilization Mission (MINUSMA) in Mali, have not been too successful. Counter-terrorist attempts by the United Kingdom (UK), the United States and France, like escalated air strikes against the Al-Shabab in Somalia by the US in 2017 and French military operations in the Sahel, too have not borne results. According to the AU's African Centre for the Study and Research on Terrorism, the number of attacks in 2020 was 2034 with fatalities numbering 2563.[17]

India's Terrorism Experience

In order to find common ground for cooperation between India and Africa, the nature of terrorism in India too, needs to be examined. Although India was also under colonial rule for centuries and emerged as an independent country only a few years before most African countries gained independence, the post-independence political trajectory of the two has been very different. India is one of the very few post-colonial countries where there has never been a military coup or seizure of power through extra-constitutional means or assassinations of presidents or prime ministers by rival Indian political-ethnic groups or the abandonment of the original Constitution for a new one or, for that matter, a civil war or a successful secessionist struggle. Indian democracy seems to have stronger foundations than most post-colonial states and democracy has become even more deeply entrenched over time. One reason could be the long non-violent mass struggle for independence under the leadership of Mahatma Gandhi, who had the political acumen to absorb dissent into the mainstream struggle. This gave India's diverse linguistic, caste and other groups enough scope to express their demands and inculcated a deeper sense of national unity among a large section of the people, particularly those involved in the freedom movement. The Indian Constitution too, was not hurriedly written; a lot of thought went into its making and it was unique for its time because despite its democratic credentials, it included the Directive Principles of State Policy for the uplift of the downtrodden. The sovereign State that came into being also had 'socialistic' elements besides being a Welfare State.

But India, like African States, was also highly diverse as well as a State-in-the-making. Despite the serious futuristic thinking that went into national development at the birth of the independent State, there were bound to be sections that had a sense of marginalisation and 'otherness.' This led to resentment that fostered insurgencies, militant action and terrorist acts against the state. Here, four factors need mention: first, the partition of India, with Pakistan, the State that the Muslim 'nation' (read, the Muslim League) had wanted desiring more, leading to wars in subsequent years, and intermittent cross-border attacks as well as the fuelling of anti-India sentiments among certain sections of the Indian populace; second, the conclusion of the unfinished business of partition – with East Pakistan opting out of Pakistan to form the largely Bengali Muslim State of Bangladesh with India's assistance, fuelling Pakistani resentment further against India; third, the almost simultaneous emergence of sub-national movements, especially in the Northeast, where the population had been deliberately kept apart from India during colonial rule and as a result, was not integrated into the mainstream (something comparable to what happened in South Sudan); sub-national movements in India's heartland, again an indirect legacy of colonial rule and partition, such as certain groups of the Sikh community wanting their own homeland, and further north, where again, some Kashmiris want separation from India; and, fourth, the dissemination of alternative ideologies like communism and Maoism which challenge the Indian State and want its overthrow. These factors have created a groundswell for the emergence of groups within and outside India that have been intermittently engaging in terrorist violence.

As in Africa in the post-1990s, there has also been a proliferation of Islamist groups with extremist tendencies in India. This has led to the emergence of retaliatory Hindu extremist groups. In earlier times, the clashes between religious groups resulted in bloody riots. These still take place, but now terrorist violence appears to be directed against symbols or members of the other community, or sometimes, when fuelled by extra-territorial organisations (sometimes sponsored by State institutions of another country), at symbols of the Indian State, like the Indian parliament. While it is true that there has been a rise in the number of extremist Islamic organisations, for example, the Students Islamic Movement in India (SIMI), the Indian Mujahideen etc., and terrorist acts are a regular occurrence, such events often have the footprint of external support or instigation, even though the apparent foreign sponsors deny these allegations. And herein lies the difference with African States: the 'foreign hand' in the Indian context has an agenda that is other than the setting up of an Islamic State in India. In fact, this is not, and has never been the issue in India. The motive seems to be a desire to destabilise the country, because India is perceived as the State that destabilised and assisted in the break-up of Pakistan. Support to Kashmiri nationalism is seen as the equivalent of a 'jihad' by some Muslim groups in Kashmir, Pakistan and elsewhere, but India views it as a covert war by Pakistan to complete what is perceived by many Pakistanis as the 'unfinished agenda' of partition. Terrorist groups using Kashmir as a rallying cry have tied the rationale for their activities to a larger Islamist movement in which India is seen variously as an anti-Muslim State, a 'Hindu nationalist' State and a friend of Western capitalism and governments, and more recently, as a friend of Israel. However, despite the appearance of a couple of ISIL flags at a rally in Srinagar a few years back, there is no indication of any ISIL-type activity in the Valley. Following the abrogation of Article 370 in 2019, the union government claims that terrorist activities in the Valley have declined. However, it is interesting that the Finance Minister Nirmala Sitharaman, while reiterating the government's views also mentioned that in 2021, 180 terrorists (148 locals and 32 foreigners including 44 top commanders) were eliminated;[18] this would imply more effective counter-terrorism efforts rather than a decline in terrorism.

However, the 26 November 2008 attacks in Mumbai on a Jewish synagogue, the Taj Mahal Hotel, which is patronised by a large number of foreign tourists, and a busy railway station, fall into a different league and mark a defining moment for terrorist activity in India. This was an attack planned on symbols of India's power by terrorists from outside its borders, since Mumbai happens to be the financial hub of India just as the twin towers of the World Trade Center were symbolic of America's financial power. The attack on the Jewish community was a first for India, as such events go. Moreover, while terrorists have targeted hotels with lots of foreign tourists in different countries including Pakistan, the attack on the Taj Mahal Hotel was again a first in India, in the genre of terror attacks. There are no Al Qaeda or ISIL-type groups in India with the kind of agenda such organisations have, but given the trend in the neighbourhood and elsewhere in the world, one cannot predict what may happen in the future.

The other, and equally important, terrorist threat is from the Maoists who are an extremist group who take advantage of the lack of development across the country's tribal heartland, starting from Bihar through Jharkhand, West Bengal, Odisha, Andhra Pradesh, and Madhya Pradesh to Maharashtra, Karnataka and Tamil Nadu, in what is called the 'Red Corridor'. The Maoists are an offshoot of the Naxalites, a far-left radical group that broke away from the Communist Party of India (Marxist) (CPI-M), and followed an alternative revolutionary brand of communist ideology whose agenda was the violent overthrow of the Indian State, of which the CPI-M had become part after it won regular elections and took office in West Bengal as part of the United Front government. The armed group of the Naxalite-Maoists is the People's Liberation Guerrilla Army (PLGA). The Maoists have carried out terror attacks killing thousands of people connected with the State apparatus over the last twenty years. The attacks have targeted district officials, military and police personnel and their installations, government buildings, road and rail bridges, trains, etc. Since their aim is overtly political (overthrow of the present system of democracy and its replacement by their version of Maoism), their targets are largely people and property connected to the government. Very rarely are ordinary people targeted, and when they are (like the kidnapping of two Italians in Odisha in 2012), the objective is to bargain for political gains like the release of imprisoned Maoists. While technically their movement has the characteristics of an insurgency, they use tactics that are essentially those used by terrorists. However, the number of incidents has come down since 2011 (from 1169 in 2010 to 342 in 2013, and three major incidents in 2015 and allegedly 53 in 2019). As such, there is hope that they may be becoming less of a menace than earlier.[19] However, they continue to be active in two cluster-areas – around the hilly areas of Dandakaranya across Chhattisgarh and neighbouring states and in the tri-border region of Jharkhand-Bihar-West Bengal, all underdeveloped tribal regions.[20]

Many analysts speak about India's vibrant democracy. India is a pluralist society with a civil society that has achieved strategic depth. It has been able to contain centripetal tendencies over the years. One reason is that the lines of communication through representative institutions are always open and an unresponsive or corrupt government can always be voted out of office in the next elections. Moreover, dissent is not smothered and thus does not get channelled to mosques, gurudwaras or churches. Political parties are omnibus organisations, which, in most cases, are not explicitly polarised on religious lines. The deepening of democracy has to an extent empowered the powerless, and there is a rapid expansion of civic bodies that are being made as representative of the common man as possible. Constitutional amendments that seek to satisfy the needs and demands of various sections of the population are put forward from time to time; in a way, flexible co-option mechanisms are embedded in the Indian Constitution which have further evolved over time to ensure the participation of all groups in the national process. Equally important, the military has never deviated from the role it was meant for – ensuring the security of the State; it has never tried to co-opt civil governance which inevitably leads to military rule.

This is not to say that there is no dissent, dissidence or subversion. All

States, even the most comprehensive and open democracies, face dissident movements and challenges from various actors as well as demands for alternative forms of government. Most States have countenanced civil wars, insurgencies, secessionist tendencies, and sometimes, acts of terrorist violence perpetrated by underground groups to propagate their ideology, advertise their presence and demonstrate the State's weakness in the face of a terror attack. India too, has been facing terrorist violence more or less since its inception, and as in the case of Africa and the rest of the world, there is an apparent change in terror methods and tactics in recent years. Strong measures for ensuring security have been in place for a long time, much before the World Trade Center attacks. Today, there is even stricter surveillance. But it should be remembered that while these can serve as pre-emptive measures for the prevention of a terror attack, they do nothing to root out the causes that lead terrorists to plan such acts. India's approach to counter-terrorism has generally been two-pronged, and contra-movements have always been dealt with politically rather than as a law-and-order problem. On the one hand, successive governments have engaged various insurgent groups to attrition, using the military to break down their resistance; on the other hand, they have also engaged them in dialogue, looking for ways to peacefully resolve issues, acceding to reasonable demands when and where necessary. So while terror attacks continue, the door for negotiations is always kept open and developmental and other agendas are pursued to meet demands or assuage grievances; India has proved itself reasonably capable of dealing with total intransigence and terrorism through military and legal means. This is one of the reasons why an extremist movement demanding a Caliphate based on the *Sharia* law or anything similar, has so far not taken root on Indian soil.

The point being made here is that the nature of terrorism in India and some of the States of Africa that are the victims of terror acts is different. Perhaps one reason for this is India's strong democratic traditions which give the country a degree of stability and its people confidence that all may not, after all, be lost – that they can depend on the State to resolve conflictual problems. Going by the definition of terror attacks given earlier, it needs to be asserted that not all countries in Africa have been subjected to terror attacks; many cases of violence are actually law and order issues rather than terrorist attacks.

III

India-Africa Cooperation on Terrorism

The earlier discussion points to the fact that terror acts are largely driven by national economic and political particularities. Western analysts, in recent years, have focussed mainly on 'Islamic' terrorism and how it has become a global scourge. It is necessary, however, to 'unpick' myths about global Islamic terrorism, examine how regional and national particularities influence terrorism and its spread, and not use only Western models to categorise terrorism. It is only then that we can come up with ideas as to how best India and Africa as a whole, as well as individual countries in Africa, can collaborate to counter international terrorism. The word 'international' is being used deliberately, because terrorist acts by local insurgents are sometimes related to law and order, civil war or insurgency issues, which are condemnable internationally, but in which a third party cannot and should not interfere unless it is specifically requested to do so. In fact, earlier, when the focus of terrorism was on the domestic power base, there was perhaps little that outside parties (read, countries) could do to cooperate to resolve issues. Today, with the globalisation of terror networks and the internationalisation of terror financing, there are spaces for cooperation that do not impinge on the sovereignty of States or the rights of groups to self-determination. Groups like the Al Qaeda – that have transnational bases and conduct operations across countries and continents, recruit from across the world and spread their ideology and resources across nations, to influence members to carry out tasks that the organization wants – can be termed international terrorist organisations. The US 'War on Terror' includes preventing terror financing, money laundering etc., which need coordinated international efforts. Unfortunately, few countries have bilateral or multilateral cooperation measures in place. While avenues have opened up for like-minded countries to work together on counter-terrorism, nothing much has been done to build on them; and that holds true for India and Africa as well.

So, how can India and Africa cooperate on counter-terrorism? The African Union is building counter-terrorism structures through its Counter-Terrorism Framework. India, too, is creating new structures after the Mumbai terror attacks of 26 November 2008 whose relative success underscored India's weaknesses in intelligence gathering, border security, information management and communications. These measures include: the creation of a new Coastal Command to secure India's 4650 miles of coastline; the establishment of 20 counter-terrorism schools; the creation of a National Intelligence Agency (NIA); an expansion of its police force; the setting up of specialised anti-terrorism squads across states; the establishment of four new units of National Security Guards (NSG) trained in counter-terrorism and counter-hijacking operations; and the strengthening of the Unlawful Activities (Prevention) Act. While the efficiency of these institutions hinges on key domestic issues like inter-agency and centre-state coordination, the fact remains that a strong counter-terrorism architecture is slowly being put in place. At the same time, these measures are generic and their objective is to prevent terrorist acts from being carried out, apprehend and punish terrorists, and in the case of a terrorist event happening despite precautions, to respond fast and effectively to minimise damage. It is the lack of 'particularity' that can provide the space for cooperation with Africa.

The Delhi Declaration of the India-Africa Forum Summit of 2008 had stated – very low in its list of priorities in Section 18 – that there was a recognition of "the need to further strengthen international cooperation to combat global terrorism" and called for the 'Expeditious finalization' of a Comprehensive Convention on International Terrorism at the UN.[21] The Addis Ababa Declaration of the India-Africa Forum Summit 2011 placed the issue of terrorism even lower at Section 22 and repeated the wording of the 2008 Declaration, adding that there was a need to ensure that cross-border terrorism does not occur and that their territories are not a base for terrorists.[22] It also condemned kidnapping, hostage-taking and ransom payments – all of which are more relevant in the African context, though such acts occur in India too. At the bilateral level, similar platitudes were voiced in the Joint Declaration issued during South African President Thabo Mbeki's visit to India in 2003[23] and also during the State visit of the President of Mozambique to India in 2010.[24] The only reference to practical cooperation was found in the Framework for Cooperation between India and Africa, 2008, under the 'Peace and Security' section of 'Political Cooperation'. It mentions technical assistance to tackle the challenges of money laundering and terror financing, as well as the sharing of information to fight international terrorism, using, among other channels, the African Centre on the Study and Research on Terrorism. In fact, there is much more cooperation between the US and Africa and the US and India in counter-terrorism than between India and Africa, though both are plagued by variations of extremist 'jihadist' Islamist terrorism, cross-border terrorism, terror attacks by home-grown groups, etc. These issues are very different from concerns that confront the US, which faces threats mainly from groups based far outside its borders who resent the United States for a variety of reasons that are beyond the scope of this chapter. Further, the US is more interested in how terrorism affects the United States and its intent is to stop attacks on its homeland, and US personnel and property abroad. It is perhaps not so pro-active in resolving terrorism issues in other countries if they do not threaten US interests. American attempts to root out terrorists that threaten the US may, in fact, have the counter-effect of aggravating problems and giving rise to resentful groups where none had existed earlier. While the nature of terrorism and the methods used by terrorists may not be the same in African countries and India, a few root causes may be similar and some of the issues involved in counter-terrorism like strengthening of borders, methods of negotiation, countering terror financing, sharing information, etc., may provide space for cooperation. India-Africa partnership and cooperation on terrorism can be based on mutual interest, which will be beneficial for both.

There was not much follow up action after the India-Africa Forum Summit of 2008, but the Ministry of Home Affairs did propose cooperation by way of having bilateral institutional mechanisms with African countries apart from building the capacity of their law enforcement officers. Subsequently, in 2013-2014, three courses were conducted, all in India, on Investigation of Economic offences including Cyber Crime (Ghaziabad), Training of Trainer Programme on Comprehensive Disaster Risk Management (New Delhi), and a Basic Course on Drug Law Enforcement (Faridabad).[25] Mutual Legal Assistance Treaties have also been signed with South Africa and Mauritius and bilateral agreements have been signed with Mauritius and Zambia. Beyond these, there has been little substantial cooperation even though the continent is a victim of terrorist violence and generator of people who indulge in such acts of violence. One of the first areas of cooperation should be to work together with greater determination to secure a final agreement on the Comprehensive Convention on International Terrorism and go beyond mere platitudes. Extra-legal and unlawful counter-terrorism methods are counter-productive in the long run, and the world is well aware of this by now. This makes it imperative to have a comprehensive international counter-terrorism regime, which, once ratified, should be enshrined into municipal law and measures should be taken to avoid its misuse to hunt down legitimate political opponents. In fact, it may be pertinent to cite UN Security Council Resolution 1373 of 2001 (following the 9/11 attacks) to explain this point:

> [All States should] Ensure that any person who participates in the financing, planning, preparation or perpetration of terrorist acts or in supporting terrorist acts is brought to justice and ensure that, in addition to any other measures against them, such terrorist acts are established as serious criminal offences in domestic laws and regulations and that the punishment duly reflects the seriousness of such terrorist acts.[26]

The purpose of this Resolution was to ensure that States, by enacting specific counter-terrorism legislation, based where possible on ratified instruments, would no longer need to rely on vague legal provisions, *ad hoc* methods, informal international cooperation or customised interpretations in order to prosecute terrorists. Instead of depending on ambiguous measures, States should establish a clear, complete and consistent legal framework that specifies terrorist acts as serious criminal offences, penalises such acts according to their gravity, and helps the courts bring terrorists to justice. There is need for an international convention, and India and Africa's many States to come together to promote the passage of such an international instrument. Cooperation in this context is also important because terrorism in the developing world has many aspects that are not manifest in the developed world. This gives the Western States a lopsided view of what is terrorism, what drives people to indulge in terror acts, and what distinguishes a common criminal bent on making monetary profit or engage in eliminating rivals, and a terrorist. It is necessary to have the alternative views of developing countries represented in such instruments.

The African Union has its own instruments, notably the 1999 Algiers Convention on the Prevention and Combating of Terrorism and its 2004 Protocol. Cooperative mechanisms are also in place, for instance, the African Centre for the Study and Research on Terrorism (ACSRT); the Nouakchott Process on the Enhancement of Security Cooperation and the Operationalisation of the African Peace and Security Architecture (APSA) in the Sahel-Saharan region; the Regional Cooperation Initiative for the Elimination of the Lord's Resistance Army (RCI-LRA); and the AU Mission in Somalia (AMISOM). In 2002, the AU also came up with a Plan of Action (PoA) that stressed on specific provisions for police and border control, legislative and judicial measures, suppression of the financing of terrorists, exchange of information, and coordination at regional, continental and international levels. Other actions have also been envisaged or undertaken, including efforts at seeking global cooperation. However, Africa continues to display significant vulnerabilities and the terrorist threat is increasing rather than decreasing. It may be noted that while 41 African countries have signed the 1999 Convention and its 2004 Protocol, only 15 countries have ratified the Protocol which strengthens coherence and coordination by clearly outlining the respective roles of the RECs/RMs (Regional Economic Communities/ Regional Mechanisms), the Commission and Council. While there is little India can do to promote AU instruments in African countries since this lies only within the scope of the AU and its member states, it is interesting to note some points made by Dr. Nkosazona Dlamini Zuma, the Chairperson of the AU Commission on Terrorism and Violent Extremism in Africa, on the main reasons for the "emergence and redeployment of terrorist groups in Africa":

> (i) poverty, illiteracy and high rate of unemployment among the youth and the general population, which render them vulnerable to the manipulative messages of terrorist groups and their promises of quick gain; (ii) poor working conditions, insufficient training and discipline of law enforcement personnel that make them easy prey for corruption; (iii) the search for safe havens and refuge by criminal networks in a zone characterized by vast territorial expanses, low and insufficient security coverage and administrative presence; (iv) the quest for new sources of funding, especially through smuggling, drug trafficking and illegal migration; (v) the need to conquer new areas for recruitment and redeployment with the objective of expanding the confrontation field beyond their traditional zone of operations; and (vi) Government institutional weaknesses and the existence of long stretches of porous, largely ill-monitored and poorly-controlled borders, which, combined with vast, ill administered spaces of territory, facilitate illegal cross-border movement of people and goods and provide fertile ground for exploitation by terrorists and transnational organized criminals.[27]

At the 16th Extraordinary Session of the AU Assembly on Terrorism and Unconstitutional Changes of Government in Africa on 28 May 2022, as mentioned earlier, the AU passed an important Declaration on Terrorism and Unconstitutional Changes in Government, which spoke, among other things, of accelerating the signing and ratification of relevant continental instruments, including the Convention on the Prevention and Combating of Terrorism; the AU Convention on Cross-Border Cooperation, and the African Charter on Maritime Security, Safety and Development in Africa; full operationalization of the African Standby Force, developing a Continental Strategic Plan of Action, and building and consolidating strategic international partnerships to reinforce and coordinate efforts to prevent and counter terrorism.[28]

It is within these points that one can find spaces for cooperation with the AU at one level by supporting its various initiatives with training (legal and otherwise), practical measures and monetary help; bilaterally, with different States through the formation of Joint Working Groups etc., and similarly, with regional organisations. Dr. Zuma's statement is quite revealing and pinpoints areas that need to be plugged to prevent terror attacks from taking place and to wean away ordinary citizens from the temptations that terrorist groups may offer. Areas where India may help lie in poverty alleviation and through the promotion of easily available and affordable high quality education to persons of all economic levels. It may also assist in the practical training of law enforcement personnel, especially specialised anti-terror squads and the strengthening of border security. It could also help in building suitable fences, as it is doing on the India-Bangladesh border, for stricter border control (since weak border controls facilitate casual cross-border operations, provision of safe havens, smuggling, illicit trade in arms, etc.). Further, assistance in promoting sustainable development may help root out one of the push factors that attract ordinary people, mired in poverty, with little commitment to ideology, to terrorist organisations. There could also be cooperation between India and Africa at all levels to tighten controls on terror financing, narcotics smuggling and arms running. There could be cooperation also in capacity-building efforts vis-à-vis the military and the police at both bilateral and regional levels (when regional policing gets a boost in Africa). Importantly, there could be extradition treaties, bilateral and multilateral treaties to counter maritime piracy, money laundering, etc. These need global efforts and cannot be done alone by a country, a region or a continent.

In July 2018, Prime Minister Narendra Modi outlined a vision of '10 Guiding Principles for India-Africa Engagement'; the seventh 'guiding principle' was "strengthen[ing] our cooperation and mutual capabilities in combating terrorism and extremism; keeping our cyberspace safe and secure; and supporting the UN in advancing and keeping peace."[29] Subsequently, India appears to have focused more on security and defence issues than on counter-terrorism *per se,* and there seems to be confusion regarding what are military cooperation issues and what is counter-terrorism cooperation. An India-Africa Field Training Exercise (AFINDEX) was held in 2019 followed by the India-Africa Defence Ministers' Conclave (IADMC) in 2020 and the India-Africa Defence Dialogue (IADD) in 2022, on the sidelines of the DefExpo at Gandhinagar, Gujarat, which led to the Gandhinagar Declaration, which emphasized capacity-building of African defence forces. The Defence Minister Rajnath Singh reiterated India's support to combating terrorism and violent extremism in Africa without outlining any details on how India plans to do this.[30] Similarly, External Affairs Minister Dr. S. Jaishankar, speaking at a book-launch at the Indian Council of World Affairs, New Delhi, said, "We are very conscious of the expanding threats posed by radicalism and fundamentalism and terrorism to African societies. These have been the subject of our contemporary agenda of cooperation. The first India-Africa Defence Ministers' Conclave in conjunction with DEFEXPO INDIA in February 2020, institutionalized defence cooperation between us";[31] here too, it appears that India is not thinking of any concrete measures so far as counter-terrorism cooperation is concerned and mixing it up with defence cooperation. It must be remembered that the two are very different things. At the third India-Africa Forum Summit, counter-terrorism appeared at the end of the document under 'Cooperation in Peace and Security', as a sub-section of point no. 48 – "Enhance cooperation and coordination between Africa and India to combat terrorism in all its forms and manifestations, including countering violent extremism and in this regard, make concerted efforts for the early adoption of the Comprehensive Convention on International Terrorism."[32] This appears more as an afterthought than anything else. Further, it should be remembered that cooperation is a two-way process; there seems to be little dialogue between India and Africa on how the AU or individual countries like Nigeria, Ghana or South Africa can help India combat cyber-terrorism, money laundering, terror financing, etc.

The idea is to move beyond platitudes to the next level of India-Africa cooperation, where counter-terrorism cooperation really matters; that is, to a more inclusive, heuristic approach focused on problem solving. That is the need of the hour, both in India and Africa, both simultaneous victims and producers of terrorism. It must be remembered that development requires an environment of peace and security, and terrorism creates an environment of instability which scares away investors, and can turn investments into rubble in seconds. At the first three forum summits, India and Africa had *spoken* of cooperation in countering terrorism; the time has come to move beyond mere talk and take actual practical steps in counter-terrorism cooperation. As Amina Mohammed, UN Deputy Secretary General, speaking on behalf of the Secretary General at the UN Security Council in November 2022, stated, "The challenges posed by terrorist and violent extremist groups can only be met through approaches that are adapted to local contexts. There are numerous regional initiatives that exist to counter terrorism in Africa, from the Multinational Joint Task Force in the Lake Chad Basin to the Joint Force of the G5 for the Sahel, the Accra Initiative and the Nouakchott Process. These regional arrangements require full support and durable commitment from the international community."[33] The time has come for a comprehensive dialogue on what the AU and African countries need from India to help combat international terrorism, and how African countries can help India through measures like extradition, information sharing, curbs on terror financing and money laundering, to prevent terrorist activities in India. It should be remembered that defence cooperation and counter-terrorism cooperation may be related, but they are not the same and the approaches are different. It is only then that there can be a meaningful dialogue and cooperation.

NOTES

1 Ajay Gondane, "Lessons from India: Confronting the Sociological Causes of Terrorism", Monograph, Henry L Stimson Center, New York, 1 July 2006.

2 Jackie Cilliers, "Terrorism and Africa" *African Security Review,* 12 (4), 2003, p. 92.

3 United Nations/Office on Drugs and Crime, "United Nations Convention against Transnational Organized Crime and the Protocols Thereto", New York, 2004. The Convention was signed in Palermo in December 2000.

4 UN General Assembly Resolutions: Resolution 54/110, 9 December 1999, Jewish Virtual Library, at http://www.jewishvirtuallibrary.org/jsource/UN/unga54_110.html, (Accessed 23 March 2015).

5 Gary LaFree, "The Global Terrorism Database: Accomplishments and Challenges", *Perspectives on Terrorism,* Terrorism Research Initiativeathttp://www.terrorismanalysts.com/pt/index.php/pot/article/view/89/html (Accessed 21 May 2015).

6 Ineke Mules, "Stemming the Flow of Illicit Arms in Africa", *Deutsche Welle,*26 July 2019at https://www.dw.com/en/stemming-the-flow-of-illicit-arms-in-africa/a-49761552, (Accessed 09 December 2022).

7 Benjamin Netanyahu, *Fighting Terrorism: How Democracies Can Defeat Domestic and International Terrorists,* Farrar, Straus and Giroux, Macmillan, New York, 1997, p xiii.

8 US Department of State, *Country Reports on Terrorism, 2007, 2008,* Washington, D.C.

9 Human Rights Watch, *Open Secret: Illegal Detention and Torture by the Anti-Terrorism Force in Uganda,* 2009.

10 Nick Ridley, *Terrorism in East and West Africa: The Under-focused Dimension*, Edward Elgar Publishing, Cheltenham, 2014, p. 36.

11 Isaac Terwase Sampson and Freedom C. Onuoha, "'Forcing the Horse to Drink or Making it Realise its Thirst?' Understanding the Enactment of Anti-Terrorism Legislation (ATL) in Nigeria", *Perspectives on Terrorism,* Terrorism Research Initiative at http://www.terrorismanalysts.com/pt/index.php/pot/article/view/154/html (Accessed 21 May 2015).

12 Eli Lake, "Boko Haram's bin Laden Connection", *The Daily Beast,* athttp://www.thedailybeast.com/articles/2014/05/11/boko-haram-s-bin-laden-connection.html, (Accessed 21 May 2015).

13 "IS Welcomes Boko Haram Allegiance: tape," AFP, 12 March 2015 at http://news.yahoo.com/accepts-allegiance-nigeria-jihadists-boko-haram-201513146.html, (Accessed 21 May 2015).

14 Joel Busher, "Introduction: Terrorism and Counter-Terrorism in Sub-Saharan Africa", *Journal of Terrorism Research,* 5 (1), Special Edition: Terrorism and Counter-Terrorism in Sub-Saharan Africa, 2014 (page number not provided in original).

15 Amina J. Mohammed, "Secretary-General's remarks to the Security Council High-Level Debate on "Counter-Terrorism in Africa - An Imperative for Peace, Security and Development" at https://www.un.org/sg/en/content/sg/statement/2022-11-10/secretary-generals-remarks-the-security-council-high-level-debate-%E2%80%9Ccounter-terrorism-africa-imperative-for-peace-security-and-develop(Accessed 10 December 2022).

16 African Union, Declaration on Terrorism and Unconstitutional Changes of Government in Africa, 28 August 2022 at https://au.int/en/pressreleases/20220528/declaration-terrorism-and-unconstitutional-changes-government-africa (Accessed 10 December 2022).

17 African Union Press Release, 'African leaders to scale up efforts against unconstitutional changes of government; terrorism and foreign mercenaries', 28 May 2022 at https://au.int/en/pressreleases/20220528/african-leaders-scale-efforts-against-unconstitutional-changes-terrorism (Accessed 10 December 2022).

18 "Post removal of Article 370, terror activities declined & investment environment created in J&K: FM", *The Economic Times,* 23 March 2022 at https://economictimes.indiatimes.com/news/india/post-removal-of-article-370-terror-activities-declined-investment-environment-created-in-jk-fm/articleshow/90397357.cms?utm_source=contentofinterest&utm_medium=text&utm_campaign=cppst, (Accessed 11 December 2022).

19 Subir Bhaumik, "Maoist Rebels Set Preconditions for Talks", BBC News,at http://news.bbc.co.uk/2/hi/south_asia/8507525.stm (Accessed 24 March 2015).

20 Sujoy Pal, "মাওবাদীএখনও 'সমস্যা'. মেনেনিলপুলিশ ! এসটিএফেচালু 'মাওবাদীদমনশাখা'" [Translation: 'The Police Accept that the Maoists are still a problem: The STF launches a Maoist section'], Left Wing Extremism Section, TV9 Bangla Digital, Edited By: Soumya Saha, Updated on: 28

May 2022, at https://tv9bangla.com/kolkata/west-bengal-stf-launches-left-wing-extremism-section-au50-572418.html, (Accessed on 11 December 2022).

21 Institute of Defence Studies and Analyses, *Delhi Declaration India-Africa Forum Summit*, at http://www.idsa.in/resources/documents/India-AfricaForumSummit2008.html, (Accessed 24 February 2015).

22 Press Information Bureau, Government of India, *Second India-Africa Forum Summit 2011: Addis Ababa Declaration*at http://pib.nic.in/newsite/erelease.aspx?relid=72319 (Accessed 24 February 2015).

23 Avtar Singh Bhasin (ed.), *India's Foreign Relations – 2003 Documents*, Geetika Publishers, New Delhi, 2006.

24 High Commission of India, Maputo,Joint Statement on State Visit of President of Mozambique 30 September 2010 at http://www.hicomind-maputo.org/maputo.php?id=Visit%20of%20President%20of%20Mozambique%20to%20India (Accessed 25 February 2015).

25 Government of India, Ministry of Home Affairs, Policy Planning Division at http://mha.nic.in/Policy_Planing_Division (Accessed 1 March 2015).

26 S/RES/1373 (2001), 28 September2001 at http://www.un.org/en/sc/ctc/specialmeetings/2012/docs/United%20Nations%20Security%20Council%20Resolution%201373%20%282001%29.pdf (Accessed 25 February 2015).

27 African Union, *Report of the Chairperson of the Commission on Terrorism and Violent Extremism in Africa at the Peace and Security Council 455th Meeting at the Level of Heads of State and Government*, Nairobi, Kenya at http://cpauc.au.int/en/content/report-chairperson-commission-terrorism-and-violent-extremism-africa-peace-and-security-co-0 (Accessed 1 May 2015).

28 African Union Press Release, no. 16.

29 Prime Minister's Office, Prime Minister's Address at Parliament of Uganda during his State Visit to Uganda, 25 July 2018 at https://pib.gov.in/PressReleasePage.aspx?PRID=1540025(Accessed 11 December 2022).

30 Press Information Bureau, Defence Wing, "India-Africa Defence Dialogue held on the sidelines of DefExpo 2022 in Gandhinagar, Gujarat; paves way for strengthening of India-Africa defence relations", 18 October 2022 at https://www.mod.gov.in/sites/default/files/sidelines-of-DefExpo-2022.pdf, (Accessed 11 December 2022).

31 Ministry of External Affairs, Government of India, Address by External Affairs Minister, Dr. S. Jaishankar, at the Launch of Book: *India-Africa Relations: Changing Horizons,*17 May 2022 at https://mea.gov.in/Speeches-Statements.htm?dtl/35322/Address_by_External_Affairs_Minister_Dr_S_Jaishankar_at_the_Launch_of_Book_IndiaAfrica_Relations_Changing_Horizons (Accessed 11 December 2022).

32 Third India-Africa Forum Summit, "India Africa Framework for Strategic Cooperation", 29 October 2015 at https://www.mea.gov.in/Uploads/PublicationDocs/25981_framework.pdf (Accessed 11 December 2022).

33 Amina J. Mohammed, no. 15.

9

India's Climate Position, Actions and Partnership

Uttam Kumar Sinha

Science of Climate Change

Scientific evidences indicate that risks and uncertainties are continuously increasing due to climate change, warmer temperatures and greater frequency of extreme events. The Intergovernmental Panel on Climate Change (IPCC)'s Sixth Assessment Report (AR6) with contributions from its three Working Groups (I, II, III) released in August 2021, February and April 2022 respectively, clearly, warned of the "adverse impacts and related losses and damages to nature and people..."[1]

The IPCC notes the following:[2]

Current State of the Environment

- It is unequivocal that human influence has warmed the atmosphere, ocean and land. Widespread and rapid changes in the atmosphere, ocean, cryosphere and biosphere have occurred.
- The scale of recent changes across the climate system as a whole – and the present state of many aspects of the climate system – are unprecedented.
- Human-induced climate change is already affecting many weather and climate extremes in every region across the globe. Evidence of observed changes in extremes such as heatwaves, heavy precipitation, droughts, and tropical cyclones, and, in particular, their attribution to human influence has strengthened.

Possible Climate Future

- Global surface temperature will continue to increase until at least mid-century under all emissions scenario considered. Global warming of 1.5°C and 2°C will be exceeded during the 21st century unless deep reductions in CO_2 and other greenhouse gas emissions occur in the coming decades.
- Continued global warming is projected to further intensify the global water cycle, including its variability, global monsoon precipitation and the severity of wet and dry events.
- Under scenarios with increasing CO_2 emissions, the ocean and land carbon sinks are projected to be less effective at slowing the accumulation of CO_2 in the atmosphere.
- Many changes due to past and future greenhouse gas emissions are irreversible for centuries to millennia, especially changes in the ocean, ice sheets and global sea level.

Limiting Future Climate Change

- From a physical science perspective, limiting human-induced global warming to a specific level requires limiting cumulative CO_2 emissions, reaching at least net zero CO_2 emissions, along with strong reductions in other greenhouse gas emissions.

The liveable world is at stake and a course correction is urgent. Solutions to curb carbon emissions by assessing mitigation options in different economic sectors as well as adaptation are critical. Without additional mitigation efforts, the world may be headed for a 3.7–4.8°C temperature increase by the end of the century. More worrying is the fact that in spite of great attention to climate change mitigation policies worldwide, the global CO_2 emissions from energy combustion and industrial processes, according to International Energy Agency (IEA), rebounded in 2021 "to reach their highest ever annual level. A 6 per cent increase from 2020 pushed emissions to 36.3 giga tonnes (Gt)..."

Some of these impacts as captured in the IPCC Report are:[3]

- Warming of the climate system is unequivocal, and since the 1950s, many of the observed changes are unprecedented over decades to millennia. The atmosphere and ocean have warmed, the amounts of snow and ice have diminished, sea level has risen, and the concentrations of greenhouse gases have increased.

- Each of the last three decades has been successively warmer at the Earth's surface than any preceding decade since.
- Ocean warming dominates the increase in energy stored in the climate system, accounting for more than 90 per cent of the energy accumulated between 1971 and 2020.
- Over the last three decades, the Greenland and Antarctic ice sheets have been losing mass, glaciers have continued to shrink almost worldwide, and Arctic sea ice and Northern Hemisphere spring snow cover have continued to decrease in extent.
- Over the past decade (2010-2020) the rate of sea level rise has increased to 3.9 mm (0.15 inches) per year. In the 1990s it was about 2.5 mm per year.

Political Ramifications

The IPCC Reports come with their share of controversies. To recall, the IPCC Fifth Assessment Report (AR5) in 2013 underlined that about half of cumulative anthropogenic CO_2 emissions between 1750 and 2010 occurred in the past 40 years and opened the Pandora's Box over the 'Anthropocene' era, which, not surprisingly, had political ramifications. First, by shrinking the emission period to a contemporary timeline of 40 years, it overly emphasised the emissions from developing countries. Second, by focusing on the time period of 40 years, it overlooked the historic emissions from 1750-1970, most of which were caused by the developed countries to meet the consumption needs of just 20 per cent of the global population. The fact remained that from 1750-2010, 6.5 out of every 10 tonnes of CO_2 was emitted by rich countries. The statistical shrinking weakened the strong claims made by developing countries for Common But Differentiated Responsibilities and Respective Capabilities (CBDR-RC), and Respective Capabilities (Article 3, UNFCCC). The IPCC Sixth Assessment Report, 2022 too has been criticised. It has been argued in India by a group of scientists from the Chennai-based M.S. Swaminathan Research Foundation and the National Institute of Advanced Studies in Bengaluru that the "modelled scenarios on how to achieve global net-zero emissions place an unfair burden on developing countries."[4]

The Food-Energy-Water Nexus

Over the years, the nexus understanding in the resource management debate has acquired greater acceptance, particularly in understanding the relationship between the three vital systems, food-energy-water (FEW) with the impact of climate change on it. The nexus is a policy approach that combines the concepts of 'security and sustainability'. The FEW perspectives have ushered a new brand of resource realism. Overall, one can see that scarcity narratives around environmental thresholds are leading to the creation of new policy configurations and responses to these crises. It will require governments, corporates and communities, to be increasingly interlinked in the process of nexus governance. The flip side is that a scarcity crisis narrative can equally push States towards control and possessiveness of resources, instead of driving them towards stability and durability solutions.

In sum, the nexus approach is leading to the identification of mutually beneficial responses, thus providing an informed and transparent framework for determining trade-offs and synergies that meet the demand without compromising sustainability. As economies expand, governments will have to choose whether to allocate water to agriculture, or to uses such as energy, industry and manufacturing. The nexus approach is now strongly linked to the emergence of the green economy idea, which also references the idea of clean energy.

There will be increasing concerns relating to the demand-side of the food-energy-water nexus in India. Various estimates suggest that the demand for food and energy will grow by 50 per cent by 2030 and the demand for fresh water by 30 per cent. Water and food management, in particular, will face major challenges due to the increasing uncertainties caused by climate change and by fast changing socio-economic conditions.

Since climate extremes are predicted to increase in frequency and intensity in the future, droughts and floods will become more severe and more frequent. This will impact food security as droughts can dramatically reduce crop yields, livestock numbers and productivity in semi-arid areas. Many parts of India with high levels of chronic undernourishment will also be exposed to the highest degree of instability in food production. This raises important concerns about achieving food security. While the impact of climate change on the biophysical aspects of production is known, its impact on food accessibility and utilisation, distribution and access is complex. The crucial issue for food security is not whether food is 'available' but whether the monetary and non-monetary resources at the disposal of the population are sufficient to allow everyone access to adequate quantities of food.[5]

Water lies at the heart of the nexus of social, economic and political issues in India. It is indisputably an economic and social good unlike any other and a crucial connector between humans, environment and all aspects of the economic system.

Demographic trends, urbanisation and increased consumption levels will drive the nexus thinking and trade-offs at the policy-making level. This will also highlight the importance of adopting an inter-sectoral approach to break the silos between various sectors.

India and Climate Change

India is among the countries that are most vulnerable to climate change. It is projected that by 2050 its population will be about 1.67 billion. Undoubtedly, there will be a commensurate increase in the demand for resources. While India's per capita consumption of energy and many minerals remains low, as it develops, it will have to balance the demand for greater resource use with the risk of exposing itself to greater environmental pressures. India thus has to confront the three interlocking challenges of sustainable development: meeting the needs for food, fuel, and water for a growing population; securing energy and other minerals to support economic growth while maximising resource efficiency; and managing the environmental constraints and strategic consequences of increased resource use and competition. The focus on access, efficiency and externalities will be critical in India's resource policies as it sets itself on the path to becoming a net-zero carbon emitter by 2070.

One of the key issues in climate change has been the lack of effective governance. The ineffectiveness stems from the challenges posed by climate variability, policy response and socio-economic issues which together strain sustainable development goals. India, given its demography, its emission profile, economic indicators and emerging power status, is a critical actor in global climate governance.

The year 2015 was particularly important because two sets of major developments were put on track: First, in respect to the Sustainable

Development Goals (SDGs), and second, the Paris Climate Summit or the COP-21 that resulted in a globally binding agreement to deal with the challenges of climate change. Its overarching goal was to hold "the increase in the global average temperature to well below 2°C above pre-industrial levels" and pursue efforts "to limit the temperature increase to 1.5°C above pre-industrial levels". Influenced by these two notable landmarks, India's domestic policy has shifted towards a proactive approach.

Climate Change Negotiations and India's Position

The history of negotiations on climate change has been about power relationships and its intricate linkages with economics, politics, security and science. The perceptible North-South divide was one of perceptions of the problem, and the perceptions of the solution. Perceptions are by no means driven only by facts and evidences (as science tells us) but also by images, narratives and values (which are unquantifiable). So far, global efforts have failed to provide answers to critical questions such as 'which' solutions will be acceptable; who will 'support' them and who will 'resist'; the 'cost' involved, etc. Briefly, what the North-South debate informs us is whether a collective need through multiple actions is achievable.

What are the reasons for climate negotiations not achieving its intended objectives? First, negotiations on climate change and development issues are highly divisive and emotive. It is difficult to arrive at a consensus. Given the structural flaw in the international system, stalling rather than reaching an agreement is the objective for many countries. Negotiations have been framed in the business-as-usual format keeping in mind the interests of the business elites. Groupings too have often clashed, rather than come to a consensus. Earlier, the affluent OECD countries could together hijack the agenda and dictate the terms. It is no longer so. Similarly, the G-77 developing countries finds it difficult to hold on to their common objectives. Likewise, the BASIC and BRICS groupings have very little in common except that Brazil, China and India are emerging economies. The G20, which has the world's most developed economies and emerging ones and accounts for 75 per cent of international trade and 60 per cent of the global population, also collectively contributes to 80 per cent of global greenhouse gas emissions. While almost all G20 countries have updated their climate pledges or the National

Determined Contributions, only "11 submitted targets are stronger than their previous ones."[6] Each of these countries has very differing interests which stymie collective climate responses.

The second reason is the inequity in the international system. The developing and emerging economies clearly perceive the past interaction with the rich and advanced developed world as being pre-determined and non-beneficial for them. For the developing and emerging economies the norms, particularly of morality and justice, remain unchanged. The rich-poor relation is perceived as being weighted in favour of the rich. With no radical restructuring of the international system, the developing countries tend to block or protest against trade, development and climate negotiations. It is crucial that any forward movement on sustainable development governance addresses the glaring gaps between rich and poor countries as well as the rich and poor within these countries. Sustainable development cannot be achieved without equitable growth.

Third, there is a dominance of the State agencies in the negotiating process. Inter-governmental structures are becoming increasingly disharmonious with the growing societal innovation and creativity. With knowledge systems expanding, it is critical to include varied stakeholders in the processes and not exclusively be government-related. The inter-governmental aspiration for a global deal on climate change or sustainable development, as the history of climate negotiations has shown, is uninspiring. A renewed attention and action at the provincial and municipal level will add substance to dealings on climate change.

Per capita emissions, an important methodology for determining equity and justice, in the climate negotiations, is another important hook on which India hangs its argument. It is similar to the 'one person, one right' principle. For example, China and the US are the top two carbon emitters but in per capita terms, China is way below the US. Likewise, India, 4th in total annual emissions, is well below even China in per capita emissions. There is a need to find 'new pathways for sustainable living', because current consumption patterns in the industrialised world are unsustainable. The equity principle, whereby everyone in the world would get the same quota of emissions, has undoubtedly helped India to firm up its global climate outlook.

For India, economic and social development is crucial in the climate debate and thus the CBDR-RC and poverty eradication remain critical in the negotiation process. The emphasis has been on 'differentiated' and not on 'common'. The principles of Agenda 21 (Rio 1992) guided by multilaterally agreed norms is fundamental to rebalance the state, society and economy and focus on consumption and production patterns. India has been upfront in its climate action and in determining a development pathway that emphasises growth but equally arrests ecological degradation.

One of India's main thrust areas at the global discussions and negotiations on 'green economy' has been to raise the pitch on financial commitment and transfer of technologies from the rich industrialised countries. Financial and technological resources are critically vital to pursue the sustainable path. India's presidency of the G20 offers a unique opportunity and 'unwavering commitment' to deal with delivery plans for economic development and a pro-poor, pro-climate-oriented growth models. Foremost, India has to enhance the legitimacy of the G20 that is not reflective of elite priorities and the machination of great power, but more people-focused and inclusive. India's approach is unlikely to tend towards support for any quantitative emissions targets. Equity and poverty eradication will continue to phrase India's climate stance. As the 'Voice of the Global South', and with CBDR as a rallying point in the climate change debate, India will call for the advanced North countries to take on emissions reduction commitment and reduce their ecological footprints through rationalisation of consumption patterns. But in view of this position and argument, India will have to equally plan how it will approach and tackle the world trading system where there will be more hostility towards an equitable global trade regime and the enforcement of the differential treatment provisions of the WTO.

India's Recent Climate Action

In the recently concluded COP-28 (Conference of the Parties to the UN Framework Convention on Climate Change) in Dubai, some resolutions were signed. The summit scored with the operationalisation of the Loss and Damage Fund. This fund aims to help the vulnerable countries from the loss and damages as a result of impact of climate change. Another achievement was the formal acknowledgement that fossil fuels are the primary reason for climate crisis in the world today. The meeting called for the need to move away from fossil fuels. The Dubai agreement also called for tripling of global renewable energy capacity by 2030.[7]

Earlier at COP-26 in Glasgow, a pact was reached to keep alive the hopes of achieving the 1.5°C goal. The main task of COP-26 was to finalise the remaining procedures, in particular the creation of new Carbon Market, for the implementation of the Paris Agreement.

However, on the issue of Loss and Damage which was introduced in the COP-19 in Warsaw in 2013, no meaningful outcome came about and it is broadly viewed as a disappointment. A dialogue mechanism, however, has been agreed upon to discuss arrangements for funding such activities. The Glasgow Pact after much deliberation called for stronger action in the current decade (2020-2030) to achieve a 1.5°C world and called on nations to:

- Strengthen their 2030 climate action plans or the NDCs (nationally determined contributions) by 2022.
- To scale-up mitigation and implementation efforts.
- Asked countries to 'phase-down' usage of 'unabated' coal power and 'phase-out' inefficient fossil fuel subsidies while providing targeted support to the poorest and the most vulnerable in line with national circumstances.

On the issue of adaptation the Glasgow Pact:

- Asked the developed countries to at least double the finance for adaptation by 2025 from the 2019 levels. In 2019, about $15 billion was made available for adaptation that was less than 20 per cent of the total climate finance flows. Developing countries have been demanding that at least half of all climate finance should be directed towards adaptation efforts.
- To create a two-year work programme to define a global goal on adaptation. The Paris Agreement had a goal on mitigation. Goal on adaptation was missing and this therefore was a significant entry for the developing countries who had been demanding adaptation goals since the Paris Agreement.

On the issue of finance:

- It reminded the developed countries of their commitment in 2009 to mobilize at least $100 billion by 2020. The Paris Agreement had asked the developed countries to scale-up this amount by 2025. Having failed on the promise of $100 billion, the developed countries have now been asked to arrange this amount by 2023.

- While setting the new target for climate finance, it called upon the developed countries to provide transparent information about the progress

On the issue of carbon markets:

- Developing countries were allowed to use carbon credits for meeting their first NDC targets but not for subsequent NDCs. That means, if a developed country wants to buy these credits to meet its own emission reduction targets, it can do so until 2025. Most countries have presented climate targets for 2025 in their first NDCs. This is seen as a major success.

India's Prime Minister Narendra Modi's presence in COP-26 Glasgow and his announcement of a *Panchamrit* (a mixture of five nectar elements) of climate action raised India's credibility as a climate conscious country. The *Panchamrit* is bold and proves the determination and value of commitment to a climate action pathway:

- India will reach its non-fossil energy capacity to 500 GW by 2030.
- India will meet 50 percent of its energy requirements from renewable energy by 2030.
- India will reduce the total projected carbon emissions by one billion tonnes from now onwards until 2030.
- By 2030, India will reduce the carbon intensity of its economy by less than 45 percent.
- By the year 2070, India will achieve the target of Net Zero.

Clearly, India has emerged as a climate leader and has taken several actions towards its mitigation since COP-21 in 2015 to reduce its emissions and adaptation measures to prepare for climate effects. The involvement of the private sector is equally important along with nature-based solutions. Having championed climate justice in the international negotiations, India is supporting just transitions especially in the coal sector while pushing hard towards renewable energy. There is also a strong emphasis on climate resilience particularly when it comes to infrastructure development.

India is the lead player in the International Solar Alliance (ISA) and Coalition for Disaster Resilient Infrastructure (CDRI). The ISA was launched by Prime Minister Modi in Paris in 2015 and now has 101 signatory countries and 80 of them have ratified the ISA framework agreement. Such has been the appeal of the ISA that the US too has found it difficult to resist and joined the solar alliance in Glasgow. It is by all accounts an important landmark proving that countries recognise the value of solar both in terms of economic and climate mitigation and importantly as a catalyst for global energy transition.

The ISA has the potential to unlock US$100 billion in public and private financing and help to promote research and development in renewable energy. The Prime Minister had put forward the idea of One Sun One World One Grid (OSOWOG) at the first ISA summit in 2018 and at Glasgow, he launched the international network of interconnected solar power grids, the Green Grids Initiative (GGI-OSOWOG) along with former British Prime Minister Boris Johnson. Likewise, the CDRI, which was first proposed by Prime Minister Modi during the Asian Ministerial Conference on Disaster Risk Reduction in 2016, has 28 member countries along with UN agencies and multilateral development banks that aim to promote resilience of critical infrastructure. India's climate pathway is based on outcomes and has taken several leads in its journey towards equitable and just transition; for example, the Lead IT initiative for industry transitions. India is all set to abolish single-use plastics and its switch to LED bulbs has helped reduce carbon emissions substantially.

The developed world needs reminding that a one-solution-suits-all-approach is not the best way forward in meeting climate challenges. Encouraging alternate successful approaches, as India has demonstrated, while providing finance and technology to support their commitments is the path, which unfortunately the developed world has failed to take. Talking about what needs to be done by 2030 instead of 2050is a vital message that India has sent across the world.

In 2022, while addressing the nation from the ramparts of the Red Fort on India's Independence Day, Prime Minister Modi said, "We have to become self-reliant in the energy sector. How long will we be dependent on others in the field of energy? We should be self-reliant in the fields of solar energy, wind energy, and various other renewable energy sources like Mission Hydrogen, bio fuel and electric vehicles." A year earlier on India's 75th Independence

Day, the Prime Minister launched the National Hydrogen Mission (NHM) with the aim to meet climate targets by producing 5 million tonnes of Green hydrogen by 2030 and bolster the development of renewable energy capacity, and as he optimistically expressed, "...a quantum leap to energy independence by 2047."

While there is no specific legislation governing renewables in India, a green hydrogen policy was notified by the Ministry of Power in February 2022. The policy has a suitable mix of incentives to attract investors; for example "Allotting land in Renewable Energy Parks to manufacture green hydrogen/ green ammonia." The policy effort is also to facilitate ease of business, for example "By proposing a single portal for all clearances related to the activities of the business". Lastly, the policy encourages export. For example, "Manufacturers of Green Hydrogen/Green Ammonia shall be allowed to set up bunkers near Ports for storage of Green Ammonia for export/use by shipping. The land for the storage for this purpose shall be provided by the respective Port Authorities at applicable charges."

Reducing carbon emissions has been a principal objective and to that effect, hydrogen and ammonia are seen as future green fuels and a catalyst for India's sustainable energy security. The objectives are interconnected – to provide clean energy to the common people, to reduce dependence on fossil fuel and cut substantially crude oil imports. As India pivots towards renewables, green hydrogen can provide significant value-creating opportunities and position India as an export hub for green fuels. Trading green hydrogen with fossil-fuel exporters like Australia and the Gulf states of Oman, Saudi Arabia and the UAE, who are looking to clean energy to diversify their economies, will add to the growing strategic partnership with these countries.

Having pledged to achieve 50 per cent of its installed electric capacity from non-fossil fuels by 2030, government policies are encouraging a "silent revolution" by laying emphasis on electric vehicles (EVs). Marking 40-years of Suzuki Motor Corporation in India, the Prime Minister expressed, "We are rapidly working on both supply and demand of EV ecosystem. From relaxation in tax to easier loan facility, we are working towards increasing the demand of EVs." The Suzuki Motor Gujarat Electric Vehicle Battery Manufacturing Facility at Hansalpur is to be set up with an investment of Rs 7500 crore to manufacture Advanced Chemistry Cell batteries for EVs. It is estimated that India will have a capacity to produce 10 lakh passenger vehicles/year.

The overall message is clear – India can aim to create energy efficient ecosystem based on technology and innovation. India's size (home to 17 per cent of world's population) and its scope for growth means that its energy demand is expected to grow by more than that of any other country in the coming decades. With policies and targets in place, much of this energy growth would be met with low-carbon energy sources. India's stated clean energy achievements this decade, including installing 500 gigawatts of renewable energy capacity, reducing the emissions intensity of its economy by 45 per cent, and reducing a billion tonnes of CO_2 by 2030, will help India achieve its net zero emissions by 2070.

India is demonstrating ability to prioritise at the policy planning and implementation levels. While it is necessary to achieve technological collaboration with different countries, it is equally crucial to strengthen national innovation. Adapting, identifying and revaluating technology and innovation, and ensuring higher budgetary resources are allocated will help India to remain both resilient and competitive in the changing landscape.

Climate Values

In November 2022, Prime Minister Modi launched the LIFE Movement. As an environment conscious lifestyle, the mission enhances the idea of 'pro-planet people' (P3), while simultaneously reinforcing Mahatma Gandhi's environment trusteeship, which claims: "The earth, the air, the land and the water are not an inheritance from our forefathers but on loan from our children." While addressing climate change requires national and international actions, communities, households and individuals, have a vital role to play too. Article 51A (g) of the Indian Constitution states, "It should be the duty of every citizen of India to protect and improve the natural environment including forests, lakes, rivers and wild life, and to have compassion for the living creatures". Where the responsibility lies has been a recurring debate in the relationship between the State and its people. With climate urgency, the time has passed about who is to blame. Clearly both are needed – system change and lifestyle change.

Studies have observed that 'lifestyle' carbon footprints are out of sync with the globally agreed goal to keeping temperature rise to 1.5°C above pre-industrial times. Some analysis in fact points out that lifestyle carbon footprints need to be reduced by 91-95 per cent by 2050 in high-income countries, compared with 76 percent in lower-middle income countries, that could account for a quarter of the emissions reductions required to keep the global heating down to 1.5°C.

What would LIFE in the true sense mean? LIFE brings in the essence of the individual, as part of the collective, to pave the way for new approaches and good habits of living by undertaking simple climate friendly actions on a daily basis. Individuals matter and they are important in affecting change by making choices about protecting the environment. The LIFE expression is simple: If democracy can work because of people's participation, then so can environment action, and since humans collectively have damaged the environment then logically they can equally fix it. Personal lifestyle exemplifies two key *jicamas* or the self-based codes of conduct. One, *shaucha* that relate to keeping the environment and natural surroundings clean in particular water and air; and *tapas* or austerity, defined by the principle of need and not greed; in other words "mindful and deliberate utilisation" instead of "mindless and wasteful consumption".

Central to LIFE, indisputably, is reining-in runaway consumption. Consumption patterns also reflect inequality between the developed, emerging economies and the developing world. But there is one common factor and that is the high-consuming lifestyle-linked greenhouse gas emissions of the rich and wealthy across the world. Addressing the way the affluent live by utilising the carbon emission space is fundamental to allowing everyone equitable opportunities for life of dignity. Food, housing and personal transport representing about four-fifths of the total lifestyle, have the largest impact on climate change. Calculations suggest that the emissions' share of the top one percent highest-income earners is greater than the total emissions of the bottom 50 per cent combined.

To reach a 'fair consumption space' a number of government actions like easing subsidies for fossil fuels and tax incentives on low-carbon technologies along with increasing the prices of carbon-intensive products and activities, can be considered and several policies have already been undertaken. Individual actions that are neither expensive nor reducing well-being can be initiated based on environmental consciousness and choice. A number of studies and surveys indicate that there are several behavioural shifts at the individual level, for example plant-based diet without wasting food, reducing buying of clothing per year, upgrading light bulbs, recycling, extending the use of electrical and electronic items, optimising public transport and holding on to personal vehicles longer. Another environment conscious approach is to trade-off individual carbon footprint. For example, if one is using personal cars then a good practice would be to offset it by other low-carbon emissions action like moving to green energy. Even at least one carbon-reducing specific action is taken at an individual level, the impact collectively will help fight climate change.

LIFE encapsulates State and society, the global and the national, the rich and poor both between and within countries, the market and regulators and all that must be done to ensure climate transition that is fair and equitable. All this will help to generate behavioural adjustments and changes. However, high impact actions require substantive even radical behaviour changes. This brings in the question of population growth, which by far has the highest impact on the climate. To gradually reduce the global population rate, the goal is to 'lower the total fertility rate from the current value of 2.4 to 2.1'. Although the fertility rate has declined since 1960, it still remains above the required level. Population control has to be a movement requiring individual awakening, change of perception, and government policies and awareness campaigns that relate family-planning decisions of the individuals, based on climate-mitigation consideration.

India and Africa

Climate change will have unimaginable consequences for livelihoods in Africa. With 96 per cent of African agriculture dependent on rainfall and 50 per cent of fisheries-related jobs estimated to be lost by 2050, climate change becomes an existential issue. Importantly, African States speak with one voice and have a unified position on climate change. Africa's demand for a climate regime that is legally binding, rules-based and transparent is forthright and genuine. African countries are responsible for less than 3 per cent of total global emissions, and yet bear the heaviest brunt of the climate impact. With the establishment of the India-Arica Forum Summit in 2008, the relationship between India and the African countries has steadily evolved with multi-dimensional issues, including climate change.

The Conference of African Heads of States on Climate Change (CAHOSCC) has consistently flagged a balance between mitigation, adaptation and finance under the Paris Agreement.[8] There is plenty of space and scope for convergence with India's position. For example, India along with the African States can strongly demand the implementation of commitments and mechanisms made under previous COPs, such as finance and technology transfer. Further, India and Africa can collectively reiterate that the obligation of developed countries to allocate public resources to support adaptation measures in developing countries should continue. India should also support the idea of an African Climate Change Fund.

Earlier, Like Minded Developing Countries (LMDC) had no African representation. From 13-member countries in 2015, it now has 20 members and includes Egypt, Sudan and Zimbabwe. This can be an important forum to raise concerns about the eligibility criteria for receiving climate finance and expanding the donor base for the Green Climate Fund on mitigation efforts. In October 2022, the Ministerial Meeting of the LMDC prepared itself for the COP-27 in Egypt. India supported the Egyptian Presidency as both "a LMDC friend and partner-nation."[9] The meeting stressed on the issues of climate adaptation, and loss and damage. Climate action can thus bring India and African countries together as a force multiplier against the developed countries on climate finance, as well as for convergence on climate mitigation and adaptation, and capacity-building and technology development.

In February 2023, the ISA with its headquarters in Gurugram hosted 13 African countries to share best practices in solar energy deployment. In 2018, the African Development Bank signed a deal with ISA to scale up solar energy in Africa. The joint declaration recognized the Bank's "New Deal on Energy for Africa, its energy policy and its leadership in working with governments, the private sector, and bilateral and multilateral energy sector initiatives to develop a Transformative Partnership on Energy for Africa."[10] Green hydrogen offers immense potential to collaborate and necessitate a sustainable energy transition, especially as Africa is becoming a bigger player in the global economy and India has proven to be a dependable partner.

Conclusion

Climate change has multitude of diverse perspectives and views. At the end of the day, there can be no better policy than the one that keeps the human ecological footprint within planetary boundaries. India is conscious of its responsibilities towards the global commons and as a climate leader, is willing to work with countries to find solutions. Technology and innovation along with values and ethics together present a range of options to transition to a climate-friendly society and ultimately to net-zero.

NOTES

1 "Climate Change 2022: Impacts, Adaptation and Vulnerability", IPCC Sixth Assessment Report at https://www.ipcc.ch/report/ar6/wg2/resources/spm-headline-statements/ (25 February 2023)

2 IPCC Working Group II, 2022 at https://www.ipcc.ch/report/ar6/wg2/downloads/report/IPCC_AR6_WGII_SummaryForPolicymakers.pdf (Accessed 25 February 2023)

3 Ibid.

4 *The Print*, 5 January 2023 at https://theprint.in/environment/why-indian-scientists-are-critiquing-ipcc-report-unfair-burden-on-developing-countries/1298871/ (Accessed 24 February, 2023)

5 Read Reena Singh and Ashok Gulati, "India's Long Term Low Carbon Strategy and Agriculture", *AgriFood Trends and Analytics Bulletin*, Vol. 2 (3), January 2023, pp. 19-24. (Accessed 24 February 2023).

6 Renita D'Souza and Debosmita Sarkar, "Climate Performance Index: A Study of the Performance of G20 Countries in Mitigation", Occasional Paper, ORF, 23 February 2023.

7 Amitabh Sinha, COP28: what were the important decisions, where they fell short" *Indian Express*, 15 December 2023 at https://indianexpress.com/article/explained/explained-climate/cop28-what-were-the-most-important-decisions-where-they-fell-short-9067358/ (Accessed 22 December 2023)

8 African Union at https://au.int/en/newsevents/20220206/meeting-committee-african-heads-state-and-government-climate-change-cahoscc (Accessed 24 February, 2023).

9 Ministry of Environment, Forests and Climate Change, Press Information Bureau, 21 October 2022at https://pib.gov.in/PressReleaseIframePage.aspx?PRID=1870125 (Accessed 24 February 2023).

10 African Development Bank Group Communiqué, 12 March 2018 at https://www.afdb.org/en/news-and-events/african-development-bank-signs-deal-with-international-solar-alliance-to-propel-solar-development-in-africa-17936 (Accessed 24 February 2023).

10

Human Security Implications of Climate Change for Sub-Saharan Africa and How India Can Assist

Ian Shanghvi

Introduction

Climate change is increasingly becoming a dominant agenda for discussion and deliberations for policy and action at national and international levels. Its prominence emanates from its perceived and experienced impact on broad human security issues and the welfare of our planet, but also from determining and influencing of the development path and balance of power in the global political economy. Climate change has caused severe and perhaps enduring alterations to the earth's geological, biological and ecological systems.[1] These changes have generated and will continue to generate large-scale environmental hazards to human health, such as extreme weather, ozone depletion, loss of biodiversity and stress on food-producing systems. It is expected that climate change will increase the risk and spread of certain infectious diseases – particularly those occurring in warm areas – including malaria, dengue fever, yellow fever and encephalitis.[2] Other concerns linked with climate change include deadly heat waves, drought, food and water shortages, and international conflicts.[3] The World Health Organization (WHO) estimates that there were 160,000 deaths per annum on account of climate change between 1950 and 2000, with the toll expected to reach about 300,000 lives by 2020.[4] Most of the climate change induced deaths that occurred in the last quarter of the 20th century were concentrated in certain regions of the world, especially Africa, the Indian subcontinent, and Southeast Asia.[5] This paper looks at the impacts of climate change on human security and welfare in Sub-Saharan Africa (SSA). The paper looks at various areas of climate change impacts on wide-ranging security issues; including human health, food security, water crisis, displacement and migration, human settlement, energy sector, and transport. It ultimately offers a suggestion on how India can assist SSA to adapt and mitigate the impacts of climate change.

Similarly, the adverse effects of climate change are experienced largely by poor and low-income communities around the world. This owes to their much higher levels of vulnerability to environmental determinants of health, wealth and other factors, and very limited capacity to cope with environmental change. The negative impacts of climate change are expected to be most experienced in the rural areas of the developing world, where agricultural production is the major sector for employment and income, due to agriculture's direct exposure to climate change.[6] Africa is particularly prone to the greatest risks of climate change due to its reliance on climate dependent sectors such as rain fed agriculture, and its history of resource, ethnic and political conflicts.[7] Conflicts were about 50 per cent more likely in Africa in years when it was unusually warm, and have increased by 50 per cent over the last two decades as a result of climate change.[8] Indeed, climate change plays a critical role in the conflicts continuously being observed in Africa, and the situation may exacerbate if effective drastic measures are not undertaken.

In fact, several longer-term impacts of climate change in Africa have been projected. The major ones include changing rainfall patterns affecting agriculture and reducing food security; worsening water security; decreasing fish resources in large lakes due to rising temperatures and overfishing; rising sea levels affecting low-lying coastal areas with large populations; and rising water stress. Figure 1 shows some of the impacts of climate change on Africa.

SSA is expected to fare worst among the developing regions of the world, as temperatures are generally already high, and most of the inhabitants (over 70 per cent) are overwhelmingly dependent on rain-fed subsistence agriculture and their livelihoods depend on natural resources.[10] Mitigation or adaptation measures in SSA will continuously be challenged by the extreme scarcity of national government funds and local incomes. These challenges, in their totality,

Figure 1: Climate Change Impacts on Africa[9]

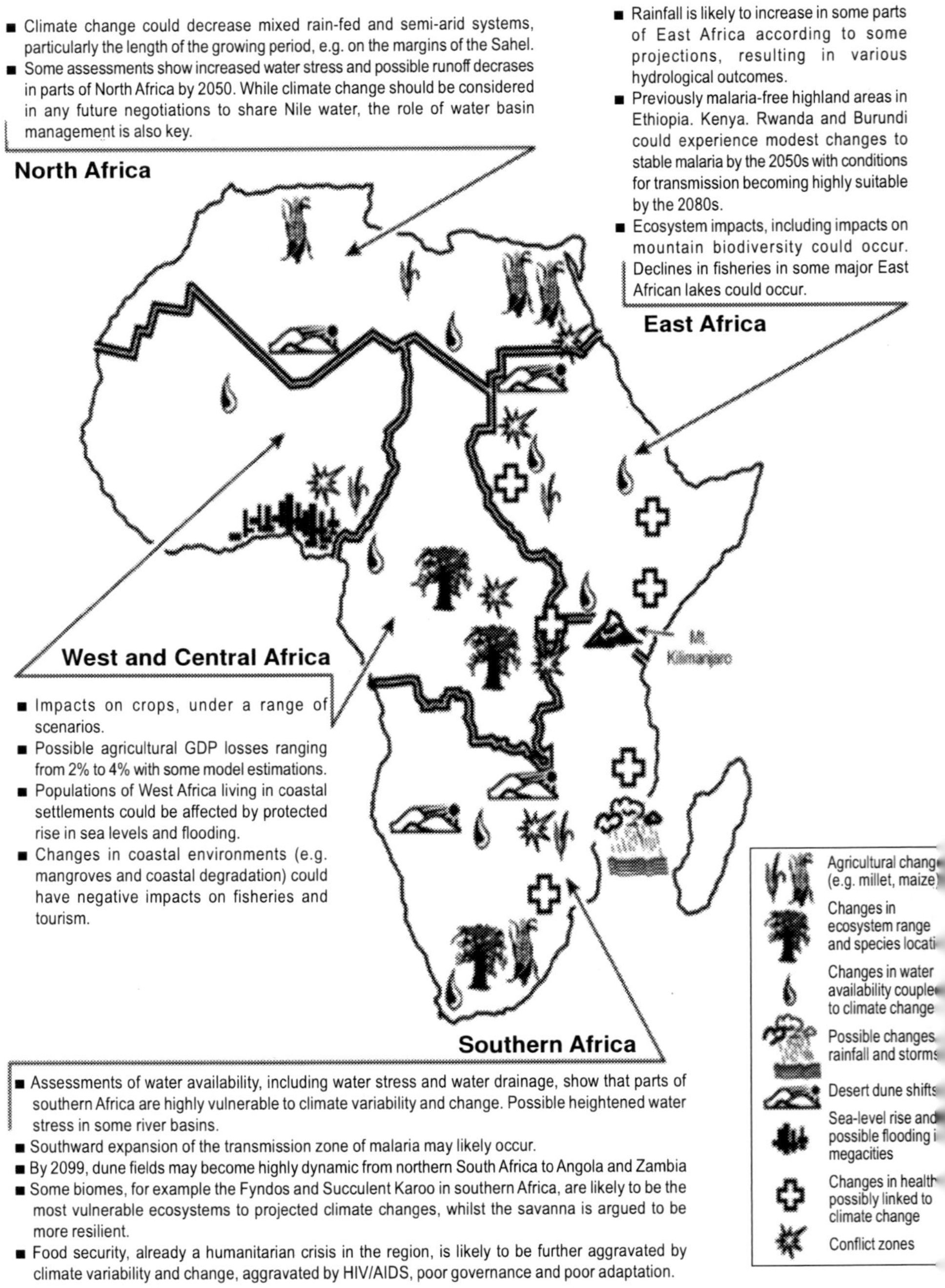

are most likely going to exacerbate the potential for violent security events. It is for this reason that climate change is particularly cited as being a *threat multiplier*. Experts have suggested links to climate change in several major conflicts, such as:

- War in Darfur, where prolonged drought encouraged conflict between herders and farmers.[11]
- Syrian Civil War, preceded by the displacement of 1.5 million people due to crop and livestock failure caused by drought.[12]
- Islamist insurgency in Nigeria, where anti-government sentiment was caused by natural resource shortages.[13]
- Somali Civil War, in which droughts and extreme high temperatures have been associated with violence.[14]
- Sahel region, where heightening competition between livestock and agricultural production due to drought led to conflicts and widespread destruction of farmland and cattle.[15]

Impacts of Climate Change on Human Security and Welfare

Most of the key vulnerabilities to climate change are related to climate phenomena that exceed the thresholds for adaptation; such as extreme weather events or abrupt climate change, as well as limited access to resources (i.e., financial, technical, human, and institutional) to cope.

Human Health

Clean air, safe water, adequate food, tolerable temperature, stable climate, and high levels of biodiversity are a prerequisite for the sustainability of health anywhere in the world. Climate change poses a threat to these requirements, thereby exposing people to health problems. The health effects are unevenly distributed, and are predominantly severe in countries with high disease burdens. SSA and Asia offer classic examples. A range of factors are already compromising Africa's resilience to the health impacts of climate change. While some African countries have already been severely affected by the worst effects of climate change on health, yet, these effects are predicted to worsen off. The Horn of Africa has suffered malnutrition specifically from the persistent food shortages. Malnutrition is the most hyped health effect resulting from climate change, yet not much has been done to arrest the situation.[16] Climate sensitive, parasitic infections like malaria, schistosomiasis, trypanosomiasis, leishmaniasis, and intestinal helminths and other climate linked epidemics such as cholera and diarrhoeal infections are already common in Africa.[17] Of these infectious diseases, malaria is the number one killer. SSA is particularly overstrained by malaria as a consequence of climate change.[18]

Children are the most vulnerable to climate change-fuelled health problems. Low-income countries, especially in SSA, continue to be adversely affected by childhood mortality due to diarrhoea notwithstanding improvements in care and the use of oral rehydration therapy.[19] It is estimated that 85 per cent of children in Africa suffer from malaria, yellow fever, diarrhoea, malnutrition, and get badly affected by natural disasters.[20] Children in poor rural and urban slum areas are at a severe risk of diarrhoeal disease mortality and morbidity.[21] The transmission of enteric pathogens has been cited to correlate with rainy seasons because of poor drainage and storm water management in low-income urban communities, as blocked drains provide a favourable environment for increased disease transmission.[22] Poor drainage systems in SSA are also linked to cholera outbreaks following flood events (an acclaimed outcome of climate change) and faecal contamination of the water supplies. Meanwhile, drought events are also associated with dust storms and respiratory health effects in SSA and worldwide.

Food Security and Food Production Systems

Global warming caused by the emissions of greenhouse gases is already warming climates and will likely cause changes in precipitation patterns. Climate change, concurrent with increasing demand for food, feed, fibre and fuel, is highly likely poised to irreversibly damage the natural resource base on which agriculture depends, with colossal ramifications for food insecurity.[23] The United Nations Security Council warns that food crisis is a threat to peace and security in Africa. Africa's high dependence on rain fed agriculture makes its food production almost entirely dependent on rainfall. The last decade saw 25 African countries affected by food shortages, which involved as many as 200 million people.[24]

At least 150,000 deaths and approximately 5 million illnesses are reported every year in SSA, attributable to climate change scenarios like global warming.[25] SSA will continuously suffer from changes in yield and area growth, higher food prices and, therefore, lower affordability of food, reduced calorie availability, and growing childhood malnutrition as a consequence of climate change.[26] This is because Africa's adaptive capacity is extremely low, which is linked to acute poverty levels and poor infrastructure, as reflected in overdependence on rain fed agriculture. In addition, climate change is happening while SSA faces growing populations, faster economic growth than in the past, and growing urbanization, coupled with insufficient improvement in agricultural productivity. Food security in SSA is further aggravated by poor prioritisation of food security issues by national and international governments, low agricultural budgets, weak institutional capacity, difficulties in coordination, and declining of resources by donors.[27] Most of the small-scale farmers who depend on food production for subsistence and income generation are already unable to meet their daily basic food needs. Certain population groups are most severely affected, especially women and children who are usually poorer, and whose daily activities include farming, fishing, and herding, among others. The economic activities of these groups depend mostly on water, which is increasingly becoming a scarce resource to support irrigation, fishing, and herding as rivers have been drying up in the recent past.

Water Crisis

While natural resources constitute the economic backbone of SSA countries, some of these natural resources are also expected to be vulnerable to climate change. The impacts of climate change on the global hydrological cycle are expected to vary the patterns of demand and supply of water for agriculture – the dominant user of freshwater. The extent and productivity of both irrigated and rain fed agriculture can be expected to change. Research has proved that conflict can be driven by natural resource degradation, scarcity and by competitive control of areas where resources are abundant.[28] Distortions of water resources by climate change have specifically been singled out for interfering with human security. National and global security can be assessed in many ways, but one underlying factor for all humanity is access to reliable sources of water for drinking, sanitation, food production and manufacturing industry. Drought and other natural incidents, in addition to political misrule and economic mismanagement, have collectively forced millions of Africans to migrate within the continent.[29] Again, further conflict may be engendered while people and their livestock are migrating in search for water and food in case of drought and floods as a result of competition.

SSA countries are now experiencing significant water stresses due to unreliable and insufficient rainfall, as well as changes in rainfall patterns. This situation will likely be aggravated by climate change, which will impose more pressure on the already scarce water supply in terms of both access and availability. And since the region is politically volatile and unstable in nature, water crisis is expected to function as a recipe for disastrous conflicts.[30]

Displacement and Migration

Large numbers of people will be forced to forsake their homes and communities as climate change makes certain parts of the world much less viable places to live: by causing flooding and unreliable water supplies, undermining livelihoods, through sea-level rise and flooding thereby reducing available land, and by increasing the frequency and destructive power of storms. In Africa, more people will continue to be affected by climate change, and migration hotspots around Africa will probably increase. Persistent environmental degradation and demographic pressures are projected to displace millions of people in Africa and create severe social upheaval.[31] Apparently, at least 30 per cent of the world's refugees and internally displaced people are accommodated by African countries.[32] North Africa has become a migration destination (for internal and cross-border migrants) and transit area for people from SSA and Asia attempting to migrate to Europe.

Furthermore, the general structure of the economies of the SSA countries will cause them to bear the most negative consequences of climate change. A third of the SSA's land area is permanently used for agriculture that employs on average two-thirds of the labour force and contributes by approximately 30% to the GDP in the region.[33] This makes the livelihoods of many people in SSA directly tied to environmental resources, hence exposing them to greater challenges of climate change. Declining resources will provoke migration and population displacement and bring antagonistic groups in competitive contact, which may stir violent clashes between them. For instance, the Horn of Africa's pastoralist areas (Ethiopia-Kenya-Somalia border) have been terribly affected by recurrent droughts, causing livestock losses that have plummeted about 11 million people who are dependent on livestock for their livelihoods into crisis and pushing large numbers of the pastoralists out of drought-affected areas.[34]

The resulting movements can cause clashes between different groups of pastoralists and between pastoralists and other land users, especially farmers.

Human Settlement

Climate variability, including extreme events such as storms, floods and sustained droughts, is causing huge impacts on human settlements and related infrastructure. The main challenge for human settlements in coastal and low-lying areas is sea-level rise, indicated by relentless declines in ice-mass balance from both Greenland and Antarctica. In countries as those situated in the SSA region, the poorest often live on floodplains mainly for extant agricultural potential. However, their settlements often lack infrastructure such as dykes and early warning systems. Poorer communities also tend to lack the insurance, savings, or access to credit needed to recover from disasters.

African populations are likely to face the challenges caused by the effects of extreme events such as tropical storms, floods, landslides, wind, cold waves, droughts, and abnormal sea-level rises that are expected as a result of climate change. These events are likely to worsen management problems associated with pollution, sanitation, waste disposal, water supply, public health, infrastructure, and technologies of production. Moreover, with the current projections that by 2015 three coastal megacities of at least 8 million inhabitants would be located in Africa, it could be feared that the rise in sea level will have significant impacts on these coastal megacities because of the concentration of poor populations in potentially hazardous areas that may be exclusively vulnerable to such changes.[35] As a matter of fact, three of the five regions shown to be at risk of flooding in coastal and deltaic areas of the world by 2080 are those located in Africa (North Africa, West Africa and Southern Africa).[36]

Energy Sector

Only a handful of studies are available that specifically examine the impacts of climate change on energy in Africa. But typically, the impacts are primarily experienced through losses or changes in hydropower potential for electricity generation and the effects of increased runoff (including consequent siltation) on hydro generation, and changes in the growth rates of trees used for fuel wood.[37] Climate change impacts on the energy sector in Africa will be most felt in the provision of energy services for rural areas and, to some extent, for urban low-income needs. The millions of cubic meters of wood harvested each year for energy purposes make Africa's dependence on biomass energy production very high. The implications of this dependence on the energy sector are formidable because the source of biomass is supported only by natural regeneration of indigenous natural forests. The eastern and southern African countries are highly dependent on charcoal.[38] As such, while climate change poses negative effects on the energy sector of Africa, the energy sector also exacerbates climate change on the continent. And even in the absence of climate change, a number of changes are expected in the energy sector. The recent and rapid urban growth in Africa is associated with increases in aggregate commercial energy demand and emission levels, let alone extensive land-use and land-cover changes.[39] These changes will alter existing surface microclimates and hydrology with a chance of aggravating the scope and scale of climate-change impacts.

Transport

It has been pointed out earlier that climate change is expected to increase the frequency and intensity of extreme weather events. Transportation and communication along the African coastal zone consist of extensive networks of roads, railways, airports, seaports and canals, which are prone to climate change impacts. As pointed out earlier, increasing sea level will result in flooding of these transportation and communication networks. Climate change will also have numerous direct effects on the road infrastructure. High temperatures easily crack the roads within a short period after their construction, while high precipitation easily causes potholes on new roads while deepening existing potholes rather fast. In fact, flooding can completely wash out or severely damage roads. This has been evidenced in the flooding in Colorado and wet-season access in SSA.[40] Repairing the roads requires huge amounts of funds that are not readily or easily available. Being the continent most vulnerable to climate change and faced with acute fiscal limitations, Africa will excruciatingly suffer from the consequences of climate change with a high potential of an enhanced criticality level for areas with a paucity of roads.[41] The direct impact of climate change on roads will have tremendous consequences on the African economic systems. Poor roads resulting from huge potholes can cause road accidents and delay the transport of foodstuffs and other goods, as well as certain services.

Way Forward: Avenues for India to Assist Sub-Saharan Africa

The pervasiveness of the climate change plights and Africa's poor position to meaningfully alleviate itself from the same calls for a collective global effort. Climate change is already having considerable impacts on Africa, and successfully adapting to these impacts is pivotal to achieving the continent's development objectives. The World Bank's development report for 2010 identifies the need for Africa to ensure that the current development impacts of climate change on its economies and populations are recognised and that a development agenda is integrated into climate negotiations.[42] African countries are already working hard to address and shield themselves from the intensifying negative impacts of climate change. The African Union (AU) also, as a lead Pan-African institution, is well aware of the criticality of climate change and devotes great efforts to address it (see Appendix 1). However, despite these efforts, Africa is still ill-placed in the face of climate change impacts. The challenges present Africa with opportunities for action, but also provide other countries around the world with entry points to assisting Africa. India, for one, can really assist Africa (especially SSA) in overcoming these challenges and paving the way for Africa to better adapt to and mitigate climate change impacts. This paper sees no need to reinvent the wheel and, therefore, considers and promotes the challenges and opportunities that are well documented in the paper by Tadesse.[43] Thus, the table below specifies the challenges facing Africa (including SSA) and opportunities for India's respective intervention.

Table 1: Climate Change Challenges Facing Africa and Assistance Opportunities for India

Challenges facing Africa (including Sub-Saharan Africa)	*Assistance opportunities for India*
1. Lack of evidence regarding both the impact of climate variability on climate-sensitive development outcomes and the benefits of climate information to improve these outcomes.	Africa needs to conduct scientific research in climate variability on climate-sensitive development outcomes and acquire evidence of the benefits of climate information to improve these outcomes. In part, this also requires raising awareness of climate information and providing evidence of its value to decision makers in climate-sensitive sectors. These activities should also target at providing the future generations in African countries with environmental education – both in the general public, primary and secondary schools, and universities.

Challenges facing Africa (including Sub-Saharan Africa)	*Assistance opportunities for India*
2. Much uncertainty about the probabilities of various possible changes occurring in specific locations. A computer-driven weather forecasting tool known as General Circulation Model can be used to understand current climate conditions and project future climate change. However, due to a lack of primary data on which to base the model, predicting Africa's climatic changes remains uncertain and the climate-observation system in Africa is in a far worse state than those of other continents, and is deteriorating.	Africa needs investments in data acquiring and improved information to reduce the degree of local uncertainty.
3. Most of the sectors on which development efforts focus are climate sensitive, including agriculture, health, energy, transport and water resources. Incorporating climate knowledge into these efforts could greatly enhance their effectiveness, yet the opportunities for doing this are largely being missed in Africa.	Africa needs an integrated approach that incorporates climate science into multidisciplinary development planning and projects. The climate tools used in such an approach will enhance stakeholders' decisions making by providing relevant new information that they can incorporate into practice.
4. The quality of the environment continues to decline in many parts of Africa. The major portion of carbon dioxide release in Africa is contributed by burning fossil fuels and the conversion of tropical forests to facilitate agricultural production, as well as lumber cutting for domestic and international industry. Yet this situation reflects the reality of energy insecurity in Africa in terms of increasing demand due to population growth and dwindling supplies of traditional fossil fuels.	Africa needs sustainable development, including a rapid move toward a low-carbon economy. New green growth investment opportunities are necessary to respond to the urgent and growing need for climate change adaptation, particularly in the area of energy security. The need becomes apparent to address the issue of alternative energy such as solar, hydro and wind power to mitigate the current problem of deforestation, overgrazing, drought and soil degradation in many parts of Africa.
5. The Secretariat of the UNFCCC estimates that US$ 220 million per year will be required by African countries to adapt to climate change by the year 2030. According to Article 4 (4) of the UNFCCC, developed countries are under a legal obligation to provide financial resources to African countries to adapt to climate change. However, despite the existence of this mechanism, limited financial resources have been made available to Africa.	India can help Africa in making an aggressive demand that developed countries meet the cost of adaptation to climate change in Africa. Such compensation should be adequate, predictable and accessible. Mobilisation, management and allocation of resources are the three main issues that must be managed to get adaptation financing right. Also, reviews of the status of international climate agreements related to adaptation, mitigation and compensation should be done.

Challenges facing Africa (including Sub-Saharan Africa)	*Assistance opportunities for India*
6. Coping with climate variability is a major challenge for the people of SSA. The high dependence of the economies and rural people of the region on rain-fed agriculture, the prevalence of poverty and food insecurity, and the limited development of institutional and infrastructural capacities in this region make coping with natural climate variability a perennial challenge. As such, climate change will exacerbate poverty unless these vulnerable populations are assisted in building climate-resilient livelihoods.	The following are required: • Adaptation measures: including water-wise irrigation systems, low-/no-till agricultural practices, income diversification and disaster risk management. • Initiatives to help small farmers and other vulnerable groups to protect and promote agricultural production, including improving agricultural extension services so as to increase yields and the establishment of independent networks of information exchange between and among communities across the region. • The empowerment of women and other marginalised social groups to overcome the additional barriers they face to adaptation. • Inclusive, transparent and accountable adaptation planning with the effective participation of especially vulnerable populations across the continent. In regard to agricultural production and water, climate adaptation may include the following: • The adoption of varieties and species of crops with increased resistance to heat stress, shocks and drought. • The modification of irrigation techniques, including amount, timing or technology (e.g., the drip irrigation system). • The adoption of water-efficient technologies to 'harvest' water, conserve soil moisture, and reduce siltation and saltwater intrusion. • Improved water management to prevent water logging, erosion and nutrient leaching. • The modification of crop calendars, i.e., the timing and location of cropping activities. • The integration of the crop, livestock, forestry and fishery sectors at farm and catchment levels. • The implementation of seasonal climate forecasting. • Additional adaptation strategies involving land-use changes that take advantage of modified agro-climate conditions.
7. The existing adaptation mechanisms and resources under the Kyoto Protocol designed to mitigate climate change's effects on Africa (and other developing regions) have been directed at limiting future carbon emissions. The Kyoto Protocol misses the facts and links between climate change and droughts, desertification, floods, coastal storms and soil erosion – contemporary disaster events that threaten lives and livelihoods and hinder Africa's economic growth and social progress.	The Kyoto Protocol fails to address Africa's vulnerability and lack of resilience to the impact of climate change on its economies and populations. A revision of the Protocol is, thus, an imperative urgent action in order to integrate the real issues pertaining to the African economies and populations.

As shown above, the challenges are numerous and the opportunities for intervention similarly abound. The solutions proposed above will play a critical role in reducing Africa's vulnerability to climate change and the consequent security outcomes. This way, Africa will be able to improve its defence against the security-related impacts of climate change, especially in the areas of human health, food security, water crisis, displacement and migration, human settlement, energy sector, and transport. African countries are willing to cooperate, and so are their regional bodies and the overarching African Union.

* * *

Appendix 1

African Union (AU)'s Commitment to Addressing Climate Change in Africa[44]

Climate Change and the AU Position

Traditionally, national development plans, poverty reduction strategy papers and sectoral strategies in climate-sensitive sectors have paid little, if any, attention to climate variability, and even less to climate change. Africa's ability to turn a threat into an opportunity hinge on actions taken today. Africans have already begun to take some steps in their region. For example, the African Union Commission (AUC) supported the Environment Initiative of the New Partnership for Africa's Development (NEPAD) and its related Action Plan, acknowledging the economic importance of climate variability and change by including a programme area on combatting climate change in Africa.

In addition, the AUC-supported NEPAD Africa Regional Strategy for Disaster Risk Reduction recognises the importance of coordination across agencies for proactive disaster prevention and response strategies.48 In addition, the AUC, in partnership with the UN Economic Commission for Africa and the African Development Bank, is supporting a major new initiative, the Global Climate Change Observing System-Africa Climate for Development, which began in 2007. The programme is designed to integrate climate information and services into development in support of Africa's progress towards the MDGs. A major objective is to mainstream climate information in national development programmes, focusing initially on the most climate-sensitive sectors.

Moreover, the recent decisions taken by African leaders at the AU Summit and the African Partnership Forum/UN Economic Commission for Africa Special Session on Climate Change, the establishment of the African Centre on Climate Policy and the statement by the AU spokesperson at the Summit on Climate Change during the session of the UN General Assembly in New York show that Africa's political leadership is sufficiently aware of the threats of climate change. African leaders are united about the need for adaptation and mitigation strategies to cope with the effects of climate change on Africa's development.

The AU, as a lead Pan-African institution, regards climate change as a very critical issue and attaches great importance to it. Several decisions relating to climate change have been taken recently at the level of African heads of state and government. On the occasion of the Twelfth Ordinary Session of the Assembly of Heads of State and Government of the AU held in Addis Ababa in February 2009 it was decided that the ongoing climate change negotiations should give Africa an opportunity to demand compensation for the damage caused to its economy due to global warming.

The AUC continues to steer efforts of AU member states and regional economic communities, as well as other stakeholders, to deal with multiple challenges facing them, including climate change.

The AU was mandated to work out the modalities of such representation. The first meeting of the Conference on Climate Change that convened on 31 August 2009 in Tripoli adopted a negotiating process, structure and coordination mechanism for Africa's common position on global climate change negotiations. A number of decisions related to climate change were also taken during the Thirteenth Ordinary Session of the Assembly of the AU in July 2009 in Sirte, Libya. The AUC has been given a clear mandate to forge ahead with the implementation of the climate change programme, in partnership with other strategic institutions. It was also decided to establish a Conference of African Heads of State and Governments on Climate Change, as well as to set up a unit to deal with climate change at the AUC.

Finally, the AU became a state party to the UNFCCC and Kyoto Protocol.

In addition, during the Twelfth African Ministerial Conference on the Environment in June 2008 the conference proposed that Africa should seek agreement on a future global emissions reduction regime under which all developed countries would by 2020 reduce their emissions to 35–40 percent below 1990 levels, and by 2050 cut emissions to targets that are what is believed to be necessary to stabilise the concentration of carbon dioxide in the atmosphere.

The AUC, through convening preparatory and consultative meetings, has mobilised all African negotiators on climate change with the aim of implementing a common negotiating position on key climate change issues. The commission has also embarked on the development of a comprehensive strategy on climate for Africa.

However, more needs to be done and the AUC needs to act aggressively in terms of creating a specialised unit on climate change and desertification control, which will strengthen its capacity to be more informed on climate change trends and to adequately plan and be better prepared to support AU member states in undertaking mitigation and adaptation measures on the continent. It will also enhance partners' coordination and the implementation of climate change activities on the continent in accordance with national, regional and international obligations.

NOTES

1 National Academy of Sciences, *America's Climate Choices*, The National Academies Press, Washington, D.C., 2011.
2 EarthShare, *Climate Change & Energy*, 2012, at http://www.earthshare.org/climate-change.html, (accessed October 2014).
3 Ibid.
4 Climate Institute, *Human Health and Climate Change*, 2010, at http://www.climate.org/topics/health.html, (accessed October 2014).
5 Ibid.
6 Oli Brown, *Climate Change Resources Migration: Securing Africa in an Uncertain Climate*, Heinrich Böll Foundation Southern Africa, Cape Town. (2010).
7 Ibid.
8 Richard Mathews, *Climate Change Exacerbates Social Tensions and Leads to Conflict*, at http://globalwarmingisreal.com/2013/08/08/climate-change-and-conflict-social-tension/, (accessed October, 2014).
9 B. Osman-Elasha, *Climate Change Impacts, Adaptation and Links to Sustainable Development in Africa*, Unasylva 231/232, Vol. 60, 2009, p. 14.
10 Claudia Ringler, Tingju Zhu, Ximing Cai, Jawoo Koo, Dingbao Wang, *Climate Change Impacts*

on Food Security in Sub-Saharan Africa: Insights from Comprehensive Climate Change Scenarios, IFPRI Discussion Paper 01042, Environment and Production Technology Division, 2010.

11 Oli Brown, n. 6.

12 Peter H. Gleick, "Water, Drought, Climate Change, and Conflict in Syria", *Wea. Climate Soc.*, 6, pp. 331–340, 2014, doi: http://dx.doi.org/10.1175/WCAS-D-13-00059.1.

13 A. Sayne, *Climate Change Adaptation and Conflict in Nigeria*, Special Report 274, United States Institute of Peace, Washington, (2011).

14 Jean-*François* Maystadt and Olivier Ecker, "Extreme Weather and Civil War: Does Drought Fuel Conflict in Somalia through Livestock Price Shocks?", *Agricultural and Applied Economics*, Association of the American Journal of Agricultural Economics, 96 (4), pp. 1157-1182, 2014, doi: 10.1093/ajae/aau010.

15 Oli Brown and Alec Crawford, *Climate Change and Security in Africa: A Study for the Nordic-African Foreign Ministers Meeting*, International Institute for Sustainable Development (IISD), 2009.

16 International Political Forum (IPF), 2014, at http://internationalpoliticalforum.com/climate-change-and-africas-health/, (accessed October, 2014).

17 Opha P. Dube and Moses J. Chimbari, *Documentation of Research on Climate Change and Human Health in Southern Africa*, Prepared on behalf of DBL – Centre for Health Research and Development Faculty of Life Sciences, University of Copenhagen, Denmark, 2009, at http://www.ddrn.dk/filer/forum/File/Climate_change_and_human_health_in_SADC_region_July09.pdf, (accessed October, 2014).

18 A Haines, R.S. Kovats, D. Campbell-Lendrum, and C. Corvalan, "Climate Change and Human Health: Impacts, Vulnerability and Public Health", *Elsevier, Public Health*, 120, 2006, pp. 585–596, doi:10.1016/j.puhe.2006.01.002.

19 U. Confalonieri, B. Menne, R. Akhtar, K.L. Ebi, M. Hauengue, R.S. Kovats, B. Revich and A. Woodward, "Human Health Climate Change 2007: Impacts, Adaptation and Vulnerability", in M.L. Parry, O.F. Canziani, J.P. Palutikof, P. J. van der Linden and C.E. Hanson (eds.), *Contribution of Working Group II to the Fourth Assessment Report of the Intergovernmental Panel on Climate Change*,Cambridge University Press, Cambridge, UK, 2007, pp. 391-431.

20 IPF, n. 16.

21 U. Confalonieri, et al., n. 19.

22 Ibid.

23 Felix Badolo and Somlanare Romuald Kinda, *Climatic Shocks and Food Security in Developing Countries*, MPRA Paper No. 43006, University Library of Munich, Germany, 2012.

24 Oli Brown and Alec Crawford, n. 15. (2012).

25 Robert Mburia, *Climate Change and Food Security Issues in Sub-Saharan Africa*, Climate Emergency Institute, 2011.

26 Claudia Ringler, et al, n. 10.

27 Robert Mburia, n. 25.

28 Oluwole Akiyode, *Conflict, Climate Change, and Water Security in Sub-Saharan Africa*, Monitor – University for Peace and Conflict, 2011.

29 Ibid.

30 Ibid.

31 Debay Tadesse, *The impact of climate change in Africa*, Institute for Security Studies (ISS), Paper 220, November 2010.

32 Oli Brown, and Alec Crawford, n. 15.

33 Kyle Clendinning, *Climate Change and Conflict: The Implications for Sub-Saharan Africa*, 2012, at http://earthreform.org/climate-change-and-conflict-the-implications-for-sub-saharan-africa/

, (accessed October, 2014).

34 Debay Tadesse, n. 31.

35 Michel Boko, Isabelle Niang, Anthony Nyong, Coleen Vogel, Andrew Githeko, Mahmoud Medany, B. Osman-Elasha, Ramaadjita Tabo and Pius Yanda, "Climate Change 2007: Impacts, Adaptation and Vulnerability", in M.L. Parry, O.F. Canziani, J.P. Palutikof, P.J. van der Linden and C.E. Hanson (eds.), *Contribution of Working Group II to the Fourth Assessment Report of the Intergovernmental Panel on Climate Change*, Cambridge University Press, Cambridge UK, 2007, pp. 433-467.

36 Ibid.

37 R.T. Watson, M.C. Zinyowera, and R.H. Moss (eds.), *The Regional Impacts of Climate Change: An Assessment of Vulnerability. Intergovernmental Panel on Climate Change (IPCC)*, Cambridge University Press, UK, 1997, p. 517.

38 Ibid.

39 Michel Boko, et al., n. 35.

40 Amy Schweikert, Paul Chinowsky, Xavier Espinet, and Michael Tarbert, "Climate Change and Infrastructure Impacts: Comparing the Impact on Roads in Ten Countries through 2100", Elsevier, *Procedia Engineering,* 78, 2014, pp. 306–316.

41 Ibid.

42 Debay Tadesse, n. 31.

43 Ibid.

44 Debay Tadesse, n. 31, pp. 8-11.

APPENDICES

Appendix 1

THIRD INDIA-AFRICA FORUM SUMMIT
29 OCTOBER 2015

Partners in Progress:
Towards a
Dynamic and Transformative Development Agenda

India-Africa Framework for Strategic Cooperation

Introduction

1. The Heads of State and Government and Heads of Delegation representing the continent of Africa, the African Union (AU) and its Institutions, and the Prime Minister of the Republic of India, met in New Delhi, India on 29 October 2015 for the Third India-Africa Forum Summit;
2. Reviewing the strategic partnership and the implementation of the Framework of Enhanced Cooperation adopted at the Second Africa-India Forum Summit held in Addis Ababa in May 2011 and the associated Plan of Action agreed upon thereafter;
3. Noting the synergies of their shared core priorities of working together towards an inclusive economic growth to eradicate poverty and allocate adequate resources for sustainable development, as defined in Africa's Agenda 2063 and its First Ten Year Implementation Plan as well as the Sustainable Development Goals under the 2030 Agenda for Sustainable Development, and the priorities of the Government of India;
4. Building on prior positive cooperation in various areas of common interest, agree to enhance their partnership with more substance, based on the aspirations of the African and Indian people to achieve development, integration and prosperity as indicated in the African Union Agenda 2063 and its First Ten Year Implementation

Plan as well as the Sustainable Development Goals under the 2030 Agenda for Sustainable Development, and the priorities of the Government of India;

5. Noting the importance of urgently fulfilling the unmet challenges of providing access to quality education, skill development and capacity building, affordable healthcare, clean modern energy sources, infrastructure, suitable employment opportunities through development of all sectors of economy including agriculture, manufacturing and services, value addition and connectivity, climate change adaptation and mitigation, blue and ocean economy, and disaster management and disaster risk reduction among others;
6. This longstanding and multifaceted Africa-India relationship has fashioned a development partnership based on equality, friendship, mutual benefit and solidarity which represents South-South Cooperation in all its dimensions. This partnership encompasses human resource development through scholarships, training, capacity building, financial assistance through grants and concessional credit to implement various public-interest projects including for education, healthcare and infrastructure, trade preferences, technology collaborations, humanitarian, financial and in kind assistance in emergency situations, deployment of peacekeeping troops, collective negotiations in multilateral fora for common causes and concerns, among others;
7. Africa and India have adopted this Framework for Strategic Cooperation between them which will comprise the following broad areas:

General Areas of Cooperation

8. The common characteristics of the African and Indian societies insofar as being multi-ethnic and multi-religious as well as the similar societal values have quite naturally cemented the bonds of friendship between the African and Indian peoples over the centuries;
9. Africa and India recognize the crucial need for gender equality for progress and sustainable development and are committed to promote empowerment of women, which will greatly support efforts towards poverty eradication, protect and promote human rights and build more non-violent and environmentally sustainable societies;
10. The Africa-India Strategic Partnership represents a multi-dimensional South-South cooperation and needs to be strengthened to render it more effective;
11. In this regard, Africa and India resolve to:
    - Facilitate greater mutual understanding of cultures, traditions and heritage and bringing our people closer through exchanges at various levels;
    - Promote gender equality and empowerment of women, which will greatly support efforts towards poverty eradication, protect and promote human rights and build more non-violent and environmentally sustainable societies;
    - Encourage use of modern social networks to build communities of mutual

interest. Linkages between academia, journalists, media entities and civil society will be further encouraged inter-alia through the Forum for Indian Development Cooperation (FIDC) to document successful development interventions by civil society among communities in developing countries;

- Promote good governance through the efficient use of emerging e-governance technologies. The empowering of peoples through enhancement of digital connectivity and access to these technologies that permeate all sectors of economy will help targeting of benefits to the needy, make delivery of services more efficient, catalyse development and increase citizen participation in governance, and promote financial inclusion and empowerment through access to banks, credit and social insurance against diseases and accidents;
- Reaffirm our strong commitment to work together for a comprehensive Reform of the United Nations system, including its Security Council, to make it more regionally representative, democratic, accountable and effective;
- Deepen ongoing cooperation and sharing of experiences in ensuring free, fair and transparent parliamentary and electoral processes, such as training and capacity building in tandem with current international best practices;
- Facilitate air and maritime connectivity and more liberal visa procedures and visa concessions to enhance tourism, trade and other people to people contacts;
- Support African Small Island States tackling the impact of climate change as well as their connectivity with mainland Africa.

Economic Cooperation

12. Africa and India emphasize their commitment to achieve sustainable prosperity and reaffirm their collaboration to promote inclusive and sustainable growth for a decent life for their peoples;
13. Africa and India acknowledge that expanded trade and economic ties would further contribute to sustainable growth and economic development in both sides and welcome the contribution by India to set up value addition and processing facilities in Africa;
14. Africa-India trade has multiplied in the last 15 years and doubled in the last five years to reach nearly US$ 72 billion in 2014-2015. There is growing investment by Indian companies, both multinational and SMEs, in Africa in a range of sectors. These include telecommunication, hydrocarbon exploration, agriculture, light manufacturing, IT and IT-enabled services, IT education, water treatment and supply management, petroleum refining and retail, chemicals, drugs & pharmaceuticals, coal, automobiles, floriculture, engineering consultancy and management, paper, textiles, among others. Such investment brings in capital and technology, assists value addition and industrialization, diversification of economic activity and most importantly generates employment and promotes skill development for local populations;

15. Both sides recognize that India was among the first emerging economies to propose a duty-free market access scheme for LDCs following the Hong Kong Ministerial Declaration of 2005. In 2014 India expanded its Duty Free Trade Preference Scheme (DFTP) for LDCs, launched in 2008 and which became fully operational in 2012, to now include 98% of tariff lines. The benefits of this unilateral scheme extend to 34 African countries to increase their exports to India. India took note of the African request to provide technical assistance to the beneficiary countries of the DFTP Scheme in order to further enhance market access of their exports to India;
16. India takes note of the request by the African side to further expand its Duty Free Tariff Preference Scheme for Least Developed Countries for greater coverage. Efforts should be made to promote private and public investment from Africa into India;
17. Both sides recognize that the Indian experience in Small, Medium and Micro enterprises offers significant avenues for further cooperation in industrialization, job creation and enhancement of local capacities of Africa, particularly in the field of managing and organizing industrial clusters, and attaching them to the feeding industries;
18. Africa and India welcome the organization, every year, of the Africa – India Project Partnership Conclave by Export Import Bank of India (EXIM Bank) and the Confederation of Indian Industry (CII); both sides further recognize the importance of the Africa – India Project Partnership Conclaves as a platform for bringing together Indian and African entrepreneurs and decision makers, and therefore call for its continuation;
19. One of the most significant forms of Africa-India partnership has been the offer of concessional credit under the Indian Development and Economic Assistance Scheme (IDEAS) for implementing a range of projects as per the economic and social priorities of African countries in areas where Indian companies have relevant expertise. In the last decade, a total of almost US$ 9 billion in concessional credit has been approved for nearly 140 projects in more than 40 African countries. So far nearly 60 projects have been completed across a range of sectors;
20. Both sides recognize that technology provides solutions to many of our common challenges and therefore there is an imperative need to enhance effective collaboration in appropriate cost effective technologies as well as in emerging and high technology areas;
21. Energy and Infrastructure form substantial part of the ongoing cooperation between Africa and India. The forms of our ongoing cooperation include training, capacity building, consultancy and project implementation through concessional credit in areas including water supply management, power generation and transmission, road and railway construction and upgradation, hydrocarbon exploration among others;

22. While underlying the importance of private investment in achieving sustainable and inclusive economic growth, the two sides decide to share experience and knowledge in this regard, and to:
    - Embark on sensitization efforts to create greater awareness of India's DFTP scheme among businesses in Africa and appeal for the extension of this duty free preference scheme to all African states;
    - Accelerate trade between Africa and India through a coordination mechanism composed of representatives of the Government of India and the African diplomatic Missions represented in India to promote investment from Africa into India and facilitate the setting up of African-owned businesses in India;
    - Enhance collaboration in technology transfer and demonstration, training and joint research and development for specific applications;
    - Explore possibilities of collaboration and training in utilising space technology for remote sensing and natural resource mapping including for water, agriculture, forest cover, mineral and marine resources, weather forecasting and disaster management and disaster risk reduction including early warning of natural disasters; and of nuclear technology for areas such as medicine, agriculture and hydrology in large installations that will have direct benefit for our peoples.

Cooperation in Trade and Industry

23. The Africa-India partnership is grounded in the core recognition that our peoples are our fundamental resource and that capable and skilled human resources are a foundation for building prosperity for all;
24. Both sides recognize the importance of developing technological capacities of the peoples towards an enhanced beneficiation and value addition to resources;
25. Africa and India take note of the importance of the capacity building institutions, which India is in the process of establishing in Africa's diverse sectors, and recognize that such efforts would greatly assist African industries and service sectors, and in the long run contribute to the growth of the continent;
26. Both sides underscore the importance of capacity building that supports industrialization and the need for establishing relevant institutions in that regard;
27. In this regard Africa and India agreed to:
    - Support establishment of Small and Medium Enterprises (SMEs) and Medium and Small Industries (MSIs) in order to promote employment creation and income generation for people of both sides;
    - Promote Public-Private Partnership (PPP) by encouraging Indian businesses to set up skills development units in African industrial zones with the aim to train African engineers, technicians, managers and workers as well as by encouraging other experts in areas such as food security and solar energy;
    - Review the functional mechanisms of the already established institutions with

a view to ensuring that the processes for their establishment, provision of material, human and financial resources and management are clearly understood and supported;

- Create a mechanism to enable women groups to access credit for productive activities and markets for their products;
- Enhance cooperation through training and collective negotiations on global trade issues, including at the WTO to protect and promote the legitimate interests of developing countries, especially the LDCs.

Cooperation in Agriculture

28. Large sections of populations in both Africa and India sustain their livelihoods from agriculture. Improving the productivity of agriculture including crop farming; animal husbandry and water management through sustainable and judicious use of inputs is vital to ensure food and nutritional security and represents a significant challenge and opportunity;
29. There has been extensive cooperation between the two sides including through sharing of experience, training, capacity building through setting up of institutions, and concessional credit in farming techniques, irrigation, soil quality assessment improvement as well as provision of farm equipment, among others;
30. Africa and India fully realize that sectors such as tourism, agriculture, fisheries, forestry and energy production are all sensitive to the adverse impacts of climate change;
31. In this regard both sides agree to:
    - Further increase cooperation in improving farming techniques through appropriate and affordable technology, organic farming, improving crop varieties, seeds, efficient use of fertilizers and other measures;
    - Enhance joint efforts for more effective and efficient management of water resources and improve irrigation techniques through transfer of technology and knowhow;
    - Support Africa's commitment to consign the hand-held hoes to the museum, as it has become a symbol of agricultural backwardness in Africa and oppression of women, who constitute the majority of agricultural workers. India will endeavour to provide tillers, cultivators, harrowers and harvesters at concessional rates and the transfer of such technologies for their production in Africa, in order to empower the African farmers;
    - Promote investment in agribusinesses and food processing industry to generate employment and greater revenue;
    - Continue to collaborate to ensure that public investment, services, and policies for agriculture give due priority to enabling, supporting and complementing smallholders' owned investment, with particular attention to women and youth food producers;

- Ensure that Indian agricultural cooperation with African countries give priority to food production and improving levels of nutrition in order to increase the resilience of local and traditional food systems and biodiversity;
- Encourage all initiatives to diversify their economies to expand climate sensitive sectors and to promote adaptation measures that are capable of increasing resilience within the sector;
- Enhance cooperation and coordination in finalizing an ambitious and comprehensive climate change agreement during the forthcoming COP 21 negotiations, which will be held in Paris, France.

Cooperation in Renewable Energy

32. Intensify our ongoing cooperation in developing renewable energy generation including solar, wind, hydro, geo-thermal and bio-mass along with building power transmission systems.

Cooperation in Blue/Ocean Economy

33. Livelihoods of large sections of our peoples are dependent on Oceans which have emerged as the new frontier for the development of the peoples of Africa and India. The significance of Oceans for global or regional trade and its marine resources as a contributor to the economic prosperity of our people is evident.
34. In this regard the two sides decide to:
    - Put special emphasis on exploring closer collaboration through training, capacity building and joint projects in developing sustainable fisheries, maritime connectivity, managing marine resources, exploring non-marine resources, promoting eco-tourism, developing renewable energy, and disaster risk reduction through modern early warning tools, pollution control and other coastal and ocean studies;
    - Pursue cooperation in port operations and marine transport, addressing illegal and unregulated fishing and hydrography surveys.

Cooperation in Infrastructure

35. Intensify ongoing cooperation in training, capacity building, consultancy and project implementation through concessional credit in infrastructure areas, including water supply management, maritime connectivity, road and railway construction and upgradation.

Cooperation in Education and Skills Development

36. Since the Second Africa-India Forum Summit (2011), over 24,000 scholarships across 300 training courses conducted at 60 training institutions have been utilized by African nationals in areas such as IT, renewable energy, agriculture, marine & aeronautical engineering, marine hydrography, SME entrepreneurship, rural development, parliamentary affairs, logistics and management, climate change

adaptation, disaster management, cyber security, forensic sciences, and defence and security, among others;

37. Both sides recognise the fundamental importance of educational cooperation and skills transfer in enhancing opportunities available to their youth in contributing to economic, scientific, technical, and social development and the need to build further through expansion of training slots in existing and newer areas in line with the opportunities and challenges arising in the African continent in key areas outlined in Agenda 2063;
38. Both sides understand that the development of Science, Technology, Research and Innovation is a crucial element and an integral part of the process of development;
39. Both sides emphasize the importance of the early introduction of ICT in educational institutions as a key enabler for capacity building, education, health, industry, poverty eradication and delivery of public services;
40. Acknowledge the importance of successful implementation of the Pan-African E-Network Project aimed at providing an efficient tool to bridge the digital divide and also offer affordable and easy access to quality education and healthcare to the peoples of Africa;
41. In this regard Africa and India agree to:
    - Continue cooperation in the areas of scientific and technological development as well as in Information and Communication Technology;
    - Explore possible joint investments to establish a robust, reliable and accessible fibre optic infrastructure in Africa, with a view to setting an enabled African information society, and integrated digital economy whereby all actors have access to reliable and affordable ICT networks and services;
    - Promote greater interaction, exchange and partnership between the tertiary institutions of Africa and India;
    - Renew, expand and upgrade the existing Pan African E-Network Project infrastructure so as to permit an innovative utilization of the E-Network Project with the view to cover newer areas of mutual interest;
    - Intensify cooperation through sharing of experiences, gender-specific training courses and capacity building measures including through skill development;
    - Provide and facilitate the access and enrolment of African students and academicians to India's premiere institutions of higher learning in an effort to boost Africa's capacity in areas such as engineering, medical, technology, agriculture as well as emerging areas;
    - Fast-track the implementation of those capacity building institutions that have been found to be feasible for continuation under IAFS-III;
    - Intensify cooperation in capacity building, joint research and development and implementation of projects in renewable energy sources including solar, wind and hydro power along with building efficient power transmission systems.

Cooperation in Health

42. Africa and India recognize that the promotion of health is critical in the development of human capital, which drives socio-economic growth;
43. They reaffirm their commitment to enhance collaboration and share experience in the application of advancement in science, technology, research and development to training in the area of HIV, TB, Malaria, Ebola and Polio;
44. Both sides recognize the need to improve nutritional and food securities of their peoples and acknowledge the right for adequate food for all and the availability and accessibility of food in quantity and quality sufficient to satisfy the dietary needs of individuals;
45. In this regard both sides agree to:
    - Collaborate in the provision of universal access to primary and public healthcare, to build resilience to fight and prevent deadly epidemics and disease control through implementing educational programme in this field, recommendation of policies, administering services and conducting research;
    - Support Africa's campaign on Accelerated Reduction of Maternal Mortality in Africa (CARMMA) and facilitate its implementation through cooperation in training and education for health professionals;
    - Ensure access to affordable and quality medicines and treatment, particularly generic medicines;
    - In this regard both sides acknowledge the importance of full use of the flexibilities provided by the agreement on trade related aspects of Intellectual Property Rights (TRIPS) administered by the World Trade Organization (WTO);
    - Train doctors and healthcare personnel, including through the deployment of telecoms and ICTs in support of tele-medicine and e-health applications;
    - Strengthen public-private sector collaboration in the areas of pharmaceutical and procurement in Africa and India in the framework of the Pharmaceutical Manufacturing Plan for Africa and the fight against counterfeit medicines;
    - Continue their dialogue on intellectual property rights, regulatory procedures and access to medicines and research and development in traditional medicine;
    - Sharing of experiences, specialized expertise and best practices in health care systems development and community health programmes;
    - Exchanges regarding food production to always meet dietary need and quality standards.

Cooperation in Peace and Security

46. Africa and India recognize the importance of peace, security and stability as a precondition for development;
47. Africa appreciates commitment of India towards supporting various African Union Missions such as those in Mali and in Somalia;

48. In this regard, Africa and India decide to:
    - Support AU Peace and Security initiative within the African Peace and Security Architecture;
    - Support programmes on conflict prevention, management and resolution;
    - Pursue cooperation on Maritime security issues through training, capacity building, sharing of information, surveillance and other measures in securing Sea Lines of Communication, preventing transnational crimes of piracy, combating terrorism, illegal and unregulated fishing, trafficking of drugs, arms and humans through surveillance, and hydrography surveys;
    - Enhance cooperation and coordination between Africa and India to combat terrorism in all its forms and manifestations, including countering violent extremism and, in this regard, make concerted efforts for the early adoption of the Comprehensive Convention on International Terrorism;
    - Share best practices and experiences in cyber security especially in combating cyber crime and use of internet for terrorist purposes.

Regional and other Forms of Cooperation

49. Appreciate the ongoing fruitful cooperation between the AU/RECs and India;
50. Take note with appreciation of the third meeting between India and the eight Regional Economic Communities (RECs) of Africa held in New Delhi in August 2014.

    The RECs have worked towards harmonization of standards and rules as well as towards creation of common markets and this has an important bearing on the development of India's trade and investment with African countries.
51. In this regard:
    - India, the African Union and RECs will enhance the ongoing cooperation in the areas of capacity building, human resource development, food and agriculture processing and soft loans for regional projects among others.

Monitoring Mechanism

52. Agree to establish a regular formal monitoring mechanism to review the implementation of the agreed areas of cooperation and identified projects by the competent bodies of the partnership. Modalities of the monitoring mechanism and the detailed Plan of Action will be jointly developed within three months.

New Delhi, 29 October 2015

भारत 2023 INDIA

वसुधैव कुटुम्बकम्

ONE EARTH • ONE FAMILY • ONE FUTURE

G20 NEW DELHI LEADERS' DECLARATION

New Delhi, India, 9-10 September 2023

Table of Contents

* * *

Preamble

1. We are One Earth, One Family, and we share One Future.
2. We, the Leaders of the G20, met in New Delhi on 9-10 September 2023, under the theme 'Vasudhaiva Kutumbakam'. We meet at a defining moment in history where the decisions we make now will determine the future of our people and our planet. It is with the philosophy of living in harmony with our surrounding ecosystem that we commit to concrete actions to address global challenges.
3. G20 cooperation is essential in determining the course the world takes. Headwinds to global economic growth and stability persist. Years of cascading challenges and crises have reversed gains in the 2030 Agenda and its Sustainable Development Goals (SDGs). Global greenhouse gas (GHG) emissions continue to increase,

with climate change, biodiversity loss, pollution, drought, land degradation and desertification threatening lives and livelihoods. Rising commodity prices, including food and energy prices are contributing to cost of living pressures. Global challenges like poverty and inequality, climate change, pandemics and conflicts disproportionately affect women and children, and the most vulnerable.

4. Together we have an opportunity to build a better future. Just energy transitions can improve jobs and livelihoods, and strengthen economic resilience. We affirm that no country should have to choose between fighting poverty and fighting for our planet. We will pursue development models that implement sustainable, inclusive and just transitions globally, while leaving no one behind.
5. As Leaders of G20, the premier global forum for international economic cooperation, we resolve to act in concrete ways through partnerships. We commit to:
   a. Accelerate strong, sustainable, balanced and inclusive growth.
   b. Accelerate the full and effective implementation of the 2030 Agenda for Sustainable Development.
   c. Pursue low-GHG/low-carbon emissions, climate-resilient and environmentally sustainable development pathways by championing an integrated and inclusive approach. We will urgently accelerate our actions to address development and climate challenges, promote Lifestyles for Sustainable Development (LiFE), and conserve biodiversity, forests and oceans.
   d. Improve access to medical countermeasures and facilitate more supplies and production capacities in developing countries to prepare better for future health emergencies.
   e. Promote resilient growth by urgently and effectively addressing debt vulnerabilities in developing countries.
   f. Scale up financing from all sources for accelerating progress on SDGs.
   g. Accelerate efforts and enhance resources towards achieving the Paris Agreement, including its temperature goal.
   h. Pursue reforms for better, bigger and more effective Multilateral Development Banks (MDBs) to address global challenges to maximise developmental impact.
   i. Improve access to digital services and digital public infrastructure, and leverage digital transformation opportunities to boost sustainable and inclusive growth.
   j. Promote sustainable, quality, healthy, safe and gainful employment.
   k. Close gender gaps and promote the full, equal, effective and meaningful participation of women in the economy as decision-makers.
   l. Better integrate the perspectives of developing countries, including LDCs, LLDCs, and SIDS, into future G20 agenda and strengthen the voice of developing countries in global decision making.

6. Through these actions today, we are building towards a system that better empowers countries to address global challenges, is human-centric, and brings prosperity and well-being to humanity.

For the Planet, People, Peace and Prosperity

7. We note with deep concern the immense human suffering and the adverse impact of wars and conflicts around the world.
8. Concerning the war in Ukraine, while recalling the discussion in Bali, we reiterated our national positions and resolutions adopted at the UN Security Council and the UN General Assembly (A/RES/ES-11/1 and A/RES/ES-11/6) and underscored that all states must act in a manner consistent with the Purposes and Principles of the UN Charter in its entirety. In line with the UN Charter, all states must refrain from the threat or use of force to seek territorial acquisition against the territorial integrity and sovereignty or political independence of any state. The use or threat of use of nuclear weapons is inadmissible.
9. Reaffirming that the G20 is the premier forum for international economic cooperation, and recognizing that while the G20 is not the platform to resolve geopolitical and security issues, we acknowledge that these issues can have significant consequences for the global economy.
10. We highlighted the human suffering and negative added impacts of the war in Ukraine with regard to global food and energy security, supply chains, macro-financial stability, inflation and growth, which has complicated the policy environment for countries, especially developing and least developed countries which are still recovering from the COVID-19 pandemic and the economic disruption which has derailed progress towards the SDGs. There were different views and assessments of the situation.
11. We appreciate the efforts of Türkiye and UN-brokered Istanbul Agreements consisting of the Memorandum of Understanding between the Russian Federation and the Secretariat of the United Nations on Promoting Russian Food Products and Fertilizers to the World Markets and the Initiative on the Safe Transportation of Grain and Foodstuffs from Ukrainian Ports (Black Sea Initiative), and call for their full, timely and effective implementation to ensure the immediate and unimpeded deliveries of grain, foodstuffs, and fertilizers/inputs from the Russian Federation and Ukraine. This is necessary to meet the demand in developing and least developed countries, particularly those in Africa.
12. In this context, emphasizing the importance of sustaining food and energy security, we called for the cessation of military destruction or other attacks on relevant infrastructure. We also expressed deep concern about the adverse impact that conflicts have on the security of civilians thereby exacerbating existing socio-economic fragilities and vulnerabilities and hindering an effective humanitarian response.

13. We call on all states to uphold the principles of international law including territorial integrity and sovereignty, international humanitarian law, and the multilateral system that safeguards peace and stability. The peaceful resolution of conflicts, and efforts to address crises as well as diplomacy and dialogue are critical. We will unite in our endeavour to address the adverse impact of the war on the global economy and welcome all relevant and constructive initiatives that support a comprehensive, just, and durable peace in Ukraine that will uphold all the Purposes and Principles of the UN Charter for the promotion of peaceful, friendly, and good neighbourly relations among nations in the spirit of 'One Earth, One Family, One Future'.
14. Today's era must not be of war.

A. Strong, Sustainable, Balanced, and Inclusive Growth

Global Economic Situation

15. Cascading crises have posed challenges to long-term growth. Facing an uneven recovery, and cognizant of the need to boost long-term growth, we will implement well-calibrated macroeconomic and structural policies. We will protect the vulnerable, through promoting equitable growth and enhancing macroeconomic and financial stability. Such an approach will help resolve the cost-of-living crisis and unlock strong, sustainable, balanced, and inclusive growth.
16. Global economic growth is below its long-run average and remains uneven. The uncertainty around the outlook remains high. With notable tightening in global financial conditions, which could worsen debt vulnerabilities, persistent inflation and geoeconomic tensions, the balance of risks remains tilted to the downside. We, therefore, reiterate the need for well-calibrated monetary, fiscal, financial, and structural policies to promote growth, reduce inequalities and maintain macroeconomic and financial stability. We will continue to enhance macro policy cooperation and support the progress towards the 2030 Agenda for Sustainable Development. We reaffirm that achieving strong, sustainable, balanced and inclusive growth (SSBIG) will require policymakers to stay agile and flexible in their policy response, as evidenced during the recent banking turbulence in a few advanced economies where expeditious action by relevant authorities helped to maintain financial stability and manage spillovers. We welcome the initial steps taken by the Financial Stability Board (FSB), Standard Setting Bodies (SSBs) and certain jurisdictions to examine what lessons can be learned from this recent banking turbulence and encourage them to advance their ongoing work. We will use macroprudential policies, where required, to safeguard against downside risks. Central banks remain strongly committed to achieving price stability in line with their respective mandates. They will ensure that inflation expectations remain well anchored and will clearly communicate policy stances to help limit negative cross-country spillovers. Central bank independence is crucial to maintaining policy credibility. We will prioritise temporary and targeted fiscal measures to

protect the poor and the most vulnerable, while maintaining medium-term fiscal sustainability. Ensuring the overall coherence of the monetary and fiscal stances remains important. We recognise the importance of supply-side policies, especially policies that increase labour supply and enhance productivity to boost growth and alleviate price pressures. We reaffirm the April 2021 exchange rate commitment made by our Finance Ministers and Central Bank Governors.

17. We recognise the critical role of private enterprise in accelerating growth and driving sustainable economic transformations. To this end, we resolve to work with private sector to:
    i. Create inclusive, sustainable, and resilient global value chains, and support developing countries to move up the value chain.
    ii. Facilitate investments including Foreign Direct Investments (FDIs) towards sustainable business models.
    iii. Devise pipelines of investible projects in developing countries, by leveraging expertise of MDBs to mobilise investments.
    iv. Promote the ease and reduce the cost of doing business.
18. We recognise that start-ups and MSMEs are natural engines of growth. They are key to socio-economic transformation by driving innovation and creating employment. We welcome the establishment of the Start-up 20 Engagement Group during India's G20 Presidency and its continuation.

Unlocking Trade for Growth

19. We reaffirm that a rules-based, non-discriminatory, fair, open, inclusive, equitable, sustainable and transparent multilateral trading system, with WTO at its core, is indispensable. We will support policies that enable trade and investment to serve as an engine of growth and prosperity for all. Today, we:
    i. Renew our commitment to ensure a level-playing field and fair competition by discouraging protectionism and market distorting practices, to foster a favourable trade and investment environment for all. We reiterate the need to pursue WTO reform to improve all its functions through an inclusive member-driven process, and remain committed to conducting discussions with a view to having a fully and well-functioning dispute settlement system accessible to all members by 2024. We commit to work constructively to ensure positive outcomes at the WTO's Thirteenth Ministerial Conference (MC13).
    ii. Recognise challenges MSMEs, particularly in developing countries, face with respect to access to information and thus, welcome Jaipur Call for Action for enhancing MSMEs' access to information to promote the integration of MSMEs into international trade.
    iii. Welcome the adoption of G20 Generic Framework for Mapping Global Value Chains (GVC) to help members identify risks and build resilience.

iv. Welcome the High-Level Principles on Digitalization of Trade Documents and will make efforts to encourage implementation, and encourage other countries to consider these principles.
v. Ensure that trade and environment policies should be mutually supportive, consistent with WTO and multilateral environmental agreements.
vi. Recognize the importance of WTO's 'Aid for Trade' initiative to enable developing countries, notably LDCs to effectively participate in global trade, including through enhanced local value creation. We welcome all efforts to mobilize necessary resources in this regard.

Preparing for the Future of Work

20. We commit to addressing skill gaps, promoting decent work and ensuring inclusive social protection policies for all. Towards this aim, we:
    i. Recognise that well-integrated and adequately skilled workers benefit origin and destination countries alike and commit to working towards ensuring well-managed, regular and skills-based migration pathways.
    ii. Welcome efforts to map global skill gaps and the development of the G20 policy priorities to address skill gaps globally, including through further strengthening our national statistical data, extending the coverage of the ILO and OECD Skills for Jobs Databases to G20 countries, as appropriate. We commit to effectively addressing global skills for sustainable and inclusive economic development.
    iii. Commit to consider the development of an international reference classification of occupations by skill and qualification requirements to facilitate cross-country comparability and mutual recognition of skills and qualifications.
    iv. Welcome the comprehensive toolkit with adaptable frameworks for designing and introducing digital upskilling and reskilling programmes.
    v. Aim to achieve sustainably financed universal social protection coverage and consider portability of social security benefits through bilateral and multilateral agreements.
    vi. Support progress on the implementation of the UN Global Accelerator on Jobs and Social Protection for Just Transitions.
    vii. Acknowledge the economic significance and societal value of the cultural and creative sector to support inclusive growth, sustainable development and decent work.
    viii. Ensure adequate social protection and decent working conditions for gig and platform workers.
    ix. Will increase our efforts for the elimination of child labour and forced labour along global value chains.

Advancing Financial Inclusion

21. We welcome the 2023 Update to Leaders on Progress towards the G20 Remittance Target and endorse the Regulatory Toolkit for Enhanced Digital Financial Inclusion of Micro, Small and Medium Enterprises (MSMEs). We endorse the voluntary and non-binding G20 Policy Recommendations for Advancing Financial Inclusion and Productivity Gains through Digital Public Infrastructure. We take note of the significant role of digital public infrastructure in helping to advance financial inclusion in support of inclusive growth and sustainable development. We also encourage the continuous development and responsible use of technological innovations including innovative payment systems, to achieve financial inclusion of the last mile and progress towards reducing the cost of remittances. We also support continuous efforts to strengthen digital financial literacy and consumer protection. We endorse the G20 2023 Financial Inclusion Action Plan (FIAP), which provides an action oriented and forward-looking roadmap for rapidly accelerating the financial inclusion of individuals and MSMEs, particularly vulnerable and underserved groups in the G20 countries and beyond.

Fighting Corruption

22. We reaffirm our commitment to zero tolerance for corruption.
    i. We endorse the three G20 High-Level Principles on:
        - o Strengthening Law Enforcement related International Cooperation and Information Sharing for Combating Corruption
        - o Strengthening Asset Recovery Mechanisms for Combating Corruption
        - o Promoting Integrity and Effectiveness of Public Bodies and Authorities responsible for Preventing and Combating Corruption

    ii. Reaffirm our support to enhance global efforts to seize, confiscate and return criminal proceeds to victims and states, in line with international obligations and domestic legal frameworks, including through support to the Financial Action Task Force (FATF) and operationalization of the GlobE Network.

    iii. Reaffirm our commitment to demonstrate and continue concrete efforts and share information on our actions towards criminalizing foreign bribery and enforcing foreign bribery legislation, in line with Article 16 of the United Nations Convention against Corruption (UNCAC), and welcome Anti-Corruption Working Group's efforts in striving towards this goal. We look forward to enlarging participation to the OECD Anti-Bribery Convention, as appropriate.

B. Accelerating Progress on Sustainable Development Goals (SDGs)

23. At the midway point to 2030, the global progress on SDGs is off-track with only 12 percent of the targets on track. During this Decade of Action, we will leverage the G20's convening power and its collective resolve to fully and effectively

implement the 2030 Agenda and accelerate progress toward the SDGs, in a timely manner, to shape the world we want to see for our future generations.

Recommitting to Achieving SDGs

24. To accelerate progress on SDGs, we commit to taking collective action for effective and timely implementation of the G20 2023 Action Plan to Accelerate Progress on the SDGs, including its High-Level Principles. We will ensure that no one is left behind. We commend the efforts of the Indian Presidency to accelerate the implementation of the 2030 Agenda. To this end, we:
    i. Recognise the role of digital transformation, AI, data advances, and the need to address digital divides. We endorse the G20 Principles on Harnessing Data for Development (D4D) and welcome the decision to launch Data for Development Capacity Building Initiative, and other existing initiatives.
    ii. We reaffirm our commitment towards the mobilisation of affordable, adequate and accessible financing from all sources to support developing countries in their domestic efforts to address bottlenecks for implementation of the 2030 Agenda and the Addis Ababa Action Agenda. We call upon developed countries to fully deliver on their respective ODA commitments that complements and encourages development financing from all other sources, including public and private, domestic and international, in a timely manner, and contribute to addressing the financing needs of developing countries.
    iii. Highlight the crucial role of tourism and culture as a means for sustainable socio-economic development and economic prosperity, and take note of the Goa Roadmap for Tourism as one of the vehicles for achieving the SDGs.
    iv. Commit to enhancing G20 cooperation and partnerships to address challenges being faced in the implementation of the 2030 Agenda. We welcome ongoing efforts at the UN, including the Secretary General's efforts to address the SDG financing gap through an SDG stimulus, and will provide full support to the United Nations 2023 SDG Summit, the United Nations Summit of the Future, and other relevant processes.
25. We reiterate our commitment to take action to scale up sustainable finance. In line with the G20 Sustainable Finance Roadmap, we welcome the analytical framework for SDG-aligned finance and voluntary recommendations for scaling up adoption of social impact investment instruments and improving nature-related data and reporting, informed by the stocktaking analyses, considering country circumstances.

Eliminating Hunger and Malnutrition

26. We commit to enhance global food security and nutrition for all in line with the G20 Deccan High-Level Principles on Food Security and Nutrition 2023. To achieve this, we:
    i. We encourage efforts to strengthen research cooperation on climate-resilient

and nutritious grains such as millets, quinoa, sorghum, and other traditional crops including rice, wheat and maize. We welcome the outcomes from the G20 members engagement in the 12th G20 Meeting of Agriculture Chief Scientists (MACS).

ii. Emphasize the importance of increasing access to, availability, and efficient use of fertilizer and agricultural inputs, including through strengthening local fertilizer production, and to improve soil health.

iii. Commit to accelerating innovations and investment focused on increasing agricultural productivity, reducing food loss and waste across the value chain, and improving marketing and storage, to build more sustainable and climate-resilient agriculture and food systems.

iv. Commit to support developing countries' efforts and capacities to address their food security challenges, and work together to enable access to affordable, safe, nutritious and healthy diets, and to foster the progressive realization of the right to adequate food.

v. Commit to facilitate open, fair, predictable, and rules-based agriculture, food and fertilizer trade, not impose export prohibitions or restrictions and reduce market distortions, in accordance with relevant WTO rules.

vi. Commit to strengthening the Agricultural Market Information System (AMIS) and the Group on Earth Observations Global Agricultural Monitoring (GEOGLAM), for greater transparency to avoid food price volatility, supporting AMIS's work on fertilizers, its expansion to include vegetable oils, and for enhancing collaboration with early warning systems.

Macroeconomic impacts of food and energy insecurity

27. While global food and energy prices have fallen from their peak levels, the potential for high levels of volatility in food and energy markets remains, given the uncertainties in the global economy. In this context, we take note of the G20 Report on Macroeconomic Impacts of Food and Energy Insecurity and their Implications for the Global Economy. We look forward to an ambitious replenishment of the International Fund for Agricultural Development (IFAD) resources at the end of the year by IFAD members to support IFAD's fight against food insecurity.

Strengthening Global Health and Implementing One Health Approach

28. We remain committed to strengthening the global health architecture, with the World Health Organization (WHO) at its core, and building more resilient, equitable, sustainable, and inclusive health systems to achieve Universal Health Coverage, implement One Health approach, enhance pandemic preparedness and strengthen existing infectious diseases surveillance systems. To achieve this, we will:

i. Focus on strengthening primary health care and health workforce and improving essential health services and health systems to better than pre-pandemic levels, ideally within the next 2-3 years, as well as continue progress towards polio eradication and ending ongoing epidemics including AIDS, tuberculosis, malaria, hepatitis and water-borne and other communicable diseases, also recognising the importance of research on long COVID.

ii. Promote the One Health-based approach driven by the Quadripartite's One Health Joint Plan of Action (2022-2026).

iii. Enhance the resilience of health systems and support development of climate-resilient and low-carbon health systems in collaboration with MDBs, and support the work of the WHO-led Alliance for Transformative Action on Climate and Health (ATACH).

iv. Implement and prioritise tackling Antimicrobial Resistance (AMR) following the One Health approach, including through research and development, infection prevention and control, as well as antimicrobial stewardship efforts within respective national action plans through AMR and antimicrobial consumption surveillance.

v. Facilitate equitable access to safe, effective, quality-assured, and affordable vaccines, therapeutics, diagnostics, and other medical countermeasures, especially in Low-and Middle-income Countries (LMICs), LDCs and SIDS.

vi. Look forward to a successful outcome of the ongoing negotiations at the Intergovernmental Negotiating Body (INB) for an ambitious, legally binding WHO convention, agreement or other international instruments on pandemic PPR (WHO CA+) by May 2024, as well as amendments to better implement the International Health Regulations (2005).

vii. Recognize the potential role of evidence-based Traditional and Complementary Medicine in health, and take note of international efforts in this direction, including WHO's global and collaborating centres, and clinical trial registries.

viii. Support the WHO-led inclusive consultative process for the development of an interim medical countermeasures coordination mechanism, with effective participation of LMICs and other developing countries, considering a network of networks approach, leveraging local and regional R&D and manufacturing capacities, and strengthening last mile delivery. This may be adapted in alignment with the WHO CA+.

ix. Promote and improve access to mental health services and psychosocial support in an inclusive manner.

x. While highlighting the public health dimension of the world drug problem, call for strong international counter-narcotics cooperation, free of unnecessary restrictions, including information sharing and capacity building to disrupt production and proliferation of illicit drugs, including synthetic drugs, and precursor chemicals at their origin, in transit and at destination points.

Finance-Health Collaboration

29. We remain committed to strengthening the global health architecture for pandemic prevention, preparedness and response (PPR) through enhanced collaboration between Finance and Health Ministries under the Joint Finance and Health Task Force (JFHTF). Under the JFHTF, we welcome the participation of invited key regional organisations in the Task Force meetings as they enhance the voice of low-income countries. We welcome the discussion on the Framework on Economic Vulnerabilities and Risks (FEVR) and the initial Report for Economic Vulnerabilities and Risks arising from pandemics, created through collaboration between World Health Organisation (WHO), World Bank, IMF, and European Investment Bank (EIB). We call on the Task Force to continue refining this Framework over its multi-year work plan in order to regularly assess economic vulnerabilities and risks due to evolving pandemic threats, taking into account country-specific circumstances. We welcome the Report on Best Practices from Finance Health Institutional Arrangements during Covid-19 that will contribute towards joint finance-health sector readiness to support our response to future pandemics. We welcome the Report on Mapping Pandemic Response Financing Options and Gaps developed by the WHO and World Bank and look forward to further deliberations on how financing mechanisms could be optimized, better coordinated and, when necessary, suitably enhanced to deploy the necessary financing quickly and efficiently, duly considering discussions in other global forums. We welcome the conclusion of the first call for proposals by the Pandemic Fund and look forward to the second Call for Proposals by the end of 2023, based on lessons learned from the first Call for Proposals. We highlight the importance of securing new donors and co-investment. We ask the Task Force to report back to Finance and Health Ministers in 2024 on its progress.

Delivering Quality Education

30. We are committed to inclusive, equitable, high-quality education and skills training for all, including for those in vulnerable situations. We recognize the importance of investment in supporting human capital development. To this end, we:
    i. Recognize the importance of foundational learning (literacy, numeracy, and socio-emotional skills) as the primary building block for education and employment.
    ii. Reiterate our commitment to harness digital technologies to overcome the digital divides for all learners.
    iii. Extend support to educational institutions and teachers to enable them to keep pace with emerging trends and technological advances including AI.
    iv. Emphasize expanding access to high-quality Technical and Vocational Education and Training (TVET).
    v. Reaffirm our commitment to promote open, equitable and secure scientific

collaboration and encourage mobility of students, scholars, researchers, and scientists across research and higher education institutions.

vi. Emphasize the importance of enabling life-long learning focused on skilling, reskilling, and upskilling especially for vulnerable groups.

Culture as a Transformative Driver of SDGs

31. We call for the full recognition and protection of culture with its intrinsic value as a transformative driver and an enabler for the achievement of the SDGs and advance the inclusion of culture as a standalone goal in future discussions on a possible post-2030 development agenda. We reiterate our commitment to strengthen our fight against illicit trafficking of cultural property at national, regional or international levels to enable its return and restitution to their countries and communities of origin as relevant, and call for sustained dialogue and action in that endeavour, with a view to strengthen cultural diplomacy and intercultural exchanges, consistent with national law and relevant UNESCO Conventions. We encourage the international community to protect the living cultural heritage, including the intellectual property, notably with regard to the impact of the over commercialization and misappropriation of such living heritage on the sustainability and on the livelihoods of practitioners and community bearers as well as Indigenous Peoples.

C. Green Development Pact for a Sustainable Future

32. Recognising that the prosperity and well-being of present and future generations depends on our current development and other policy choices and actions, we resolve to pursue environmentally sustainable and inclusive economic growth and development in an integrated, holistic and balanced manner.

33. We commit to urgently accelerate our actions to address environmental crises and challenges including climate change. We recognize that the impacts of climate change are being experienced worldwide, particularly by the poorest and the most vulnerable, including in LDCs and SIDS. Mindful of our leadership role, we reaffirm our steadfast commitments, in pursuit of the objective of UNFCCC, to tackle climate change by strengthening the full and effective implementation of the Paris Agreement and its temperature goal, reflecting equity and the principle of common but differentiated responsibilities and respective capabilities, in light of different national circumstances. We note with concern that global ambition and implementation to address climate change remain insufficient to achieve the temperature goal of the Paris Agreement to hold the increase in the global average temperature to well below 2°C above pre-industrial levels, and pursue efforts to limit the temperature increase to 1.5°C above pre-industrial levels. We highlight the importance of ambitious action on all pillars of the Paris Agreement, taking into account the best available science. Noting the IPCC assessments, that the impacts of climate change will be much lower at a temperature increase of 1.5°C compared with 2°C, we reiterate our resolve to pursue further efforts to limit the

increase to 1.5°C. This will require meaningful and effective actions and commitment by all countries, taking into account different approaches, through the development of clear national pathways that align long term ambition with short and medium-term goals, and with international cooperation and support, including finance and technology and sustainable and responsible consumption and production as critical enablers, in the context of sustainable development. We recognize that limiting global warming to 1.5°C requires rapid, deep and sustained reductions in global GHG emissions of 43% by 2030 relative to the 2019 levels. We also take note of the finding of the IPCC AR6 Synthesis Report, based on global modelled pathways and assumptions, stating that "Global GHG emissions are projected to peak between 2020 and at the latest before 2025 in global modelled pathways that limit warming to 1.5°C with no or limited overshoot and in those that limit warming to 2°C and assume immediate action." This does not imply peaking in all countries within this timeframe; timeframes for peaking may be shaped by sustainable development, poverty eradication needs, equity, and in line with different national circumstances. We further recognize that technology development and transfer on voluntary and mutually agreed terms, capacity building and financing can support countries in this regard.

34. We urge all countries that have not yet aligned their NDCs with the temperature goal of the Paris Agreement, to revisit and strengthen the 2030 targets in their NDCs, as necessary, by the end of 2023, taking into account different national circumstances, and we welcome those who have already done so. We recall the nationally determined nature of NDCs and Article 4.4 of the Paris Agreement, which provides that "Developed country Parties should continue taking the lead by undertaking economy-wide absolute emission reduction targets. Developing country Parties should continue enhancing their mitigation efforts, and are encouraged to move over time towards economy-wide emission reduction or limitation targets in the light of different national circumstances." In this context, we commend those countries whose NDCs include economy-wide targets covering all GHGs, and others are encouraged to include such economy-wide targets in their upcoming NDC cycle(s), in the light of different national circumstances. We will contribute to a successful conclusion of the first global stocktake at COP28 in Dubai, that drives enhanced climate action across mitigation, adaptation, and means of implementation and support. We reiterate our commitment to achieve global net zero GHG emissions/carbon neutrality by or around mid-century, while taking into account the latest scientific developments and in line with different national circumstances, taking into account different approaches including the Circular Carbon Economy, socio-economic, technological, and market development, and promoting the most efficient solutions.

Macroeconomic risks stemming from climate change and transition pathways

35. The macroeconomic costs of the physical impacts of climate change are significant both at aggregate and country levels, and the cost of inaction substantially outweighs that of orderly and just transitions. We recognise the importance of international dialogue and cooperation, including in the areas of finance and technology, and timely policy action consistent with country-specific circumstances. It is also critical to assess and account for the short, medium and long-term macroeconomic impact of both the physical impact of climate change and transition policies, including on growth, inflation, and unemployment. We endorse the G20 Report on Macroeconomic Risks Stemming from Climate Change and Transition Pathways. Building on analysis in this Report, we will consider further work on the macroeconomic implications, as appropriate, particularly as relevant for fiscal and monetary policies, drawing on the inputs from a diverse set of stakeholders.

Mainstreaming Lifestyles for Sustainable Development (LiFE)

36. Based on the G20 High-Level Principles on Lifestyles for Sustainable Development, we commit to robust collective actions that will enable the world to embrace sustainable production and consumption patterns and mainstream Lifestyles for Sustainable Development. Relevant studies on it show that it could contribute to significant emission reduction by 2030 for a global net-zero future. We support the creation of an enabling policy environment to promote sustainable lifestyles for climate action. Towards this end, we:
    i. Commit to implement the G20 High-Level Principles on Lifestyles for Sustainable Development.
    ii. Support the implementation of the High-Level Principles (HLPs) through international cooperation, financial support, and development, deployment and dissemination of technology. We encourage International Organizations to incorporate the HLPs into their programs, as appropriate.
    iii. Note the launch of "Travel for LiFE" and support the development of smart destinations that are responsible and sustainable.

Designing a Circular Economy World

37. In order to endeavour to decouple our economic growth from environmental degradation and enhance sustainable consumption and production, including primary resource consumption while supporting economic growth, we acknowledge the critical role played by circular economy, extended producer responsibility and resource efficiency in achieving sustainable development. We thank the Indian presidency in launching Resource Efficiency and Circular Economy Industry Coalition (RECEIC). We commit to enhance environmentally sound waste management, substantially reduce waste generation by 2030, and highlight the importance of zero waste initiatives.

Implementing Clean, Sustainable, Just, Affordable & Inclusive Energy Transitions

38. We commit to accelerating clean, sustainable, just, affordable and inclusive energy transitions following various pathways, as a means of enabling strong, sustainable, balanced and inclusive growth and achieve our climate objectives. We recognise the needs, vulnerabilities, priorities and different national circumstances of developing countries. We support strong international and national enabling environments to foster innovation, voluntary and mutually agreed technology transfer, and access to low-cost financing. To this end, we:

    i. Emphasise the importance of maintaining uninterrupted flows of energy from various sources, suppliers and routes, exploring paths of enhanced energy security and market stability, including through inclusive investments to meet the growing energy demand, in line with our sustainable development and climate goals, while promoting open, competitive, non-discriminatory and free international energy markets.

    ii. Recognizing that developing countries need to be supported in their transitions to low carbon/emissions, we will work towards facilitating low-cost financing for them.

    iii. Support the acceleration of production, utilization, as well as the development of transparent and resilient global markets for hydrogen produced from zero and low-emission technologies and its derivatives such as ammonia, by developing voluntary and mutually agreed harmonising standards as well as mutually recognised and inter-operable certification schemes. To realise this, we affirm the 'G20 High Level Voluntary Principles on Hydrogen', to build a sustainable and equitable global hydrogen ecosystem that benefits all nations. We take note of the Presidency's initiative to establish the Green Hydrogen Innovation Centre steered by the International Solar Alliance (ISA).

    iv. Will work towards facilitating access to low-cost financing for developing countries, for existing as well as new and emerging clean and sustainable energy technologies and for supporting the energy transitions. We note the report on "Low-cost Financing for the Energy Transitions" prepared under the Indian Presidency and its estimation that the world needs an annual investment of over USD 4 trillion, with a high share of renewable energy in the primary energy mix.

    v. Will pursue and encourage efforts to triple renewable energy capacity globally through existing targets and policies, as well as demonstrate similar ambition with respect to other zero and low-emission technologies, including abatement and removal technologies, in line with national circumstances by 2030. We also note the 'Voluntary Action Plan for Promoting Renewable Energy to Accelerate Universal Energy Access'.

    vi. Pledge to advance cooperation initiatives to develop, demonstrate and deploy clean and sustainable energy technologies and solutions and other efforts for innovation.

vii. Take note of the 'Voluntary Action Plan on Doubling the Rate of Energy Efficiency Improvement by 2030'.

viii. Recognize the importance of sustainable biofuels in our zero and low-emission development strategies, and note the setting up of a Global Biofuels Alliance.

ix. Support reliable, diversified, sustainable and responsible supply chains for energy transitions, including for critical minerals and materials beneficiated at source, semi-conductors and technologies. We take note of the Presidency's "Voluntary High-Level Principles for Collaboration on Critical Minerals for Energy Transitions".

x. For countries that opt to use civil nuclear energy, will collaborate on voluntary and mutually agreed terms, in research, innovation, development & deployment of civil nuclear technologies including advanced and Small Modular Reactors (SMRs), in accordance with national legislations. These countries will promote responsible nuclear decommissioning, radioactive waste and spent fuel management and mobilizing investments, and share knowledge and best practices, through strengthening international cooperation to promote nuclear safety globally.

xi. Recognize the role of grid interconnections, resilient energy infrastructure and regional/cross-border power systems integration, where applicable in enhancing energy security, fostering economic growth and facilitating universal energy access for all.

xii. Will increase our efforts to implement the commitment made in 2009 in Pittsburgh to phase-out and rationalise, over the medium term, inefficient fossil fuel subsidies that encourage wasteful consumption and commit to achieve this objective, while providing targeted support for the poorest and the most vulnerable.

xiii. Recognise the importance to accelerate the development, deployment and dissemination of technologies, and the adoption of policies, to transition towards low-emission energy systems, including by rapidly scaling up the deployment of clean power generation, including renewable energy, as well as energy efficiency measures, including accelerating efforts towards phasedown of unabated coal power, in line with national circumstances and recognizing the need for support towards just transitions.

Delivering on Climate and Sustainable Finance

39. We welcome the Sustainable Finance Working Group (SFWG) recommendations on the mechanisms to support the timely and adequate mobilisation of resources for climate finance while ensuring support for transition activities in line with country circumstances. We also recognise the significant role of public finance as an important enabler of climate actions, such as leveraging much-needed private

finance through blended financial instruments, mechanisms and risk-sharing facilities to address both adaptation and mitigation efforts in a balanced manner for reaching ambitious Nationally Determined Contributions (NDCs), carbon neutrality and net-zero considering different national circumstances. We welcome the SFWG recommendations for scaling up blended finance and risk-sharing facilities, including the enhanced role of MDBs in mobilizing climate finance. We underscore the importance of maximizing the effect of concessional resources, such as those of the multilateral climate funds, to support developing countries' implementation of the Paris Agreement and call for an ambitious second replenishment process of the Green Climate Fund for its upcoming 2024-2027 programming period We will undertake work to facilitate access to multilateral climate funds and enhance their leverage and ability to mobilize private capital. Recognizing the importance of supporting the commercialization of early-stage technologies that avoid, abate and remove greenhouse gas emissions and facilitate adaptation, we note the recommendations on financial solutions, policies, and incentives to encourage greater private flows for the rapid development, demonstration, and deployment of green and low-emission technologies. We reiterate the importance of a policy mix consisting of fiscal, market and regulatory mechanisms, including, as appropriate, the use of carbon pricing and non-pricing mechanisms and incentives toward carbon neutrality and net zero.

40. We endorse the multi-year G20 Technical Assistance Action Plan (TAAP) and the voluntary recommendations made to overcome data-related barriers to climate investments. We encourage the implementation of TAAP by relevant jurisdictions and stakeholders in line with the national circumstances. We look forward to reporting on the progress made in the implementation of the G20 Sustainable Finance Roadmap, which is voluntary and flexible in nature, and call for further efforts to advance the Roadmap's recommended actions that will scale up sustainable finance, including, among others, the implementation of the Transition Finance Framework. We look forward to the 2023 G20 Sustainable Finance Report. We welcome the finalization of the sustainability and climate-related disclosure standards published by the International Sustainability Standards Board (ISSB) in June 2023, which provide the mechanisms that address proportionality and promote interoperability. It is important that flexibility, to take into account country-specific circumstances, is preserved in the implementation of those standards. When put into practice as above, those standards will help support globally comparable and reliable disclosures.

41. We recognise the need for increased global investments to meet our climate goals of the Paris Agreement, and to rapidly and substantially scale up investment and climate finance from billions to trillions of dollars globally from all sources. In this regard, it is essential to align all relevant financial flows with these objectives while scaling up finance, capacity building and technology transfer on voluntary and mutually agreed terms, taking into account the priorities and needs of developing countries. To achieve this, we:

i. Note the need of USD 5.8-5.9 trillion in the pre-2030 period required for developing countries, in particular for their needs to implement their NDCs, as well as the need of USD 4 trillion per year for clean energy technologies by 2030 to reach net zero emissions by 2050.

ii. We recall and reaffirm the commitment made in 2010 by the developed countries to the goal of mobilizing jointly USD 100 billion climate finance per year by 2020, and annually through 2025, to address the needs of the developing countries, in the context of meaningful mitigation action and transparency in implementation. Developed country contributors expect this goal to be met for the first time in 2023.

iii. We will work to successfully implement the decision at COP27 on funding arrangements for responding to loss and damage for assisting developing countries that are particularly vulnerable to the adverse effects of climate change, including establishing a fund. We will support the Transitional Committee established in this regard, and look forward to its recommendations on operationalization of the new funding arrangements including a fund at COP28.

iv. Call on Parties to set an ambitious, transparent and trackable New Collective Quantified Goal (NCQG) of climate finance in 2024, from a floor of USD 100 billion a year, taking into account the needs and priorities of developing countries in fulfilling the objective of the UNFCCC and implementation of the Paris Agreement.

v. Recalling para 18 of the Glasgow Climate Pact, we urge the developed countries to fulfil their commitment to at least double their collective provision of adaptation finance from 2019 levels by 2025, in the context of achieving scaled up financial resources.

vi. Call on all relevant financial institutions, such as MDBs and multilateral funds to further strengthen their efforts including by setting ambitious adaptation finance targets and announcing, where appropriate, revised and enhanced 2025 projections.

vii. Acknowledge the vital role of private climate finance in supplementing public climate finance and encourage the development of financing mechanisms such as blended finance, de-risking instruments and green bonds for projects in developing countries.

Conserving, Protecting, Sustainably Using and Restoring Ecosystems

42. We emphasize the importance of healthy ecosystems in addressing climate change, biodiversity loss, desertification, drought, land degradation, pollution, food insecurity and water scarcity. We commit to restoring by 2030 at least 30% of all degraded ecosystems and scaling up efforts to achieve land degradation neutrality. To achieve this, we:

i. Commit to the swift, full and effective implementation of the Kunming-

Montreal Global Biodiversity Framework (GBF), and encourage others to do the same, and encourage actions to halt and reverse biodiversity loss by 2030. We also call for enhanced financial resources from all sources. To this end, we welcome the recent establishment of the Global Biodiversity Framework Fund within the Global Environment Facility (GEF).

ii. Support the G20 ambition to reduce land degradation by 50% by 2040 on a voluntary basis, as committed under the G20 Global Land Initiative (GLI) and note the discussions on the Gandhinagar Implementation Roadmap and the Gandhinagar Information Platform.

iii. Recognize that forests provide crucial ecosystem services, as well as for climate purposes acting as sinks, at the global and local levels for the environment, climate and people. We will scale up efforts to protect, conserve and sustainably manage forests and combat deforestation, in line with internationally agreed timelines, highlighting the contributions of these actions for sustainable development and taking into account the social and economic challenges of local communities and indigenous peoples. In the context of forests, we will avoid discriminatory green economic policies, consistent with WTO rules and multilateral environmental agreements. We are committed to mobilizing new and additional finance for forests from all sources, including concessional and innovative financing, in particular for developing countries. We commit to prevention and mitigation of wildfires and remediation of mining-degraded lands.

iv. Call for enhancing global cooperation and sharing of best practices on water, and welcome the deliberations at the UN 2023 Water Conference and G20 Dialogue on Water.

Harnessing and Preserving the Ocean-based Economy

43. We commit to conserving, protecting, restoring and sustainably using the world's ocean, marine ecosystems, and look forward to make progress and in this regard, contribute to the 2025 UN Ocean Conference. To this end, we:

i. Welcome the Chennai High-Level Principles for a Sustainable and Resilient Blue/Ocean-based Economy.

ii. Note the adoption of the new international legally binding instrument under the UN Convention on the Law of the Sea (UNCLOS) on the conservation and sustainable use of marine Biological diversity of areas Beyond National Jurisdiction (BBNJ) and call on all countries for its early entry into force and implementation.

iii. Support the Commission for the Conservation of Antarctic Marine Living Resources (CCAMLR), within the Antarctic Treaty system, to establish a representative system of Marine Protected Areas (MPAs) in the CCAMLR Convention area based on the best available scientific evidence.

iv. Reiterate our commitment to ending illegal, unreported, and unregulated

(IUU) fishing, as well as destructive fishing methods in accordance with international law.

v. Support the role of Ocean 20 Dialogue in making progress to achieve this agenda.

Ending Plastic Pollution

44. We are determined to end plastic pollution. In this context, we welcome the resolution UNEP/EA.5/Res.14 which established an Intergovernmental Negotiating Committee (INC) to develop an international legally binding instrument on plastic pollution, including the marine environment, with the ambition of completing its work by the end of 2024. We will also build on the G20 Marine Litter Action Plan as elucidated in the Osaka Blue Ocean Vision.

Financing Cities of Tomorrow

45. We emphasise the need for enhanced mobilisation of finances and efficient use of existing resources in our efforts to make the cities of tomorrow inclusive, resilient, and sustainable. To this effect, we endorse the G20 Principles for Financing Cities of Tomorrow, which are voluntary and non-binding in nature and the G20/OECD Report on Financing Cities of Tomorrow, which provides a financing strategy as well as presents a compendium of innovative urban planning and financing models. We encourage stakeholders, including the Development Financial Institutions and the MDBs, to explore the potential of drawing upon these principles in their planning and financing of urban infrastructure wherever applicable and share experiences from early pilot cases. We note the progress in outlining the enablers of inclusive cities. We also note the customisable G20/ADB Framework on Capacity Building of Urban Administration to guide local governments in assessing and enhancing their overall institutional capacity for the effective delivery of public services. We note the ongoing pilot application of the voluntary and non-binding Quality Infrastructure Investment (QII) Indicators and look forward to further discussion on their application considering country circumstances.

Reducing Disaster Risk and Building Resilient Infrastructure

46. This year, the G20 Presidency has catalysed efforts on disaster risk reduction in the G20 through institutionalization of the Disaster Risk Reduction (DRR) Working Group as noted by UNGA res. 77/289. We reaffirm the Sendai Framework for Disaster Risk Reduction (SFDRR) and recognize the need for accelerating its full implementation. To this end, we:

i. Urge for accelerating progress on Early Warning and Early Action through strengthening national and local capacities, innovative financing tools, private sector investment, and knowledge sharing.

ii. Continue to support augmentation of capabilities of all countries, including emerging economies, in particular developing countries, LDCs and SIDS, for promoting disaster and climate resilience of infrastructure systems. We welcome the Global Platform for DRR and take note of initiatives such as the Coalition for Disaster Resilient Infrastructure (CDRI) in furtherance of such collaboration and sharing.

iii. Promote mutual learning of recovery experiences applying all the principles of Sendai Framework.

D. Multilateral Institutions for the 21st Century

Reinvigorating Multilateralism

47. The global order has undergone dramatic changes since the Second World War due to economic growth and prosperity, decolonization, demographic dividends, technological achievements, emergence of new economic powers and deeper international cooperation. The United Nations must be responsive to the entire membership, faithful to its founding purposes and principles of its Charter and adapted to carrying out its mandate. In this context, we recall the Declaration on the Commemoration of the 75th anniversary of the United Nations (UNGA 75/1) which reaffirmed that our challenges are inter-connected and can only be addressed through reinvigorated multilateralism, reforms and international cooperation. The need for revitalized multilateralism to adequately address contemporary global challenges of the 21st Century, and to make global governance more representative, effective, transparent and accountable, has been voiced at multiple fora. In this context, a more inclusive and reinvigorated multilateralism and reform aimed at implementing the 2030 agenda is essential.

Reforming International Financial Institutions

48. The 21st century also requires an international development finance system that is fit for purpose, including for the scale of need and depth of the shocks facing developing countries, in particular the poorest and most vulnerable. We are working to deliver better, bigger and more effective MDBs by enhancing operating models, improving responsiveness and accessibility, and substantially increasing financing capacity to maximise development impact. Stronger MDBs will be important to our efforts to mobilize financing from all sources for a quantum jump from billions to trillions of dollars for development. We underscore the need for enhancing representation and voice of developing countries in decision-making in global international economic and financial institutions in order to deliver more effective, credible, accountable and legitimate institutions. The international finance system must deliver significantly more financing to help developing countries and EMEs to fight poverty, tackle global challenges and maximise development impact.
49. We remain committed to pursuing ambitious efforts to evolve and strengthen MDBs to address the global challenges of the 21st century with a continued focus on addressing the development needs of low- and middle-income countries.
50. We endorse the G20 Roadmap for Implementing the Recommendations of the

G20 Independent Review of MDBs Capital Adequacy Frameworks (CAFs) and call for its ambitious implementation, within MDBs' own governance frameworks while safeguarding their long-term financial sustainability, robust credit ratings and preferred creditor status. We also call for a regular review of the progress of implementation on a rolling basis including through engaging with MDBs, subject experts and shareholders. We commend the MDBs for their progress in implementing the CAF recommendations, especially with respect to adapting definitions of risk appetite and financial innovation. We appreciate the ongoing collaboration among MDBs on the timely release of Global Emerging Markets (GEMs) data and the launch of GEMs 2.0 as a stand-alone entity by early 2024. Going forward, we also encourage MDBs to collaborate in areas such as hybrid capital, callable capital, and guarantees. We appreciate the enhanced dialogue between the MDBs, Credit Rating Agencies and shareholders and encourage continued transparency in the exchange of information and rating methodologies. We take note that initial CAF measures, including those under implementation and consideration, could potentially yield additional lending headroom of approximately USD 200 billion over the next decade, as estimated in the G20 CAF Roadmap. While these are encouraging first steps, we will need to give an additional push for continued and further impetus on CAF implementation.

51. Furthermore, we call on the MDBs to undertake comprehensive efforts to evolve their vision, incentive structures, operational approaches and financial capacities so that they are better equipped to maximize their impact in addressing a wide range of global challenges while being consistent with their mandate and commitment to accelerate progress towards Sustainable Development Goals (SDGs). We welcome the World Bank's progress on their Evolution Roadmap and look forward to further steps by the IMF/WBG Annual Meetings in Marrakesh and beyond. Recognising the urgent need to strengthen and evolve the MDB ecosystem for the 21st century, we appreciate the efforts of the G20 Independent Expert Group on Strengthening MDBs in preparing Volume 1 of the Report and look forward to its examination in conjunction with Volume 2 expected in October 2023. We take note of Volume 1's recommendations and the MDBs may choose to discuss these recommendations as relevant and appropriate, within their governance frameworks, in due course, with a view to enhancing the effectiveness of MDBs. We support the upcoming G20 High-Level Seminar, on the sidelines of the Fourth G20 FMCBG in October 2023 on strengthening the financial capacity of MDBs. Scaling up investment to meet development needs and global challenges requires a big push on investments and, in this context, we ask the IMF and the World Bank, in coordination with other relevant international institutions, to support efforts at enhancing domestic resource mobilisation in EMDEs. We call on the MDBs to also leverage private capital through innovative financing models and new partnerships to maximise their development impact. Recognizing other multilateral efforts, we take note of the Summit for a New Global Financing Pact.

52. Recognizing the imperative of achieving the SDGs, we will collectively mobilize more headroom and concessional finance to boost the World Bank's capacity to support low and middle-income countries that need help in addressing global challenges, with a clear framework for the allocation of scarce concessional resources, and to provide strong support for the poorest countries. Therefore, we are exploring options that will deliver a powerful boost to IBRD headroom, reduce the cost of investments addressing global challenges, and increase the capacity of the IDA crisis response window. We also look forward to an ambitious IDA21 replenishment to increase IDA financing capacity. We acknowledge the concluding report on the 2020 Shareholding Review of the International Bank for Reconstruction and Development (IBRD) and look forward to the 2025 Shareholding Review.
53. We reiterate our commitment to a strong, quota-based, and adequately resourced IMF at the centre of the global financial safety net. We remain committed to revisiting the adequacy of quotas and will continue the process of IMF governance reform under the 16th General Review of Quotas (GRQ), including a new quota formula as a guide, and ensure the primary role of quotas in IMF resources, to be concluded by December 15, 2023. In this context, we support at least maintaining the IMF's current resource envelope. We welcome the landmark achievement of the global ambition of USD 100 billion of voluntary contributions (in SDRs or equivalent) and USD 2.6 billion of grants in pledges for countries most in need and call for the swift delivery of pending pledges. We welcome the progress achieved under the Resilience and Sustainability Trust (RST) and Poverty Reduction and Growth Trust (PRGT). We call for further voluntary subsidy and loan pledges to the PRGT and will continue to monitor the effectiveness of RST supported programs. We look forward to the preliminary analysis by the IMF of the range of options to put the PRGT on a sustainable footing with a view to meeting the growing needs of low-income countries in the coming years. The G20 reiterates its continued support to Africa, including through the G20 Compact with Africa. We look forward to further progress on the exploration of viable options for voluntary channelling of SDRs through MDBs, while respecting relevant legal frameworks and the need to preserve the reserve asset character and status of SDR. We look forward to review of precautionary arrangements and take note of the discussions held on the IMF surcharge policy.

Managing Global Debt Vulnerabilities

54. We re-emphasise the importance of addressing debt vulnerabilities in low and middle-income countries in an effective, comprehensive and systematic manner. We continue to stand by all the commitments made in the Common Framework for Debt Treatments beyond the DSSI, including those in the second and final paragraphs, as agreed on November 13, 2020, and step up the implementation of the Common Framework in a predictable, timely, orderly and coordinated manner. To this end, we call for continued discussion on policy-related issues

linked to the implementation of the Common Framework for making appropriate recommendations. We welcome the recent agreement between the Government of Zambia and the official creditor committee on debt treatment and look forward to a swift resolution. We welcome the formation of the official creditor committee for Ghana and look forward to an agreement on a debt treatment as soon as possible. We also call for a swift conclusion of the debt treatment for Ethiopia. Beyond the Common Framework, we welcome all efforts for timely resolution of the debt situation of Sri Lanka, including the formation of the official creditor committee, and we call for the resolution as soon as possible. We encourage the efforts of the Global Sovereign Debt Roundtable (GSDR) participants to strengthen communication and foster a common understanding among key stakeholders, both within and outside the Common Framework, for facilitating effective debt treatments. We welcome joint efforts by all stakeholders, including private creditors, to continue working towards enhancing debt transparency. We note the results of the voluntary stocktaking exercise of data sharing with International Financial Institutions. We welcome the efforts of private sector lenders who have already contributed data to the joint Institute of International Finance (IIF)/OECD Data Repository Portal and continue to encourage others to also contribute on a voluntary basis.

E. Technological Transformation and Digital Public Infrastructure

55. Technology can enable rapid transformations for bridging the existing digital divides and accelerate progress for inclusive and sustainable development. Digital public infrastructure (DPI), as an evolving concept and as a set of shared digital systems, built and leveraged by both the public and private sectors, based on secure and resilient infrastructure, and can be built on open standards and specifications, as well as opensource software can enable delivery of services at societal-scale. In our voluntary efforts to make digital public infrastructure interoperable, we recognize the importance of data free flow with trust and cross-border data flows while respecting applicable legal frameworks. We also reaffirm the role of Data for Development.

Building Digital Public Infrastructure

56. We recognize that safe, secure, trusted, accountable and inclusive digital public infrastructure, respectful of human rights, personal data, privacy and intellectual property rights can foster resilience, and enable service delivery and innovation. To this end, we:
    i. Welcome the G20 Framework for Systems of Digital Public Infrastructure, a voluntary and suggested framework for the development, deployment and governance of DPI.
    ii. Welcome India's plan to build and maintain a Global Digital Public Infrastructure Repository (GDPIR), a virtual repository of DPI, voluntarily shared by G20 members and beyond.

iii. Take note of the Indian Presidency's proposal of the One Future Alliance (OFA), a voluntary initiative aimed to build capacity, and provide technical assistance and adequate funding support for implementing DPI in LMICs.

Building Safety, Security, Resilience and Trust in the Digital Economy

57. An enabling, inclusive, open, fair, non-discriminatory and secure digital economy is increasingly important for all countries and stakeholders while respecting applicable legal frameworks. We will share our approaches and good practices to build a safe, secure and resilient digital economy. To this extent, we:
    i. Welcome the non-binding G20 High-level Principles to Support Businesses in Building Safety, Security, Resilience, and Trust in the Digital Economy.
    ii. Welcome the G20 Toolkit on Cyber Education and Cyber Awareness of Children and Youth.

Crypto-assets: Policy and Regulation

58. We continue to closely monitor the risks of the fast-paced developments in the crypto-asset ecosystem. We endorse the Financial Stability Board's (FSB's) high-level recommendations for the regulation, supervision and oversight of crypto-assets activities and markets and of global stablecoin arrangements. We ask the FSB and SSBs to promote the effective and timely implementation of these recommendations in a consistent manner globally to avoid regulatory arbitrage. We welcome the shared FSB and SSBs workplan for crypto assets. We welcome the IMF-FSB Synthesis Paper, including a Roadmap, that will support a coordinated and comprehensive policy and regulatory framework taking into account the full range of risks and risks specific to the emerging market and developing economies (EMDEs) and ongoing global implementation of FATF standards to address money laundering and terrorism financing risks. Our Finance Ministers and Central Bank Governors will discuss taking forward the Roadmap at their meeting in October 2023. We also welcome the BIS Report on The Crypto Ecosystem: Key Elements and Risks.

Central Bank Digital Currency

59. We welcome discussions on the potential macro-financial implications arising from the introduction and adoption of Central Bank Digital Currencies (CBDCs), notably on cross-border payments as well as on the international monetary and financial system. We welcome the BIS Innovation Hub (BISIH) Report on Lessons Learnt on CBDCs and look forward to the IMF Report on Potential macro-financial implications of widespread adoption of CBDCs to advance the discussion on this issue.

Fostering Digital Ecosystems

60. We resolve to deploy all available digital tools and technologies and spare no

effort in fostering safe and resilient digital ecosystems, and ensuring that every citizen on our planet is financially included. To support this, we:

i. Commit to promote responsible, sustainable and inclusive use of digital technology by farmers and an ecosystem of Agri-Tech start-ups and MSMEs.
ii. Welcome the establishment of the Global Initiative on Digital Health (GIDH) within a WHO-managed framework to build a comprehensive digital health ecosystem in compliance with respective data protection regulations.
iii. Will leverage digital technologies for the protection and promotion of culture and cultural heritage and adopt digital frameworks for the development of cultural and creative sectors and industries.

Harnessing Artificial Intelligence (AI) Responsibly for Good and for All

61. The rapid progress of AI promises prosperity and expansion of the global digital economy. It is our endeavour to leverage AI for the public good by solving challenges in a responsible, inclusive and human-centric manner, while protecting people's rights and safety. To ensure responsible AI development, deployment and use, the protection of human rights, transparency and explainability, fairness, accountability, regulation, safety, appropriate human oversight, ethics, biases, privacy, and data protection must be addressed. To unlock the full potential of AI, equitably share its benefits and mitigate risks, we will work together to promote international cooperation and further discussions on international governance for AI. To this end, we:

i. Reaffirm our commitment to G20 AI Principles (2019) and endeavour to share information on approaches to using AI to support solutions in the digital economy.
ii. Will pursue a pro-innovation regulatory/governance approach that maximizes the benefits and takes into account the risks associated with the use of AI.
iii. Will promote responsible AI for achieving SDGs.

F. International Taxation

62. We reaffirm our commitment to continue cooperation towards a globally fair, sustainable and modern international tax system appropriate to the needs of the 21st century. We remain committed to the swift implementation of the two-pillar international tax package. Significant progress has been made on Pillar One including the delivery of a text of a Multilateral Convention (MLC), and work on Amount B (framework for simplified and streamlined application of the arm's length principle to in-country baseline marketing and distribution activities) as well as the completion of the work on the development of the Subject to Tax Rule (STTR) under Pillar Two. We call on the Inclusive Framework to resolve swiftly the few pending issues relating to the MLC with a view to preparing the MLC for signature in the second half of 2023 and completing the work on Amount B by the end of 2023. We welcome the steps taken by various countries to implement

the Global Anti-Base Erosion (GloBE) Rules as a common approach. We recognise the need for coordinated efforts towards capacity building to implement the two-pillar international tax package effectively and, in particular, welcome a plan for additional support and technical assistance for developing countries. We note the 2023 update of the G20/OECD Roadmap on Developing Countries and International Taxation. We call for the swift implementation of the Crypto-Asset Reporting Framework ("CARF") and amendments to the CRS. We ask the Global Forum on Transparency and Exchange of Information for Tax Purposes ("Global Forum") to identify an appropriate and coordinated timeline to commence exchanges by relevant jurisdictions, noting the aspiration of a significant number of these jurisdictions to start CARF exchanges by 2027 and to report to our future meetings on the progress of its work. We note the OECD Report on Enhancing International Tax Transparency on Real Estate and the Global Forum Report on Facilitating the Use of Tax-Treaty-Exchanged Information for Non-Tax Purposes.

G. Gender Equality and Empowering All Women and Girls

63. The G20 reaffirms that gender equality is of fundamental importance, and that investing in the empowerment of all women and girls, has a multiplier effect in implementing the 2030 Agenda.

Enhancing Economic and Social Empowerment

64. We encourage women-led development and remain committed to enhancing women's full, equal, effective, and meaningful participation as decision makers for addressing global challenges inclusively and in contributing as active participants in all spheres of society, across all sectors and at all levels of the economy, which is not only crucial for achieving gender equality, but also for contributing to global GDP growth. To this end, we:
    i. Reaffirm our commitment to achieving the Brisbane Goal to reduce the gap in labour force participation and implementing the G20 Roadmap Towards and Beyond the Brisbane Goal '25 by 25' and ask the ILO and OECD to report progress annually.
    ii. Ensure equal access to affordable, inclusive, equitable, safe and quality education from early childhood through higher education to lifelong learning and support the greater enrolment, participation and leadership of all women and girls, including those with disabilities, in STEM fields and in emerging digital technologies.
    iii. Take steps to promote the full and meaningful participation of women in a transitioning world of work by enabling inclusive access to employment opportunities, with a focus on closing the gender pay gap and ensuring women's equal access to decent work and quality jobs.
    iv. Promote investment in the availability and accessibility of social protection,

and to affordable care infrastructure to address the unequal distribution in paid and unpaid care and domestic work and to promote the continued participation of women in education and employment.

v. Commit to eliminate gender-based violence including sexual violence, harassment, discrimination and abuse against women and girls both online and offline, and ensure safe workplaces in this regard.

vi. Promote women's inclusion into the formal financial system by strengthening their access to economic resources, particularly through digital finance and microfinance.

vii. Eliminate gender stereotypes and biases, and change norms, attitudes and behaviours that perpetuate gender inequality.

Bridging the Gender Digital Divide

65. We commit to halve the digital gender gap by 2030. To this end, we will:

i. Address gender norms and barriers to accessibility, affordability, adoption, and usage of digital technologies.

ii. Promote regulatory policy frameworks that enable all women and girls to actively participate in the formulation and implementation of national digital strategies, including enhancing digital literacy and skills.

iii. Identify and eliminate all potential risks that women and girls encounter from increased digitalization, including all forms of online and offline abuse, by encouraging the adoption of safety-by-design approaches in digital tools and technologies.

iv. Promote and implement gender-responsive policies to create an enabling, inclusive, and non-discriminatory digital economy for women-led and -owned businesses, including MSMEs.

v. Encourage and support initiatives by identifying, funding, and accelerating proven solutions, thereby improving women's livelihoods and income security.

vi. Welcome initiatives to support women empowerment in the digital economy.

Driving Gender Inclusive Climate Action

66. Acknowledging the disproportionate impact of climate change, biodiversity loss, desertification and pollution on all women and girls, accelerating climate action must have gender equality at its core. To this end, we will:

i. Support and increase women's participation, partnership, decision-making and leadership in climate change mitigation and adaptation, and disaster risk reduction strategies and policy frameworks on environmental issues.

ii. Support gender-responsive and environment-resilient solutions, including water, sanitation and hygiene (WASH) solutions, to build resilience to the impact of climate change and environmental degradation.

Securing Women's Food Security, Nutrition, and Well-Being

67. Women's food security and nutrition is the cornerstone of individual and community development as it lays the foundation for women's health, as well as that of her children, family and general well-being of the community. To this end, we will:
    i. Encourage investments in inclusive, sustainable and resilient agriculture and food systems. Support accessible, affordable, safe and nutritious food and healthy diets in school meal programmes. Promote innovation for inclusive agri-value chains and systems by and for women farmers.
    ii. Support gender-responsive and age-sensitive nutrition and food system interventions by leveraging innovative financing instruments and social protection systems in ending hunger and malnutrition.

Creation of a Working Group on the Empowerment of Women

68. We agree to create a new Working Group on Empowerment of Women to support the G20 Women's Ministerial and look forward to the convening of its first meeting during the Brazilian G20 Presidency.

H. Financial Sector Issues

69. We continue to strongly support the work of the FSB and SSBs to address vulnerabilities and enhance the resilience of non-bank financial intermediation (NBFI) from a systemic perspective while monitoring evolving developments in NBFI. We welcome the FSB's consultation report on revisions to the FSB 2017 recommendations on addressing liquidity mismatch in open-ended funds and the FSB report on the financial stability implications of leverage in NBFI, and we support work to promote implementation of the FSB money market fund proposals. We welcome the FSB's recommendations to achieve greater convergence in cyber incident reporting, updates to the Cyber Lexicon and Concept Note for a Format for Incident Reporting Exchange (FIRE). We look forward to the FSB's further work on FIRE and ask the FSB to develop an action plan with appropriate timelines. We welcome the FSB's consultation Report on Enhancing Third-party Risk Management and Oversight. We expect the toolkit to support efforts in enhancing the operational resilience of financial institutions, addressing the challenges arising from their growing reliance on critical third-party service providers, including BigTechs and FinTechs, as well as reducing fragmentation in regulatory and supervisory approaches across jurisdictions and in different areas of the financial services sector.
70. We reaffirm our commitment to the effective implementation of the prioritised actions for the next phase of the G20 Roadmap for Enhancing Cross-border Payments to achieve global targets for faster, cheaper, more transparent and inclusive cross-border payments by 2027 and welcome the initiatives undertaken by SSBs and international organisations in this direction. We welcome the

successful conclusion of the G20 TechSprint 2023, a joint initiative with the BIS Innovation Hub, which will promote innovative solutions aimed at improving cross-border payments.

71. We welcome the annual progress report on the FSB's Roadmap for Addressing Financial Risks from Climate Change. We endorse the revised G20/OECD Principles of Corporate Governance with the aim to strengthen policy and regulatory frameworks for corporate governance that support sustainability and access to finance from capital markets, which in turn can contribute to the resilience of the broader economy. We reiterate our commitment to promote sustainable capital flows. To this effect, we take note of the OECD's Report, "Towards Orderly Green Transition – Investment Requirements and Managing Risks to Capital Flows".

I. Countering Terrorism and Money laundering

72. We condemn terrorism in all its forms and manifestations, including those on the basis of xenophobia, racism and other forms of intolerance, or in the name of religion or belief, recognizing the commitment of all religions to peace. It constitutes one of the most serious threats to international peace and security.
73. We strongly condemn all terrorist acts against critical infrastructure, including critical energy facilities, and against other vulnerable targets. All acts of terrorism are criminal and unjustifiable, regardless of their motivation, wherever, whenever and by whomsoever committed. Effective counterterrorism measures, support for the victims of terrorism and the protection of human rights are not conflicting goals, but complementary and mutually reinforcing. A holistic approach on the basis of international law can effectively counter terrorism. Efforts to increase the effectiveness of international cooperation should be strengthened to deny terrorist groups safe haven, freedom of operations, movement and recruitment, as well as financial, material or political support.
74. We also express concern about illicit trafficking and diversion of small arms and light weapons. International cooperation among States is critical to combat these phenomena, including export, import controls, and tracing.
75. We commit to supporting the increasing resource needs of the Financial Action Task Force (FATF) and FATF Style Regional Bodies and encourage others to do the same, including for the next round of mutual evaluations. We remain committed to the timely and global implementation of the revised FATF Standards on the transparency of beneficial ownership of legal persons and legal arrangements to make it more difficult for criminals to hide and launder ill-gotten gains. We welcome the ongoing work of the FATF to enhance global efforts to recover criminal proceeds, in particular, the progress made by the FATF towards revising its standards on asset recovery and reinforcing global asset recovery networks. We reiterate the importance of countries developing and implementing effective regulatory and supervisory frameworks to mitigate risks associated with virtual

assets in line with FATF Standards, especially for terrorism financing, money laundering, and proliferation financing risks. In this regard, we support the FATF's initiative to accelerate the global implementation of its standards, including the "travel rule", and its work on risks of emerging technologies and innovations, including decentralised finance (DeFi) arrangements and peer-to-peer transactions.

J. Creating a More Inclusive World

76. We welcome the African Union as a permanent member of the G20 and strongly believe that inclusion of the African Union into the G20 will significantly contribute to addressing the global challenges of our time. We commend the efforts of all G20 members which paved the way for accession of the African Union as a permanent member during India's Presidency of the G20. Africa plays an important role in the global economy. We commit to strengthen our ties with and support the African Union realise the aspirations under Agenda 2063. We also reiterate strong support to Africa, including through the G20 Compact with Africa and G20 Initiative on supporting industrialization in Africa and LDCs. We are supportive of further discussing the deepening of cooperation between the G20 and other regional partners.
77. We reaffirm our commitment to support migrants, including migrant workers and refugees in our efforts towards a more inclusive world, in line with national policies, legislations and circumstances, ensuring full respect for the human rights and their fundamental freedoms regardless of their migration status. We also recognize the importance of preventing irregular migration flows and the smuggling of migrants, as part of a comprehensive approach for safe, orderly and regular migration while responding to humanitarian needs and the root causes of displacement. We support strengthening cooperation between countries of origin, transit and destination. We will continue the dialogue on migration and forced displacement during future Presidencies.
78. We note the UNGA Resolution A/RES/77/318, particularly its commitment to promote respect for religious and cultural diversity, dialogue and tolerance. We also emphasize that freedom of religion or belief, freedom of opinion or expression, the right to peaceful assembly, and the right to freedom of association are interdependent, inter-related and mutually reinforcing and stress the role that these rights can play in the fight against all forms of intolerance and discrimination based on religion or belief. In this regard, we strongly deplore all acts of religious hatred against persons, as well as those of a symbolic nature without prejudice to domestic legal frameworks, including against religious symbols and holy books.
79. We will continue to integrate the perspectives of the developing countries into the G20 agendas and appreciate the G20 members' initiatives in this regard.

Conclusion

80. We thank India for successfully hosting the 18th G20 Summit in New Delhi, for

its warm welcome to delegates, and for its valuable contributions to the strengthening of the G20. We appreciate the successful conclusion of various G20 Working Groups and Ministerial meetings and welcome their outcomes as annexed. We also congratulate India on the successful landing on the moon on 23 August 2023.

81. We reiterate our commitment to the G20 as the premier forum for global economic cooperation and its continued operation in the spirit of multilateralism, on the basis of consensus, with all members participating on an equal footing in all its events including Summits. We look forward to meeting again in Brazil in 2024 and in South Africa in 2025, as well as in the United States in 2026 at the beginning of the next cycle. We welcome Saudi Arabia's ambition to advance its turn for hosting the G20 Presidency in the next cycle. We also look forward to the Paris Olympic and Paralympic Games in 2024 as a symbol of peace, dialogue amongst nations and inclusivity, with participation of all.

82. We thank international organizations for their participation and support. We thank the Engagement Groups of B20, S20, SAI20, Startup20, T20, U20, W20, Y20, C20, P20 and L20 and the Initiatives, namely, EMPOWER, Research Initiative, Space Economy Leaders Meeting (SELM), Chief Science Advisers' Roundtable (CSAR) and the G20 Cybersecurity Conference for their valuable recommendations.

83. Recalling our collective actions to stem earlier global crises, we are determined to steer the world out of its current challenges and build a safer, stronger, more resilient, inclusive and healthier future for our people and the planet.

LIST OF DOCUMENTS ANNEXED TO THE G20 NEW DELHI LEADERS' DECLARATION, 2023

Ministerial Meetings and Working Group Documents

1. G20 Agriculture Ministers' Meeting Outcome Document and Chair's Summary (16-17 June 2023, Hyderabad)
   i. G20 Deccan High Level Principles on Food Security and Nutrition 2023
   ii. Stocktaking of G20 Initiatives in Agriculture - Presidency's Summary Statement
2. G20 Anti-Corruption Ministers' Meeting Outcome Document and Chair's Summary (12 August 2023, Kolkata)
   i. G20 High-Level Principles on Strengthening Law Enforcement related International Cooperation and Information Sharing for Combatting Corruption
   ii. G20 High-Level Principles on Strengthening Asset Recovery Mechanisms for Combatting Corruption
   iii. G20 High-Level Principles on Promoting Integrity and Effectiveness of Public

Bodies and Authorities Responsible for Preventing and Combatting Corruption

iv. Accountability Report 2023 on Mutual Legal Assistance (MLA)

v. Compendium of Good Practices in Enhancing the Role of Auditing in Tackling Corruption

3. G20 Culture Ministers' Meeting Outcome Document and Chair's Summary - Kashi Culture Pathway (26 August 2023, Varanasi)
   i. G20 Culture Working Group Terms of Reference
4. G20 Development Ministers' Meeting Outcome Document and Chair's Summary (12 June 2023, Varanasi)
5. G20 2023 Action Plan on Accelerating Progress on the SDGs (12 June 2023, Varanasi)
   i. G20 High Level Principles on Harnessing Data for Development (D4D) to Accelerate Progress on the SDGs
   ii. Implementing Sustainable, Inclusive and Just Transitions Globally, while leaving no one behind
   iii. G20 Action Plan on Sustainable Development through Gender Equality on Sustainable Development through Gender Equality and Empowerment of Women
6. G20 High Level Principles on Lifestyles for Sustainable Development (12 June 2023, 6. Varanasi)
7. 2023 G20 New Delhi Update
8. G20 Digital Economy Ministers' Meeting Outcome Document and Chair's Summary (19 August 2023, Bengaluru)
   i. G20 Framework for systems of Digital Public Infrastructure
   ii. G20 High Level Principles to Support Business in Building Safety, Security, Resilience, and Trust in the Digital Economy
   iii. G20 Toolkit on Cyber Education and Cyber Awareness of Children and Youth
   iv. G20 Toolkit for Designing and Introducing Digital Upskilling and Reskilling Programs
   v. G20 Roadmap to Facilitate the Cross-Country Comparison of Digital Skills
9. G20 Disaster Risk Reduction Working Group Meeting Outcome Document and Chair's Summary (24-25 July 2023, Chennai)
10. G20 Environment & Climate Ministers' Meeting Outcome Document and Chair's Summary (28 July 2023, Chennai)
    i. Chennai High Level Principles for a Sustainable and Resilient Blue/Ocean-Based Economy
    ii. Presidency's Gandhinagar Implementation Roadmap (GIR) And Gandhinagar

Information Platform (GIP) For strengthening the G20 Global Land Initiative.

iii. Compendium of Best Practices on Restoration of Mining Affected Areas.
iv. Compendium of Best Practices on Restoration of Forest Fire Affected Areas
v. Best Practices for Water Management
vi. Technical Study on Accelerating the Transition to a Sustainable and Resilient Blue Economy
vii. G20 Report on Actions Against Marine Plastic Litter – Fifth Information Sharing Based on G20 Implementation Framework
viii. Knowledge Exchange on Circular Economy in Steel Sector
ix. Knowledge Exchange on Extended Producer Responsibility for Circular Economy
x. Knowledge Exchange on Circular Bioeconomy
xi. Resource Efficiency and Circular Economy Industry Coalition (RECEIC)

11. G20 Education Ministers' Meeting Outcome Document and Chair's Summary (22 June 2023, Pune)
    i. G20 EdWG Report: Education Policies and Programmes in G20 Countries
    ii. G20 EdWG Compendium: Education Policies and Programmes in G20 Countries
12. G20 Energy Transitions Ministers' Meeting Outcome Document and Chair's Summary (22 July 2023, Goa)
    i. G20 High-Level Voluntary Principles on Hydrogen
    ii. Voluntary High-Level Principles for Collaboration on Critical Minerals for Energy Transitions
    iii. Voluntary Action Plan on Doubling the Global Rate of Energy Efficiency Improvement by 2030
    iv. Voluntary Action Plan for Lowering the Cost of Finance for Energy Transitions
    v. Voluntary Action Plan for Promoting Renewable Energy to Accelerate Universal Energy Access.
13. G20 Foreign Ministers' Meeting Chair's Summary and Outcome Document (1-2 March 2023, New Delhi)
14. First G20 Finance Ministers and Central Bank Governors Meeting Chair's Summary and Outcome Document (24-25 February 2023, Bengaluru)
    i. IMF G20 Note on the Macro financial Implications of Crypto Assets
    ii. FSB Chair's Letter to G20 Finance Ministers and Central Bank Governors, February 2023
    iii. FSB Report on the Financial Stability Risks of Decentralised Finance
    iv. FSB Report on the Financial Stability Aspects of Commodities Markets
    v. FSB report: G20 Roadmap for Enhancing Cross-border Payments - Priority actions for achieving the G20 targets

   vi. OECD Secretary-General's Tax Letter to G20 Finance Ministers and Central Bank Governors, February 2023.
   vii. OECD Secretary-General Tax Report to G20 Finance Ministers and Central Bank Governors

15. Third G20 Finance Ministers and Central Bank Governors Meeting Outcome Document and Chair's Summary (17-18 July 2023, Gandhinagar)
   i. G20 Report on Macroeconomic Impacts of Food and Energy Insecurity and their implications for the global economy
   ii. G20 Report on Macroeconomic risks stemming from climate change and transition pathways
   iii. G20 Roadmap for implementing the recommendations of the G20 Independent Review of MDBs Capital Adequacy Frameworks (CAFs)
   iv. Volume 1 of the G20 Expert Group on Strengthening MDBs
   v. IMF Report on potential macro-financial implications of widespread adoption of CBDCs
   vi. BIS Innovation Hub (BISIH) Report on "Lessons learnt on CBDCs"
   vii. OECD's report on "Towards Orderly Green Transition – Investment Requirements and Managing Risks to Capital Flows
   viii. G20 note on the total global ambition of USD 100bn of voluntary contributions for countries most in need
   ix. G20 Principles for Financing Cities of Tomorrow: inclusive, resilient and sustainable
   x. G20/OECD Report on Financing Cities of Tomorrow
   xi. G20/ADB Framework on Capacity Building of Urban Administration
   xii. G20 Sustainable Finance Working Group Deliverables, 2023
   xiii. Framework on Economic Vulnerabilities and Risks (FEVR) and the initial Report for economic vulnerabilities and risks arising from pandemics
   xiv. Report on Best Practices from Finance Health Institutional Arrangements during Covid-19
   xv. Report on Mapping Pandemic Response Financing Options and Gaps developed by the WHO and World Bank
   xvi. G20/OECD Roadmap on Developing Countries and International Taxation Update 2023
   xvii. OECD Report on 'Enhancing International Tax Transparency on Real Estate'
   xviii. Global Forum Report on 'Facilitating the Use of Tax-Treaty-Exchanged Information for Non-Tax Purposes'
   xix. Global Forum Update on the implementation of the 2021 Strategy on Unleashing the Potential of Automatic Exchange of Information for Developing Countries

xx. FSB Chair's Letters to G20 Finance Ministers and Central Bank Governors, April and July 2023

xxi. FSB's global regulatory framework for crypto-asset activities: Umbrella public note to accompany final framework

xxii. FSB's high-level recommendations for the regulation, supervision, and oversight of crypto-asset activities and markets

xxiii. FSB's high-level recommendations for the regulation, supervision, and oversight of global stablecoin arrangements

xxiv. BIS Report on "The crypto ecosystem: key elements and risks"

xxv. FSB Consultation Report on addressing liquidity mismatch in open-ended funds-Revisions to the FSB 2017 policy recommendations

xxvi. FSB Consultative document on Enhancing Third-Party Risk Management and Oversight: A toolkit for financial institutions and financial authorities

xxvii. FSB Roadmap for Addressing Financial Risks from Climate Change: 2023 Progress Report

xxviii. FSB Recommendations to Achieve Greater Convergence in Cyber Incident Reporting: Final Report

xxix. FSB Concept Note on Format for Incident Reporting Exchange (FIRE) - A possible way forward

xxx. Revised G20/OECD Principles of Corporate Governance

xxxi. IMF-FSB Synthesis Paper: Policies for Crypto-Assets

xxxii. FSB progress report on enhancing the resilience of NBFI

xxxiii. FSB report on the financial stability implications of leverage in NBFI

xxxiv. G20 Policy Recommendations for Advancing Financial Inclusion and Productivity Gains through Digital Public Infrastructure

xxxv. 2023 Update to Leaders on Progress towards the G20 Remittance Target

xxxvi. Regulatory Toolkit for Enhanced Digital Financial Inclusion of Micro, Small and Medium Enterprises (MSMEs)

xxxvii. G20 2023 Financial Inclusion Action Plan

xxxviii. 2023 Updated GPFI Terms of Reference

xxxix. 2023 GPFI Progress Report to G20 Leaders

xl. G20 Financial Inclusion Action Plan Progress Report 2021-23

xli. FATF Report- Countering Ransomware Financing Report (March 2023)

xlii. Targeted Update on the Implementation of the FATF Standards for Virtual Assets (June 2023)

xliii. FATF Report on Guidance on Beneficial Ownership Transparency for Legal Persons (March 2023)

16. G20 Health Ministers' Meeting Outcome Document and Chair's Summary (18-19 August 2023, Gandhinagar)

17. G20 Labour & Employment Ministers' Outcome Document and Chair's Summary (21 July 2023, Indore)
    i. List of reports prepared by International Organizations
18. G20 Policy Priorities on Strategies to Address Skill Gaps Globally (21 July 2023, Indore)
19. G20 Policy Priorities on Adequate and Sustainable Social Protection and Decent Work for Gig and Platform Workers (21 July 2023, Indore)
20. G20 Policy Options for Sustainable Financing of Social Protection (21 July 2023, Indore)
21. G20 Meeting of Agricultural Chief Scientists (MACS) Chair's Summary and Outcome Document (17-19 April 2023, Varanasi)
    i. G20 Millet and other Ancient Grains International Research Initiative (MAHARISHI)
22. G20 Tourism Ministers' Meeting Outcome Document and Chairs' Summary (21 June 2023, Goa)
    i. G20 Goa Roadmap for Tourism as a Vehicle for Achieving the Sustainable Development Goals
23. G20 Trade & Investment Ministers' Meeting Outcome Document and Chairs' Summary (25 August 2023, Jaipur)
    i. G20 Generic Framework for Mapping GVCs
    ii. Jaipur Call for Action for enhancing MSMEs' Access to Information
    iii. High Level Principles on Digitalization of Trade Documents
24. G20 Ministerial Conference on Women Empowerment - Chair's Statement (2-4 August 2023, Gandhinagar)
25. G20 Chief Science Advisers Round Table – Outcome Document and Chairs' Summary (28 August 2023, Gandhinagar)
26. G20 Research Ministerial Meeting - Outcome Document and Chairs' Summary (5 July 2023, Mumbai)

Index